£2.50

KU-515-360

The Complete Book of
Everyday Classics

THE AUSTRALIAN
Women's Weekly

The Complete Book of
Everyday Classics

acp
books

contents

From Sunday morning scrambled eggs to delicious buckwheat pancakes with caramelised banana, the most important meal of the day is now one you'll really look forward to sharing with friends over a long, leisurely weekend morning.

breakfast
and brunch

toasted muesli

bircher muesli

high fibre muesli

porridge with apple compote

toasted muesli

preparation time 15 minutes
cooking time 45 minutes (plus cooling time)
serves 2

1 cup (90g) rolled oats
¼ cup (15g) unprocessed bran
¼ cup (35g) finely chopped dried apricots
¼ cup (20g) finely chopped dried apples
2 tablespoons sultanas
1 tablespoon honey
1 tablespoon water
1 cup (250ml) skimmed milk

1 Preheat oven to low.
2 Combine oats, bran and fruit in medium bowl; stir in combined honey and water.
3 Spread mixture onto oven tray. Bake in low oven about 45 minutes or until toasted, stirring occasionally; let cool.
4 Serve muesli with milk, and fresh fruit, if desired.
per serving 4.4g fat; 1433kJ (343 cal)
TIP Muesli can be refrigerated in an airtight container for several weeks.

bircher muesli

preparation time 15 minutes (plus refrigeration time)
serves 6

3 cups (270g) rolled oats
2 cups (500ml) fresh orange juice
400g plain yogurt
1 cup (160g) pitted dried dates, chopped coarsely
½ cup (85g) raisins
½ cup (150g) dried apricots, sliced thinly
⅓ cup (115g) honey
1 cup (250ml) milk
1 large apple (200g), peeled, grated coarsely
⅓ cup (45g) toasted slivered almonds

1 Combine oats, juice and yogurt in large bowl. Cover tightly; refrigerate overnight.
2 Stir dates, raisins, apricot, honey, milk and apple into oat mixture. Cover; refrigerate 30 minutes.
3 Serve muesli in individual serving bowls; top with almonds and fresh mixed berries, if desired.
per serving 12.6g fat; 2000kJ (478 cal)
TIPS Try to find plain full-cream yogurt, sometimes called country-style or greek-style yogurt, for this recipe. Other types, especially the low-fat kind, are not suitable. Additional milk can be added if muesli is too thick. Use a tart, crisp green apple, such as a granny smith, for this recipe.

high-fibre muesli

preparation time 15 minutes
cooking time 5 minutes
makes about 9 cups (1.25kg)

½ cup (50g) desiccated coconut
2 tablespoons (30g) sesame seeds
2 cups (185g) rolled oats
1 cup (140g) rolled rice
1 cup (100g) rolled triticale
½ cup (80g) oat bran
½ cup (60g) wheatgerm
2 tablespoons (40g) sunflower seed kernels
2 tablespoons (40g) pumpkin seed kernels
½ cup (70g) pecans or walnuts, chopped coarsely
½ cup (80g) hazelnuts, chopped coarsely
¾ cup (100g) dried apricots
½ cup (45g) dried apples
½ cup (90g) sultanas

1 Combine coconut and sesame seeds in small frying pan; stir constantly over medium heat until both ingredients are browned lightly. Place in large bowl; mix in rolled oats, rice and triticale, then oat bran, wheatgerm, sunflower seed kernels, pepitas and nuts.
2 Chop apricots and apples into small pieces using scissors; stir into oat mixture with sultanas. Transfer mixture to airtight container.
3 Serve topped with raspberries, if desired.

TOASTED MUESLI
Preheat oven to moderate; complete step 1, above. Heat 60g butter and 2 tablespoons oil in baking dish. Add mixture; stir well. Bake, uncovered, in moderate oven 10 minutes. Remove mixture from oven; stir well. Return to oven; bake further 50 minutes, stirring every 10 minutes, or until browned. Remove from oven; stir in fruit. Cool muesli to room temperature; transfer to storage jar.
per ¼-cup serving 6.8g fat; 514kJ (123 cal)

porridge with apple compote

preparation time 10 minutes
cooking time 15 minutes
serves 4

1 cup (90g) rolled oats
1 cup (250ml) skimmed milk
1½ cups (375ml) boiling water
2 tablespoons brown sugar

APPLE COMPOTE
2 medium apples (300g)
¼ cup (55g) caster sugar
¼ teaspoon ground cinnamon
¼ cup (60ml) water
8 dried apricots
1 tablespoon sultanas

1 Combine oats, milk and the water in medium saucepan; bring to a boil. Reduce heat; simmer, uncovered, about 5 minutes or until mixture thickens.
2 Serve porridge with apple compote, sprinkled with brown sugar.

APPLE COMPOTE
Peel, core and slice apples thickly; combine apple with sugar, cinnamon and the water in medium saucepan. Cook, stirring, over low heat until sugar dissolves. Bring apple mixture to a boil. Reduce heat; simmer, uncovered 5 minutes. Add apricots and sultanas; simmer, uncovered, about 5 minutes or until apple is tender.
per serving 2.1g fat; 1019kJ (244 cal)
TIP Any other dried fruit, such as prunes, pears or peaches, may be used instead of the apricots

buttermilk pancakes with ricotta cream

preparation time 10 minutes (plus standing time)
cooking time 10 minutes
serves 4

1 cup (150g) self-raising flour
½ teaspoon ground cinnamon
1 tablespoon caster sugar
2 eggs, beaten lightly
1¼ cups (310ml) buttermilk
125g reduced-fat smooth ricotta cheese
½ cup (125ml) maple syrup
1 medium lemon (140g), cut into wedges

1 Sift flour, cinnamon and sugar into medium bowl. Whisk in combined egg and buttermilk, gradually, until smooth. Cover; stand 30 minutes.
2 Pour ¼ cup (60ml) of the batter into heated oiled non-stick frying pan; cook until bubbles start to appear. Turn pancake; cook until browned underneath. Remove pancake from pan; cover to keep warm. Repeat with remaining batter to make eight pancakes.
3 Combine ricotta with a tablespoon of the maple syrup in small bowl.
4 Serve pancakes with ricotta mixture, remaining maple syrup and lemon.
per serving 7.6g fat; 1599kJ (382 cal)
TIPS This recipe is best made just before serving. Pancakes are suitable to freeze.

fruit salad with honey yogurt

preparation time 15 minutes
serves 4

¾ cup (200g) low-fat yogurt
2 tablespoons honey
200g peeled, coarsely chopped pineapple
200g cantaloupe melon, deseeded, peeled,
    coarsely chopped
250g strawberries, halved
250g blueberries
1 large banana (230g), sliced thinly
2 tablespoons passionfruit pulp
2 teaspoons lime juice
12 fresh mint leaves

1 Combine yogurt and honey in small bowl.
2 Just before serving, combine remaining ingredients
in large bowl; serve with honey yogurt.
per serving 2g fat; 749kJ (179 cal)
TIPS Lime juice not only adds flavour to this recipe
but also prevents the banana from discolouring.
Honey yogurt can be made a day ahead and
refrigerated, covered.

buckwheat pancakes with caramelised banana

preparation time 10 minutes (plus refrigeration time)
cooking time 20 minutes
serves 4

¼ cup (35g) self-raising flour
¼ cup (35g) buckwheat flour
1 tablespoon caster sugar
¼ teaspoon ground cinnamon
1 egg
¾ cup (180ml) skimmed milk
20g butter
¼ cup (50g) firmly packed brown sugar
4 medium bananas (800g), sliced thickly
2 tablespoons water

1 Combine flours, caster sugar and cinnamon in
medium bowl; gradually whisk in combined egg and
milk until smooth. Cover; refrigerate 30 minutes.
2 Meanwhile, melt butter in large frying pan. Add brown
sugar; cook, stirring, until dissolved. Add banana and
the water; cook, uncovered, stirring occasionally, about
2 minutes or until banana is caramelised.
3 Pour ¼ cup (60ml) of the batter into heated 20cm
non-stick frying pan; cook pancake until browned
both sides. Repeat with remaining batter to make four
pancakes; cover to keep warm. Just before serving,
halve each pancake; divide halves among serving
plates. Spoon banana mixture onto each half; fold to
enclose filling. Drizzle with remaining caramel sauce.
per serving 6.1g fat; 1285kJ (307 cal)
TIPS Fresh strawberries may be used as a filling instead
of caramelised bananas.
Dust pancakes with icing sugar before serving.

boiled eggs

corned beef hash with poached eggs

scrambled eggs

eggs with pancetta

boiled eggs

preparation time 5 minutes
cooking time 5 minutes (plus cooling time)

eggs

BOILING EGGS
Store eggs in refrigerator with ends pointing down so the yolk is less likely to break when egg is used. As eggshells are porous they should not be washed before storing or stored near strong-smelling foods.
Use the freshest eggs possible. To test freshness, place egg in enough cold water to cover. If the egg sinks, it is fresh; if it floats, don't use it.

1 Choose saucepan to suit the number of eggs you are boiling; one egg in small saucepan, up to four eggs in medium saucepan; more eggs in large saucepan (there should be enough room to move eggs around). Add enough cold water to cover eggs. Stir constantly using wooden spoon over high heat until water boils; this will centralise each yolk. Boil, uncovered, until yolks are as soft or as firm as you like. As a guide, 3 minutes will give you set egg white and soft yolk. After 5 minutes, the yolk will be set.
2 Place saucepan of eggs under cold running water about 1 minute or until eggs are cool. This will stop a dark ring forming around the yolk.
3 Serve boiled eggs with toast soldiers, if desired.
per egg 6.4g fat; 373kJ (89 cal)
TIP To peel eggs, crack shells gently and leave eggs immersed in cold water for at least 5 minutes or until cold. Remove shells, starting from broad end. Wash eggs; pat dry using absorbent paper.

corned beef hash with poached eggs

preparation time 10 minutes
cooking time 10 minutes
serves 2

1 medium brown onion (150g), chopped finely
3 medium potatoes (600g), grated
500g cooked corned beef, shredded
2 tablespoons finely chopped fresh flat-leaf parsley
2 tablespoons plain flour
2 eggs, beaten lightly
1 tablespoon vegetable oil
4 eggs, extra

POACHING EGGS
Poaching is a gentle method of cooking food in simmering liquid. Eggs should be lowered into the simmering water. Water should almost cover the eggs, not submerge them. The pan may be covered or uncovered. When covered, the eggs are cooked by the trapped steam as well as the simmering water. When uncovered, the water can be spooned over the top of the eggs until cooked to suit your taste.

1 Combine onion, potato, beef, parsley, flour and egg in large bowl; mix well. Divide mixture into four portions; flatten to form patties.
2 Heat oil in large heavy-base frying pan; cook patties, uncovered, until browned both sides and potato is tender.
3 Put a little butter or oil on index finger; grease inside egg rings or spray lightly with non-stick spray. Place about 1cm water in frying pan so egg will not be covered. Bring water to a boil; reduce heat until water is barely simmering. Place rings into water; gently pour extra eggs, one at a time, into rings.
4 Egg white will start to set. If eggs are large, a little white may seem to puff up around top of rings. Make sure water doesn't boil or white will toughen. Now start spooning water over yolks until set enough to suit your taste. It is not possible to give a time as this depends on type and size of pan, amount and heat of water, size and temperature of eggs and, most important, individual preferences.
5 Carefully lift rings away from eggs; lift eggs from water using egg slide.
6 Serve hash patties topped with poached eggs; top with shredded basil, if desired.
per serving 37.8g fat; 3263kJ (779 cal)

scrambled eggs

preparation time 3 minutes
cooking time 3 minutes
serves 2

4 eggs, beaten lightly
⅓ cup (80ml) milk
1 tablespoon finely chopped fresh chives
1 teaspoon butter

1 Place egg in small bowl with milk and chives; whisk to combine.
2 Melt butter in medium saucepan over low heat; add egg mixture. When egg mixture starts to 'catch' on bottom of pan, stir continuously with wooden spoon. Cook only until egg is just firm. Serve with toasted brioche and smoked salmon, sprinkled with chopped fresh chives, if desired.
per serving 15g fat; 837kJ (200 cal)
TIPS Whisk eggs just long enough to combine the yolks and whites; excessive beating will aerate the mixture too much.
Cook eggs just before serving.
Any chopped herb can be substituted for the chives.

eggs with pancetta

preparation time 15 minutes
cooking time 20 minutes
serves 4

2 teaspoons olive oil
1 small red pepper (150g), chopped finely
6 slices pancetta (90g), chopped finely
100g mushrooms, chopped finely
4 spring onions, chopped finely
⅓ cup (25g) finely grated parmesan cheese
8 eggs
2 teaspoons coarsely chopped fresh flat-leaf parsley

1 Preheat oven to moderately hot (200°C/180°C fan-assisted). Lightly oil four ¾-cup (180ml) ovenproof dishes.
2 Heat oil in medium frying pan; cook pepper and pancetta, stirring, until pepper is just tender. Add mushroom and onion; cook, stirring, until onion just softens. Remove from heat; stir in half the cheese.
3 Divide pepper mixture among dishes; break two eggs into each dish. Bake, uncovered, in moderately hot oven 5 minutes. Sprinkle remaining cheese over eggs; bake further 5 minutes or until eggs are just set. Sprinkle with parsley just before serving.
per serving 18g fat; 1074kJ (257 cal)

bacon and eggs

preparation time 5 minutes
cooking time 10 minutes
serves 2

4 bacon rashers (280g)
1 tablespoon vegetable oil
4 eggs
1 medium tomato (190g), halved

FRYING EGGS

Use a heavy-base frying pan; the size doesn't matter.
Gentle cooking is the secret; use either a little butter or oil
in the pan, a pan sprayed with non-stick spray, or a pan
with a non-stick surface.

If you want a nice round egg, use an egg ring; grease it
first with a little butter or oil on your index finger or use a
non-stick spray.

Butter should be hot but not browned when you add the
egg; if butter is too hot, the egg will burn around the edge
and underneath before the centre is cooked. Spoon a little
hot oil or butter over egg to help cook it.

Some people prefer a fried egg which is a little crispy on
the base. To attain this, increase the heat carefully until the
white is as crisp as you like.

You should serve the egg immediately it is cooked, as a
fried egg cannot be reheated successfully.

Remember to always choose the freshest egg available so
the white will set in a good shape when cooked; a stale
egg will result in a watery white when cooked.

1 Cook bacon in medium frying pan, uncovered, until
browned and cooked as desired. Remove from pan;
keep warm.
2 Place oil in pan; break eggs into pan or into greased
egg rings in pan. Cook, uncovered, until egg white has
set and yolk is cooked as desired.
3 Meanwhile, place tomato, cut-side up, onto baking
tray; season with salt and pepper, if desired. Place
under heated grill; cook tomato until browned lightly and
just tender.
4 Serve fried eggs, bacon and tomato with toast, if
desired
per serving 47.9g fat; 2476kJ (591 cal)

Pouring egg into pan

Spooning a little hot butter over egg

Serve egg immediately it is cooked

courgette and mushroom omelette

preparation time 10 minutes
cooking time 10 minutes
serves 1

10g butter
1 clove garlic, crushed
25g button mushrooms, sliced thinly
¼ cup (50g) coarsely grated courgettes
1 spring onion, chopped finely
2 eggs
1 tablespoon water
¼ cup (30g) coarsely grated cheddar cheese

1 Heat half of the butter in small non-stick frying pan; cook garlic and mushroom, stirring, over medium heat about 2 minutes or until mushroom is lightly browned. Add courgette and onion; cook, stirring, about 1 minute or until courgette begins to soften. Remove vegetable mixture from pan; cover to keep warm.
2 Beat eggs and the water in small bowl. Add cheese; whisk until combined.
3 Heat remaining butter in same pan; swirl pan so butter covers base. Pour egg mixture into pan; cook, tilting pan, over medium heat until almost set.
4 Place vegetable mixture evenly over half of the omelette; using spatula, flip other half over vegetable mixture. Slide omelette gently onto serving plate.
per serving 29.2g fat; 1502kJ (359 cal)

mushroom, pepper and cheese omelette

preparation time 15 minutes
cooking time 15 minutes
serves 4

20g butter
1 small red pepper (150g), sliced thinly
200g mushrooms, sliced thinly
2 tablespoons finely chopped fresh chives
8 eggs
1 tablespoon milk
4 spring onions, sliced thinly
½ cup (60g) coarsely grated cheddar cheese

1 Melt butter in large frying pan; cook pepper, mushroom and chives, stirring occasionally, until vegetables soften. Drain vegetable filling on absorbent-paper-lined plate; cover with foil to keep warm.
2 Whisk eggs until well combined, then whisk in milk and onion.
3 Pour half the egg mixture into same pan used for the vegetables; tilt pan to cover base with egg mixture. Cook over medium heat about 4 minutes or until omelette is just set.
4 Carefully spoon half the vegetable filling onto one half of the omelette; sprinkle half the cheese over vegetable filling. Use a spatula to lift and fold unfilled omelette half over vegetable filling. Carefully slide omelette onto plate; cover with foil to keep warm.
5 Make one more omelette with remaining egg mixture, vegetable filling and cheese. Cut each omelette in half; place one half on each serving plate.
per serving 19.7g fat; 1087kJ (260 cal)
TIPS Vegetable filling can be prepared up to a day ahead. Reheat gently over low heat when required. Omelettes are best made at time of serving.
We used button mushrooms for our omelettes, but you can choose any variety you like.

spanish tortilla

preparation time 10 minutes
cooking time 15 minutes
serves 4

1 tablespoon olive oil
1 large brown onion (200g), sliced thinly
750g canned tiny new potatoes, drained,
  sliced thickly
6 eggs, beaten lightly
100g feta cheese, chopped coarsely
⅓ cup (25g) finely grated parmesan cheese
⅓ cup (40g) coarsely grated cheddar cheese

1 Heat oil in medium frying pan; cook onion, stirring, until onion softens.
2 Combine onion, potato, egg and cheeses in large bowl.
3 Pour potato mixture into heated oiled medium non-stick frying pan. Cover; cook over low heat 10 minutes or until egg sets.
4 Carefully invert tortilla onto plate and slide back into frying pan. Cook further 5 minutes or until cooked through.
5 Remove from heat; allow to cool in pan. Serve with baby rocket, if desired.
per serving 23.8g fat; 1560kJ (373 cal)
TIP Tortilla can be eaten hot or cold and makes great picnic fare.

butternut squash, spinach and feta frittata

preparation time 10 minutes
cooking time 35 minutes
serves 4

4 cups (640g) coarsely chopped butternut squash
1 large potato (300g), chopped coarsely
125g baby spinach leaves, chopped coarsely
200g feta cheese, crumbled
¾ cup (90g) coarsely grated cheddar cheese
8 eggs, beaten lightly
1 small red onion (100g), sliced thinly

1 Preheat oven to very hot. Grease deep 23cm-square cake tin; line base and two opposite sides with baking parchment.
2 Place squash in large microwave-safe bowl. Cover; cook on HIGH (100%), stirring halfway through cooking time, about 5 minutes or until just tender. Place potato in small microwave-safe bowl. Cover; cook on HIGH (100%) 4 minutes or until just tender.
3 Combine squash and potato in large bowl. Add spinach, cheeses and egg; stir to combine. Transfer egg mixture to prepared tin; top with onion.
4 Bake in very hot oven about 25 minutes or until firm. Stand 5 minutes before serving.
per serving 30.6g fat; 2032kJ (486 cal)
TIP If you don't have a microwave oven, boil or steam squash and potato, separately, until just tender; drain.

french toast

preparation time 5 minutes
cooking time 10 minutes
serves 4

3 eggs, beaten lightly
⅓ cup (80ml) cream
⅓ cup (80ml) milk
¼ teaspoon ground cinnamon
1 tablespoon caster sugar
12 x 2cm slices french bread stick
50g butter

1 Combine egg, cream, milk, cinnamon and sugar in large bowl. Dip bread slices into egg mixture.
2 Melt half of the butter in large frying pan; cook half of the bread slices until browned both sides. Repeat with remaining butter and bread. Serve sprinkled with sifted icing sugar, if desired.
per serving 25.1g fat; 1505kJ (359 cal)
TIP This recipe is best made close to serving.

smoked salmon on rösti

preparation time 20 minutes
cooking time 20 minutes
serves 4

4 medium potatoes (800g)
2 tablespoons vegetable oil
½ cup (120g) spreadable light cream cheese
1 tablespoon finely chopped fresh flat-leaf parsley
1 tablespoon finely chopped fresh chives
1 tablespoon lemon juice
150g sliced smoked salmon

1 Coarsely grate peeled potatoes; use hands to squeeze out as much excess liquid as possible. Measure ¼ cups of grated potato, placing each portion on long sheet of baking parchment.
2 Heat 2 teaspoons of the oil in large non-stick frying pan; place two portions of the grated potato in pan, flattening each with a spatula. Cook rösti over medium heat until browned; turn with spatula to cook other side. Drain rösti on absorbent paper; make six more rösti with remaining oil and grated potato.
3 Combine cream cheese, chopped herbs and juice in small bowl.
4 Divide rösti among serving plates, top with herbed cream cheese and smoked salmon.
per serving 16.1g fat; 1275kJ (305 cal)
TIP Rösti are Swiss pan-fried potato cakes, and are best made from 'starchy' potatoes.

smoked salmon and mascarpone crepe cake

preparation time 30 minutes
(plus standing and refrigeration time)
cooking time 30 minutes
serves 12

¾ cup (110g) plain flour
3 eggs
1 tablespoon vegetable oil
1⅓ cups (330ml) milk
2 cups (500g) mascarpone
2 tablespoons horseradish sauce
2 tablespoons drained capers, rinsed, chopped
  coarsely
2 tablespoons finely chopped fresh tarragon
1 tablespoon finely grated lemon rind
500g sliced smoked salmon

1 Line base and side of deep 22cm-round cake tin with cling film.
2 Place flour in medium bowl. Make well in centre; gradually whisk in combined eggs, oil and milk. Strain batter into large jug, cover; stand 30 minutes.
3 Heat oiled 22cm non-stick frying pan; pour about ¼ cup of the batter into pan, tilting pan so batter coats base evenly. Cook crepe, over low heat, loosening around edge with spatula, until browned lightly. Turn crepe; brown other side. Remove from pan; repeat with remaining batter to make a total of eight crepes.
4 Combine mascarpone, horseradish, capers, tarragon and rind in medium bowl. Place one crepe in prepared cake pan; spread with about ⅓ cup of the mascarpone mixture, cover with slices of salmon. Continue layering with remaining crepes, mascarpone mixture and salmon, finishing with crepe layer. Cover; refrigerate 3 hours or until firm.
5 Cut crepe cake into 12 wedges.
per serving 33.1g fat; 1739kJ (416 cal);
TIP Crepes can be made up to two days ahead; wrap in cling film and refrigerate until required. Crepe cake can be assembled the day before; store, covered, in refrigerator.

apricot muffins

wholemeal fig muffins

bacon and fresh herb muffins

cheese muffins

apricot muffins

preparation time 15 minutes
cooking time 20 minutes (plus cooling time)
makes 12

1 cup (150g) coarsely chopped dried apricots
3 cups (450g) self-raising flour
½ cup (110g) caster sugar
125g butter, chopped coarsely
½ cup (125ml) milk
2 eggs

1 Place apricot in small bowl; cover with boiling water. Cover; stand 30 minutes. Drain well.
2 Sift flour and sugar into large bowl; rub in butter using fingertips.
3 Add apricot to flour mixture.
4 Place milk and eggs in medium jug. Mix using fork; add to flour mixture. Mix using fork until ingredients are just combined; do not over-mix. Mixture should be coarse and lumpy.
5 Divide mixture into greased 12-hole (⅓ cup/80ml) muffin tray. Bake in moderately hot oven 20 minutes. Turn onto wire racks to cool.
per muffin 10.3g fat; 1176kJ (281 cal)
TIP Muffins are at their best freshly cooked and eaten warm with butter. Muffins can be stored in airtight container 2 days or frozen for up to 2 months.

wholemeal fig muffins

preparation time 10 minutes
cooking time 20 minutes (plus cooling time)
makes 12

2 cups (320g) wholemeal self-raising flour
1 cup (150g) self-raising flour
½ cup (110g) raw sugar
125g butter, chopped coarsely
1 cup (190g) coarsely chopped dried figs
2 eggs, beaten lightly
1 cup (250ml) milk

1 Place flours in large bowl. Add sugar; rub in butter.
2 Add figs, then combined eggs and milk. Mix using fork until ingredients are just combined; do not over-mix. Mixture should be coarse and lumpy.
3 Divide mixture into greased 12-hole (⅓ cup/80ml) muffin tray. Bake in moderately hot oven 20 minutes. Turn onto wire racks to cool. Serve with butter and a drizzle of honey, if desired.
per muffin 11.1g fat; 1258kJ (300 cal)
TIP Muffins can be stored in airtight container 2 days or frozen for up to 2 months.

bacon and fresh herb muffins

preparation time 15 minutes
cooking time 25 minutes (plus cooling time)
makes 12

6 bacon rashers, chopped finely
3 cups (450g) self-raising flour
60g butter, chopped coarsely
1 tablespoon coarsely chopped fresh basil
2 tablespoons coarsely chopped fresh chives
2 teaspoons coarsely chopped fresh oregano
¾ cup (60g) grated parmesan cheese
2 eggs, beaten lightly
1 cup (250ml) milk

1 Cook bacon in small frying pan until crisp. Drain on absorbent paper; cool.
2 Place flour in large bowl; rub in butter. Add bacon, herbs and cheese, then combined eggs and milk. Mix using fork until ingredients are just combined; do not over-mix. Mixture should be coarse and lumpy.
3 Divide mixture into greased 12-hole (⅓ cup/80ml) muffin tray. Bake in moderately hot oven 20 minutes. Turn onto wire racks to cool.
per muffin 9.5g fat; 1010kJ (241 cal)
TIP Can be kept in airtight container 2 days or frozen for up to 2 months.

cheese muffins

preparation time 10 minutes
cooking time 25 minutes
makes 12

3 cups (450g) self-raising flour
40g butter, chopped coarsely
1¾ cups (430ml) buttermilk
2 tablespoons basil pesto
¾ cup (90g) coarsely grated cheddar cheese
¼ teaspoon sweet paprika
1 tablespoon plain flour

1 Preheat oven to moderately hot. Grease 12-hole (⅓-cup/80ml) muffin tray.
2 Place self-raising flour in large bowl; rub in butter with fingertips. Using fork, stir in buttermilk to form a soft, sticky dough. Swirl pesto and cheese through; do not over-mix.
3 Divide mixture among holes of prepared tray. Sprinkle with combined paprika and plain flour.
4 Bake in moderately hot oven 25 minutes.
5 Stand muffins in pan 5 minutes before turning out onto wire rack.
per muffin 7.8g fat; 929kJ (222 cal)
TIP Use bottled pesto to save time. A sun-dried tomato pesto can also be used.

day-before muffins

preparation time 15 minutes (plus refrigeration time)
cooking time 30 minutes
makes 4

⅔ cup (100g) coarsely chopped dried apricots
½ cup (95g) coarsely chopped dried figs
1⅓ cups (95g) All-Bran breakfast cereal
1½ cups (375ml) skimmed milk
1¼ cups (250g) firmly packed brown sugar
1½ tablespoons golden syrup
1¼ cups (185g) self-raising flour
½ cup (60g) pecans, chopped coarsely

1 Combine apricot, fig, cereal, milk, sugar and syrup in large bowl; mix well. Cover; refrigerate overnight.
2 Preheat oven to moderately hot. Lightly grease four holes only of a six-hole large (¾-cup/180ml) muffin tray.
3 Stir flour and nuts into apricot mixture. Spoon mixture into prepared tray; bake in moderately hot oven 30 minutes.
4 Serve muffins hot or cold. Dust with sifted icing sugar and top with dried apricots, if desired.
per muffin 11.1g fat; 2941kJ (704 cal)
TIP Muffins can be frozen for up to 2 months.

banana bread

preparation time 10 minutes
cooking time 30 minutes
makes 12 slices

1¼ cups (185g) self-raising flour
1 teaspoon ground cinnamon
20g butter
½ cup (100g) firmly packed brown sugar
1 egg, beaten lightly
¼ cup (60ml) milk
½ cup mashed banana

1 Preheat oven to hot. Grease 14cm x 21cm loaf tin; line base with baking parchment.
2 Sift flour and cinnamon into large bowl; rub in butter.
3 Stir in sugar, egg, milk and banana. Do not overmix, the batter should be lumpy. Spoon mixture into prepared tin. Bake in hot oven about 30 minutes or until cooked when tested; cool.
4 Cut bread into 12 slices; toast lightly. Spread each with a tablespoon of cream cheese and drizzle with a teaspoon of honey, if desired.
per slice 2.6g fat; 497kJ (119 cal)
TIP Bread can be made a day ahead and is also suitable to freeze.

Every meal should begin with something delicious. Fresh rice paper rolls with prawns perhaps, or a steaming bowl of clam chowder? Whatever your preference, you'll find the perfect prelude to any main course here.

soups, starters
and dips

speedy minestrone

lamb and vegetable soup

beefy black-eyed bean and spinach soup

scotch broth

speedy minestrone

preparation time 10 minutes
cooking time 40 minutes
serves 6

30g butter
1 medium brown onion (150g), sliced thinly
1 clove garlic, crushed
2 bacon rashers (140g), chopped coarsely
1 trimmed celery stalk (100g), chopped coarsely
1 medium carrot (120g), chopped coarsely
400g can chopped tomatoes
310g can red kidney beans, rinsed, drained
3 cups (750ml) chicken stock
⅓ cup pasta spirals
¼ cup (20g) flaked parmesan
2 tablespoons finely chopped fresh flat-leaf parsley

1 Heat butter in large saucepan, add onion, garlic and bacon; stir over medium heat until onion is soft. Add celery and carrot; stir over heat 2 minutes.
2 Stir in undrained tomatoes, beans, stock and pasta. Bring to a boil, reduce heat; simmer, covered, 30 minutes. Serve topped with cheese and parsley.
per serving 7.9g fat; 752kJ (180 cal)
TIPS Minestrone can be made up to two days ahead; keep, covered, in refrigerator, or freeze for up to two months.

lamb and vegetable soup

preparation time 20 minutes
cooking time 1 hour 45 minutes
serves 4

4 lamb shanks (1kg)
2 medium carrots (240g), chopped coarsely
2 medium white onions (300g), chopped coarsely
2 cloves garlic, crushed
2 medium potatoes (400g), chopped coarsely
2 trimmed celery stalks (200g), chopped coarsely
400g can chopped tomatoes
1.5 litres (6 cups) beef or chicken stock
½ cup (125ml) tomato paste
2 medium courgettes (240g), chopped coarsely

1 Combine lamb, carrot, onion, garlic, potato, celery, undrained tomatoes, stock and paste in large saucepan. Bring to a boil, reduce heat; simmer, covered, 1 hour.
2 Add courgettes, simmer, uncovered, further 30 minutes or until lamb is tender.
3 Remove lamb from soup. When cool enough to handle, remove meat from bones, discard bones. Return meat to soup, stir until heated through.
per serving 9.2g fat; 1513kJ (362 cal)
TIP Recipe can be made three days ahead; keep, covered, in refrigerator.

beefy black-eyed bean and spinach soup

preparation time 5 minutes (plus standing time)
cooking time 1 hour 50 minutes
serves 4

1 cup (200g) black-eyed beans
1 tablespoon olive oil
1 medium brown onion (150g), chopped finely
1 clove garlic, crushed
2.5 litres beef stock (10 cups)
¼ cup (60ml) dry red wine
2 tablespoons tomato paste
500g piece beef braising steak
250g trimmed spinach, chopped coarsely

1 Place beans in medium bowl, cover with water, stand overnight, drain. Rinse under cold water; drain.
2 Heat oil in large saucepan; cook onion and garlic, stirring, until onion softens. Add stock, wine, paste and beef to pan; bring to a boil. Reduce heat; simmer, covered, 40 minutes. Uncover; simmer 30 minutes.
3 Remove beef from pan. Add beans to pan; bring to a boil. Reduce heat; simmer, uncovered, until beans are tender.
4 Meanwhile, when beef is cool enough to handle, remove and discard fat and sinew. Chop beef coarsely; return to pan with spinach; simmer, uncovered, until soup is hot.
per serving 13.9g fat; 2199kJ (526 cal)

scotch broth

preparation time 30 minutes
cooking time 1 hour 45 minutes
serves 4

2.25 litres (9 cups) water
1kg lamb neck chops
¾ cup (150g) pearl barley
1 large brown onion (200g), diced into 1cm pieces
2 medium carrots (240g), diced into 1cm pieces
1 medium leek (350g), sliced thinly
2 cups (160g) finely shredded savoy cabbage
½ cup (60g) frozen peas
2 tablespoons coarsely chopped fresh flat-leaf
  parsley

1 Place the water in large saucepan with lamb and barley; bring to a boil. Reduce heat; simmer, covered, 1 hour, skimming fat from surface occasionally. Add onion, carrot and leek; simmer, covered, about 30 minutes or until carrot is tender.
2 Remove lamb from pan. When cool enough to handle, remove and discard bones; shred lamb coarsely.
3 Return lamb to soup with cabbage and peas; cook, uncovered, about 10 minutes or until cabbage is just tender.
4 Serve bowls of hot soup sprinkled with parsley.
per serving 24.4g fat; 2274kJ (544 cal)

hearty lamb and barley soup

preparation time 40 minutes (plus refrigeration time)
cooking time 2 hours 50 minutes
serves 6

2 tablespoons olive oil
2 small carrots (140g), chopped finely
2 trimmed celery stalks (200g), chopped finely
2 cloves garlic, crushed
¾ cup (150g) pearl barley
3 sprigs fresh oregano
½ cup coarsely chopped fresh flat-leaf parsley
1 tablespoon lemon juice, approximately

LAMB STOCK
2 tablespoons olive oil
1.2kg lamb neck chops
3 medium brown onions (450g), chopped coarsely,
   skins left on
2 medium carrots (240g), chopped coarsely
2 trimmed celery stalks (200g), chopped coarsely
2 bay leaves
1 teaspoon black peppercorns
8 stalks fresh flat-leaf parsley
2 sprigs fresh thyme
4 litres (16 cups) water

1 Make lamb stock.
2 Pull meat off bones; reserve meat, discard bones.
3 Heat oil in large, clean saucepan; add carrot, celery and garlic, cook, stirring, until softened. Add barley; stir to coat in mixture.
4 Add oregano and prepared lamb stock; bring to a boil. Reduce heat, simmer, covered, about 30 minutes or until barley is tender. Blend or process one-third of the soup until smooth. Return processed soup to pan.
5 Add reserved lamb meat; simmer, covered, about 5 minutes or until meat is hot.
6 Just before serving, stir in parsley and juice to taste.

LAMB STOCK
Heat half of the oil in large saucepan. Add lamb; cook, in batches, until well browned. Heat remaining oil in same pan, add vegetables; cook, stirring, until well browned. Return lamb to pan with remaining ingredients. Bring to a boil, then reduce heat, skim surface; simmer, uncovered, 2 hours, skimming surface occasionally. Strain stock through muslin-lined strainer into large, clean bowl, reserving lamb neck chops; discard vegetables. Refrigerate stock for several hours or overnight, then discard solidified fat from stock surface.
per serving 31.4g fat; 2119kJ (507 cal)
TIP The lamb stock can be made up to two days ahead.

chiang mai noodle soup

preparation time 20 minutes
cooking time 25 minutes
serves 4

vegetable oil, for deep-frying
500g fresh egg noodles
1 large brown onion (200g), sliced thinly
2 spring onions, sliced thinly
¼ cup loosely packed fresh coriander leaves
¼ cup (75g) thai red curry paste
2 cloves garlic, crushed
¼ teaspoon ground turmeric
2 cups (500ml) water
400ml can coconut milk
500g chicken breast fillets, sliced thinly
¼ cup (60ml) fish sauce
1 tablespoon soy sauce
2 tablespoons grated palm sugar
2 teaspoons lime juice
2 tablespoons coarsely chopped fresh coriander
1 fresh long red thai chilli, sliced thinly

1 Heat oil in wok; deep-fry 100g of the noodles, in batches, until crisp. Drain on absorbent paper.
2 Using same heated oil, deep-fry brown onion, in batches, until browned lightly and crisp. Drain on absorbent paper. Combine fried noodles, fried onion, spring onion and coriander leaves in small bowl. Cool oil; remove from wok, reserve for another use.
3 Place remaining noodles in large heatproof bowl, cover with boiling water; use fork to separate noodles, drain well.
4 Cook paste, garlic and turmeric in same cleaned wok, add the water and coconut milk; bring to a boil. Reduce heat; simmer, stirring, 2 minutes. Add chicken; cook, stirring, about 5 minutes or until chicken is cooked through. Add sauces, sugar and juice; cook, stirring, until sugar dissolves. Stir in chopped coriander.
5 Divide drained noodles among serving bowls; spoon chicken curry mixture into each bowl, top with fried noodle mixture. Sprinkle chilli slices over each bowl.
per serving 34.7g fat; 3394kJ (812 cal)
TIP Substitute brown sugar for the palm sugar, if desired.

asian chicken broth

preparation time 30 minutes
cooking time 20 minutes
serves 4

1 litre (4 cups) water
1 litre (4 cups) chicken stock
10cm stick (20g) fresh lemongrass, chopped finely
4cm piece fresh ginger (20g), sliced thinly
2 fresh small red thai chillies, sliced thinly
2 tablespoons soy sauce
1 tablespoon lime juice
1 tablespoon fish sauce
500g chinese cabbage, chopped coarsely
3 spring onions, sliced thinly
⅓ cup loosely packed fresh coriander leaves

CHICKEN DUMPLINGS
400g minced chicken
1 tablespoon finely chopped fresh coriander
2 cloves garlic, crushed

1 Combine the water, stock, lemongrass, ginger, chilli and soy sauce in large saucepan; bring to a boil. Reduce heat; simmer, uncovered, about 5 minutes.
2 Meanwhile, make chicken dumplings.
3 Add chicken dumplings to simmering broth; simmer, covered, about 5 minutes or until dumplings are cooked through.
4 Add juice, fish sauce, chinese cabbage and onion to broth; cook, uncovered, until chinese cabbage just wilts. Stir in coriander just before serving.

CHICKEN DUMPLINGS
Combine ingredients in medium bowl. Using hands, roll level tablespoons of the mixture into balls.
per serving 9.5g fat; 849kJ (203 cal)

beef noodle soup

Preparation time 40 minutes
cooking time 2 hours 30 minutes
serves 6

1.5kg beef bones
2 medium brown onions (300g), chopped coarsely
2 medium carrots (240g), chopped coarsely
4 trimmed celery stalks (400g), chopped coarsely
2 cinnamon sticks
4 star anise
6 cardamom pods, bruised
10 black peppercorns
2 tablespoons fish sauce
6 cloves
12cm piece fresh ginger (60g), sliced thinly
6 cloves garlic, sliced thinly
500g piece braising steak
4 litres (16 cups) water
2 tablespoons soy sauce
200g bean thread vermicelli
½ cup loosely packed fresh vietnamese mint leaves
4 fresh small red thai chillies, sliced thinly
1 medium brown onion (150g), sliced thinly, extra
½ cup loosely packed fresh coriander leaves
1¼ cups (100g) beansprouts

1 Preheat oven to hot (220°C/200°C fan-assisted).
2 Combine beef bones, onion, carrot and celery in large baking dish; roast, uncovered, about 45 minutes or until browned all over. Drain excess fat from dish.
3 Combine beef mixture, cinnamon, star anise, cardamom, peppercorns, fish sauce, cloves, ginger, garlic, braising steak and the water in large saucepan. Bring to a boil; simmer, uncovered, 1½ hours, skimming occasionally. Strain through muslin-lined strainer into large bowl. Reserve broth and beef; discard bones and spices. When beef is cool enough to handle, shred finely; return with soy sauce and broth to cleaned pan.
4 Just before serving, place vermicelli in large heatproof bowl; cover with boiling water, stand 3 minutes, drain.
5 Divide vermicelli among serving bowls; top with broth and beef mixture, mint, chilli, extra onion and coriander. Serve with sprouts.
per serving 4.7g fat; 1074kJ (257 cal)
TIP Chicken can be substituted for the beef, if preferred.

combination wonton soup

preparation time 30 minutes
cooking time 10 minutes
serves 4

150g minced chicken
1 spring onion, sliced thinly
2 tablespoons light soy sauce
16 wonton wrappers
24 medium uncooked prawns (600g)
1.5 litres (6 cups) chicken stock
100g chinese barbecued pork, sliced thinly
100g fresh shiitake mushrooms, sliced thinly
150g baby pak choy, chopped coarsely
4 spring onions, sliced thinly, extra

1 Combine chicken, onion and half of the sauce in small bowl.
2 Place a heaped teaspoon of chicken mixture in centre of each wonton wrapper. Brush edges with a little water; pinch edges together to seal.
3 Shell and devein prawns, leaving tails intact.
4 Bring stock to a boil in large saucepan. Add wontons; cook, uncovered, about 3 minutes or until wontons are just cooked through.
5 Add prawns, remaining sauce, pork and mushroom; cook, uncovered, until prawns just change in colour. Add pak choy and extra onion; cook, uncovered, until pak choy just wilts.
per serving 9.1g fat; 1155kJ (276 cal)
TIP Uncooked wontons are suitable to freeze for up to 3 months. You don't have to defrost them; just remove from freezer and simmer in stock until cooked through.

hot and sour soup

preparation time 10 minutes
cooking time 15 minutes
serves 4

2cm piece galangal (10g), chopped coarsely
2 tablespoons coarsely chopped lemongrass
2 spring onions, chopped coarsely
3 kaffir lime leaves
1 clove garlic, quartered
2 teaspoons groundnut oil
1½ cups (375ml) vegetable stock
1.125 litres (4½ cups) water
2cm piece fresh ginger, sliced thinly
2 fresh red thai chillies, sliced thinly
425g can straw mushrooms, drained, rinsed
2 teaspoons sugar
⅓ cup (80ml) lime juice
2 teaspoons soy sauce
2 tablespoons coarsely chopped fresh coriander

1 Blend or process galangal, lemongrass, onion, lime leaves and garlic until chopped finely.
2 Heat oil in large saucepan; cook galangal mixture, stirring, until mixture is fragrant.
3 Add stock and the water; bring to a boil. Reduce heat; simmer, covered, 10 minutes. Strain stock mixture into large bowl; discard solids. Return stock mixture to same pan.
4 Return stock mixture to heat. Add ginger, chilli, mushrooms, sugar, juice and sauce; cook, uncovered, until hot. Just before serving, stir coriander through soup. Accompany soup with jasmine rice and wilted Asian greens, if desired.
per serving 3g fat; 251kJ (60 cal)
TIPS For a milder flavour, remove seeds from the chillies.
The broth can be made ahead and frozen until required.

chicken, chorizo and okra gumbo

preparation time 30 minutes
cooking time 2 hours 45 minutes
serves 8

3 litres (12 cups) water
1.5kg whole chicken
2 medium carrots (240g), chopped coarsely
2 trimmed celery stalks (200g), chopped coarsely
1 medium brown onion (150g), chopped coarsely
12 black peppercorns
1 bay leaf
60g butter
1 small brown onion (80g), chopped finely, extra
2 cloves garlic, crushed
1 medium red pepper (200g), chopped finely
2 teaspoons dried oregano
1 teaspoon sweet paprika
¼ teaspoon cayenne pepper
¼ teaspoon ground clove
¼ cup (35g) plain flour
¼ cup (70g) tomato paste
400g can crushed tomatoes
100g fresh okra, halved diagonally
1 cup (200g) long grain rice
1 chorizo sausage (170g), sliced thinly

1 Place the water in large saucepan with chicken, carrot, celery, onion, peppercorns and bay leaf; bring to a boil. Reduce heat; simmer, covered, 1½ hours.
2 Remove chicken from pan. Strain broth through muslin-lined sieve or colander into large heatproof bowl; discard solids. When chicken is cool enough to handle, remove and discard skin and bones; shred meat coarsely.
3 Melt butter in large saucepan; cook extra onion and garlic, stirring, until onion softens. Add pepper, herbs and spices; cook, stirring, until mixture is fragrant. Add flour and paste; cook, stirring, 1 minute. Gradually stir in reserved broth and undrained tomatoes; bring to a boil, stirring. Stir in okra and rice, reduce heat; simmer, uncovered, about 15 minutes, stirring occasionally, or until rice is tender.
4 Meanwhile, heat large oiled frying pan; cook sausage until browned; drain. Add sausage with chicken to gumbo; stir over medium heat until hot.
per serving 26.8g fat; 2011kJ (481 cal)

chicken and risoni soup with herbed meatballs

preparation time 30 minutes (plus refrigeration time)
cooking time 2 hours 45 minutes
serves 4

2.5 litres (10 cups) water
1.6kg whole chicken
1 large tomato (220g), halved
2 trimmed celery stalks (200g), halved
1 medium brown onion (150g), halved
2 fresh flat-leaf parsley stalks
5 black peppercorns
300g minced chicken
½ cup (50g) packaged breadcrumbs
2 tablespoons finely chopped fresh flat-leaf parsley
2 tablespoons finely grated parmesan cheese
1 egg
1 tablespoon olive oil
¾ cup (165g) risoni
2 tablespoons lemon juice
⅓ cup coarsely chopped fresh flat-leaf parsley

1 Place the water in large saucepan with whole chicken, tomato, celery, onion, parsley stalks and peppercorns; bring to a boil. Reduce heat; simmer, covered, 2 hours.
2 Remove chicken from pan. Strain broth through muslin-lined sieve or colander into large heatproof bowl; discard solids. Allow broth to cool, cover; refrigerate overnight. When chicken is cool enough to handle, remove and discard skin and bones. Shred meat coarsely; cover, refrigerate overnight.
3 Combine mince, breadcrumbs, finely chopped parsley, cheese and egg in medium bowl; roll rounded teaspoons of mixture into balls. Heat oil in medium saucepan; cook meatballs, in batches, until browned all over.
4 Skim and discard fat from surface of broth. Return broth to large saucepan; bring to a boil. Reduce heat; simmer, uncovered, 20 minutes. Add meatballs and pasta; simmer, uncovered, about 10 minutes or until meatballs are cooked through and pasta is just tender. Add 2 cups of the reserved chicken (keep remaining chicken for another use), juice and coarsely chopped parsley to pan; stir soup over medium heat until hot.
per serving 45.8g fat; 3536kJ (846 cal)

chicken, lemon and rice soup

preparation time 10 minutes
cooking time 35 minutes
serves 4

2 teaspoons olive oil
1 small brown onion (80g), chopped finely
1 litre (4 cups) chicken stock
400g chicken breast fillets, chopped coarsely
⅓ cup (65g) white short-grain rice
2 eggs
⅓ cup (80ml) lemon juice
2 tablespoons finely chopped fresh flat-leaf parsley

1 Heat oil in large saucepan; cook onion, stirring, until soft. Add stock, chicken and rice; bring to a boil. Reduce heat; simmer, covered, about 20 minutes or until rice is tender.
2 Whisk eggs and juice in small bowl until smooth. Gradually whisk ½ cup hot soup into egg mixture then stir warmed egg mixture into soup.
3 Serve bowls of soup sprinkled with parsley.
per serving 8.4g fat; 1099kJ (263 cal)

cream of chicken soup with cheese and herb scone

preparation time 35 minutes
cooking time 2 hours 30 minutes
serves 4

2 litres (8 cups) water
1 litre (4 cups) chicken stock
1.8kg whole chicken
1 medium carrot (120g), chopped coarsely
1 trimmed celery stalk (100g), chopped coarsely
1 medium brown onion (150g), chopped coarsely
40g butter
⅓ cup (50g) plain flour
2 tablespoons lemon juice
½ cup (125ml) cream
¼ cup finely chopped fresh flat-leaf parsley

1 Place the water and stock in large saucepan with chicken, carrot, celery and onion; bring to a boil. Reduce heat; simmer, covered, 1½ hours. Remove chicken from pan; simmer broth, covered, 30 minutes.
2 Strain broth through muslin-lined sieve or colander into large heatproof bowl; discard solids. Remove and discard chicken skin and bones; shred meat coarsely.
3 Preheat oven to 200°C/180°C fan-assisted. Make herb and cheese scone.
4 Melt butter in large saucepan, add flour; cook, stirring, until mixture thickens and bubbles. Gradually stir in broth and juice; bring to a boil, stirring. Add cream, reduce heat; simmer, uncovered, about 25 minutes, stirring occasionally. Add chicken; stir soup over medium heat until hot.
5 Serve bowls of soup sprinkled with parsley, accompanied with scone.
per serving 58.6g fat; 3327kJ (796 cal)

CHEESE AND HERB SCONE
Heat 2 teaspoons olive oil in small saucepan; cook 1 finely chopped small brown onion, stirring, until soft. Cool 5 minutes. Place 1⅓ cups self-raising flour in medium bowl; add onion, ⅓ cup coarsely grated cheddar cheese and 2 tablespoons each finely chopped fresh flat-leaf parsley and chives. Stir in as much of ⅔ cup milk required to mix to a soft, sticky dough. Turn dough onto floured surface; knead until smooth. Divide dough into four pieces, shape into rounds. Place on oiled oven tray; sprinkle with 2 tablespoons coarsely grated parmesan cheese. Bake for about 20 minutes or until browned lightly.
serves 4 per serving 8.9g fat; 1133kJ (271 cal)

cauliflower soup with cheese and bacon toasts

preparation time 20 minutes
cooking time 20 minutes
serves 6

1 tablespoon olive oil
1 medium brown onion (150g), chopped coarsely
2 cloves garlic, crushed
1 large potato (300g), chopped finely
1kg cauliflower, trimmed, chopped coarsely
3 cups (750ml) salt-reduced chicken stock
3 cups (750ml) water
2 tablespoons coarsely chopped fresh chives

CHEESE AND BACON TOASTS
3 thin bacon rashers (210g), quartered
1 thin crusty Italian-style bread
1 tablespoon wholegrain mustard
120g thinly sliced cheddar cheese

1 Heat oil in large saucepan; cook onion and garlic over low heat, stirring, until soft, but not coloured.
2 Add potato, cauliflower, stock and the water, bring to a boil. Reduce heat; simmer, covered, about 15 minutes or until vegetables are very soft.
3 Meanwhile, make cheese and bacon toasts.
4 Blend or process cauliflower mixture, in batches, until smooth; return to pan, stir gently over low heat until hot.
5 Divide soup among serving bowls; sprinkle with chives. Serve with cheese and bacon toasts.

CHEESE AND BACON TOASTS
Place bacon on foil-covered oven tray; grill until browned and crisp. Slice bread diagonally into 12 thin slices. Grill bread slices until browned lightly; spread with mustard, top with cheese. Grill until cheese melts; top with bacon.
per serving 14.3g fat; 1404kJ (336 cal)
TIPS The soup can be made two days ahead. The bacon toasts are best made close to serving.

potato and leek soup

preparation time 30 minutes (plus cooling time)
cooking time 55 minutes
serves 4

2 medium potatoes (400g), chopped coarsely
2 medium carrots (240g), chopped coarsely
1 large brown onion (200g), chopped coarsely
1 medium tomato (150g), chopped coarsely
1 trimmed celery stalk (100g), chopped coarsely
1.5 litres (6 cups) water
1 tablespoon olive oil
50g butter
4 medium potatoes (800g), chopped coarsely, extra
1 large leek (500g), sliced thickly
300ml cream
2 tablespoons finely chopped fresh chives
1 tablespoon finely chopped fresh basil
1 tablespoon finely chopped fresh dill

1 Combine potato, carrot, onion, tomato, celery and the water in large saucepan; bring to a boil. Reduce heat; simmer, uncovered, 20 minutes. Strain broth through muslin-lined sieve or colander into large heatproof bowl; discard solids.
2 Heat oil and butter in same cleaned pan; cook extra potato and leek, covered, 15 minutes, stirring occasionally. Add broth; bring to a boil. Reduce heat; simmer, covered, 15 minutes. Cool 15 minutes.
3 Meanwhile, make croûtons.
4 Blend or process soup, in batches, until smooth. Return soup to same cleaned pan, add cream; stir over medium heat until hot.
5 Serve bowls of soup sprinkled with combined herbs then topped with croûtons.
per serving 47.9g fat; 2822kJ (675 cal)

CROÛTONS
Cut and discard crusts from 2 slices wholemeal bread; cut bread into 1cm pieces. Melt 50g butter in medium frying pan. Add bread; cook, stirring, until croûtons are browned lightly. Drain on absorbent paper.
serves 4 per serving 10.7g fat); 535kJ (128 cal)

bouillabaisse

preparation time 45 minutes
cooking time 40 minutes
serves 6

6 uncooked small crabs (2kg)
2 tablespoons olive oil
4 cloves garlic, crushed
2 medium white onions (300g), chopped finely
¼ cup (70g) tomato paste
¾ cup (180ml) dry white wine
2 x 400g cans chopped tomatoes
½ teaspoon ground turmeric
2 bay leaves
2 teaspoons white sugar
1½ cups (375ml) water
1kg firm white fish fillets, chopped coarsely
500g uncooked large prawns
250g scallops
250g calamari (squid) rings

1 Remove and discard triangular flap from underside of each crab. Remove and discard the whitish gills, liver and brain matter; rinse crab well. Crack nippers slightly; chop down centre of each crab to separate body into 2 pieces.

2 Heat oil in large saucepan, add garlic and onion; cook, stirring, until onion is soft.

3 Stir in tomato paste, wine, undrained tomatoes, turmeric, bay leaves, sugar and the water. Bring to a boil, reduce heat, simmer, uncovered, 10 minutes.

4 Add crab and fish to tomato mixture, bring to a boil; reduce heat, simmer, covered, 5 minutes.

5 Meanwhile, shell and devein prawns leaving tails intact. Remove vein from scallops.

6 Stir prawns, scallops and calamari into tomato mixture, bring to a boil, reduce heat, simmer until prawns just change colour.

7 Serve bouillabaisse immediately, with fresh crusty bread, if desired.

per serving 11.7g fat; 1843kJ (441 cal)

TIPS Recipe must be made and served immediately, as seafood does not reheat successfully.

You will need to use an extra large saucepan to fit in all the seafood.

clam chowder

preparation time 25 minutes
cooking time 35 minutes
serves 6

1.5kg clams
1 cup (250ml) dry white wine
40g butter
1 medium brown onion (150g), chopped finely
2 bacon rashers (140g), chopped finely
2 trimmed sticks celery (150g), chopped finely
¼ cup (35g) plain flour
3 cups (750ml) fish stock
400g can tomatoes
3 cups (750ml) water
1 tablespoon fresh thyme leaves
2 bay leaves
4 large potatoes (1.2kg), cut into 1cm cubes
¼ cup chopped fresh flat-leaf parsley

1 Rinse clams under cold running water. Combine with wine in medium saucepan having a tight-fitting lid; bring to a boil. Steam, covered tightly, about 5 minutes or until clams have opened; discard any that do not open. Strain clams over large bowl; reserve ¼ cup (60ml) of the cooking liquid.

2 Melt butter in large saucepan; cook onion, stirring, until soft. Add bacon and celery; cook, stirring, 5 minutes. Add flour; cook, stirring, until mixture thickens and bubbles. Gradually stir in stock. Add undrained crushed tomatoes and the water; cook, stirring, until mixture boils and thickens. Stir in thyme, bay leaves and potato; cook, covered, stirring occasionally, about 15 minutes or until potato is tender.

3 Just before serving, stir clams, reserved cooking liquid and parsley into chowder.

per serving 8g fat; 1190kJ (285 cal)

TIPS Dry red wine can be substituted for the white wine but be certain that whatever wine you use you would also consider drinking.

Cubed raw potato won't discolour if submerged in cold water until required.

prawn laksa

preparation time 45 minutes
cooking time 1 hour 20 minutes
serves 6

2kg medium uncooked prawns
100g fresh coriander
4 trimmed sticks celery (300g), chopped coarsely
2 medium carrots (240g), chopped coarsely
2 large brown onions (400g), chopped coarsely
3 litres (12 cups) water
2 stalks lemongrass, chopped coarsely
3 fresh red thai chillies, seeded, chopped coarsely
1 teaspoon ground turmeric
¼ cup chopped fresh vietnamese mint
2 cloves garlic, crushed
1 tablespoon grated fresh ginger
1 tablespoon grated fresh galangal
1 tablespoon shrimp paste
1 tablespoon ground coriander
2 tablespoons groundnut oil
400ml coconut milk
100g fresh singapore egg noodles
200g fried tofu
100g beansprouts
4 spring onions, sliced thinly

1 Shell and devein prawns; reserve prawns and shells. Cut roots from coriander. Wash leaves and roots well; reserve both but keep separate.
2 Combine reserved shells and coriander roots, celery, carrot and half of the brown onion with the water in large saucepan; bring to a boil. Reduce heat; simmer, uncovered, 30 minutes. Strain through muslin-lined strainer into large bowl. Reserve broth; discard shells and vegetables.
3 Blend or process remaining brown onion with ¼ cup loosely packed reserved coriander leaves, lemongrass, chilli, turmeric, mint, garlic, ginger, galangal, shrimp paste, ground coriander and half of the oil until mixture forms a paste.
4 Heat remaining oil in large saucepan; cook laksa paste, stirring, about 2 minutes or until fragrant. Stir in reserved broth and coconut milk; bring to a boil. Reduce heat; simmer, uncovered, 20 minutes. Stir in reserved prawns; cook, stirring, about 10 minutes or until prawns change in colour.
5 Meanwhile, place noodles in large heatproof bowl; cover with boiling water. Stand 3 minutes; drain. Cut tofu into 2cm cubes.
6 Just before serving, stir noodles, tofu, 2 tablespoons finely chopped reserved coriander leaves, beansprouts and spring onion into laksa.
per serving 25.6g fat; 1926kJ (461 cal)
TIP If you don't have access to packaged fried tofu, use fresh – cut tofu into cubes, then shallow-fry it in vegetable oil until browned lightly; drain on absorbent paper.

creamy crab and tomato bisque

preparation time 1 hour
cooking time 1 hour 20 minutes
serves 4

4 uncooked medium crabs (1.3kg)
60g butter
1 medium brown onion (150g), chopped coarsely
1 medium carrot (120g), chopped coarsely
1 medium leek (350g), chopped coarsely
2 cloves garlic, crushed
1 tablespoon tomato paste
2 tablespoons brandy
1 cup (250ml) dry white wine
1.25 litres (5 cups) fish stock
1 bay leaf
2 sprigs fresh thyme
2 medium tomatoes (300g), chopped finely
20g butter, extra
1 tablespoon plain flour
½ cup (125ml) cream

1 Slide knife under top of crab shells at back, lever off and discard. Discard gills; rinse crabs under cold water. Using cleaver or heavy knife, chop each body into quarters.
2 Melt butter in large saucepan; cook onion, carrot, leek and garlic, stirring, until vegetables soften. Add crab, in batches; cook, stirring, until changed in colour.
3 Add paste to pan; cook, stirring, 2 minutes. Return crab to pan with brandy; stir over heat about 2 minutes or until alcohol evaporates.
4 Add wine, stock, bay leaf, thyme and tomato; bring to a boil. Reduce heat; simmer, uncovered, 45 minutes.
5 Meanwhile, using back of teaspoon, work extra butter into flour in small bowl.
6 Strain soup through muslin-lined sieve or colander into large heatproof bowl; extract as much meat as possible from crab, add to soup. Discard shells, claws and other solids.
7 Return soup to same cleaned pan; bring to a boil. Stir in flour mixture and cream; stir until soup boils and thickens slightly.
per serving 32g fat; 2152kJ (515 cal)

mediterranean fish soup

preparation time 25 minutes
cooking time 30 minutes
serves 4

1 tablespoon olive oil
1 clove garlic, crushed
1 small leek (200g), halved, sliced thinly
1 small red pepper (150g), cut into 1cm pieces
1 small red onion (100g), halved, sliced thinly
1 trimmed celery stalk (100g), cut into 1cm pieces
1 small carrot (70g), cut into 1cm pieces
½ teaspoon finely grated orange rind
¼ teaspoon dried chilli flakes
2 tablespoons tomato paste
2 cups (500ml) water
3 cups (750ml) fish stock
¼ cup (60ml) dry white wine
2 large plum tomatoes (180g), chopped coarsely
200g uncooked small king prawns
200g skinless white fish fillet, chopped coarsely
200g skinless ocean trout fillet, chopped coarsely
¼ teaspoon finely chopped fresh thyme
1 tablespoon finely chopped fresh dill

1 Heat oil in large saucepan; cook garlic, leek, pepper, onion, celery, carrot, rind and chilli, stirring, until vegetables soften.
2 Add paste, the water, stock, wine and tomato; bring to a boil. Reduce heat; simmer, uncovered, 20 minutes.
3 Meanwhile, shell and devein prawns; chop meat coarsely. Add prawn meat, fish, thyme and half the dill to soup; simmer, uncovered, about 3 minutes or until prawn and fish are cooked.
4 Serve bowls of soup sprinkled with remaining dill.
per serving 7.7g fat; 978kJ (234 cal)

french onion soup with gruyère croûtons

preparation time 30 minutes
cooking time 50 minutes
serves 4

50g butter
4 large brown onions (800g), halved, sliced thinly
¾ cup (180ml) dry white wine
3 cups (750ml) water
1 litre (4 cups) beef stock
1 bay leaf
1 tablespoon plain flour
1 teaspoon fresh thyme leaves

1 Melt butter in large saucepan; cook onion, stirring, about 30 minutes or until caramelised.
2 Meanwhile, bring wine to a boil in large saucepan; boil 1 minute. Stir in the water, stock and bay leaf; return to a boil. Remove from heat.
3 Stir flour into onion mixture; cook, stirring, 2 minutes. Gradually add hot broth mixture, stirring, until mixture boils and thickens slightly. Reduce heat; simmer, uncovered, stirring occasionally, 20 minutes. Discard bay leaf; stir in thyme.
4 Meanwhile, make gruyère croûtons.
5 Serve bowls of soup topped with croûtons.
per serving 1.1g fat; 96kJ (23 cal)

GRUYÈRE CROÛTONS
Preheat grill. Finely grate 60g gruyère cheese. Cut 1 small french bread stick into 1.5cm slices; discard end pieces. Toast slices one side then turn and sprinkle equal amounts of cheese over untoasted sides; grill croûtons until cheese browns lightly.
serves 4 per serving 5.7g fat; 623kJ (149 cal)

gazpacho

preparation time 25 minutes (plus refrigeration time)
serves 4

3 cups (750ml) tomato juice
8 medium plum tomatoes (600g), chopped coarsely
1 medium red onion (170g), chopped coarsely
1 clove garlic, quartered
½ cucumber (130g), chopped coarsely
1 small red pepper (150g), chopped coarsely
2 teaspoons Tabasco
4 spring onions, chopped finely
¼ cucumber (65g), chopped finely
½ small yellow pepper (75g), chopped finely
2 teaspoons olive oil
1 tablespoon vodka
2 tablespoons finely chopped fresh coriander

1 Blend or process juice, tomato, red onion, garlic, coarsely chopped cucumber and red pepper, in batches, until pureed. Strain through sieve into large bowl, cover; refrigerate 3 hours.
2 Combine remaining ingredients in small bowl.
3 Serves bowls of soup topped with vegetable salsa.
per serving 2.6g fat; 560kJ (134 cal)

chilled yogurt, cucumber and mint soup

preparation time 10 minutes (plus refrigeration time)
serves 4

3 medium cucumbers (510g), peeled and coarsely
  grated
1 clove garlic, quartered
1 tablespoon lemon juice
1 tablespoon coarsely chopped fresh mint
500g greek-style plain yogurt

1 Place cucumber in sieve over bowl, cover; refrigerate 3 hours or overnight. Reserve cucumber liquid in bowl. Squeeze excess liquid from cucumber.
2 Blend or process cucumber, garlic, juice and mint until mixture is smooth; transfer to large bowl. Stir yogurt into cucumber mixture then add reserved cucumber liquid, a little at a time, stirring, until soup is of desired consistency.
3 Serve bowls of soup topped with extra mint and toasted turkish bread, if desired.
4 Serve bowls of soup sprinkled with remaining dill.
per serving 8.9g fat; 715kJ (171 cal)

smoked seafood and mixed vegetable antipasti

preparation time 35 minutes
serves 4

⅓ cup (80g) soured cream
2 teaspoons raspberry vinegar
1 tablespoon coarsely chopped fresh chives
1 clove garlic, crushed
1 large yellow courgette (150g)
1 tablespoon raspberry vinegar, extra
¼ cup (60ml) extra virgin olive oil
⅓ cup (45g) slivered almonds, toasted
1 cup (150g) drained semi-dried tomatoes
1 large avocado (320g)
1 tablespoon lemon juice
300g hot-smoked ocean trout portions
200g sliced smoked salmon
16 drained caperberries (80g)
1 large lemon (180g), cut into wedges
170g packet roasted garlic bagel crisps

1 Combine soured cream, vinegar, chives and garlic in small bowl, cover; refrigerate until required.
2 Meanwhile, using vegetable peeler, slice courgette lengthways into ribbons; combine courgette in small bowl with extra vinegar and 2 tablespoons of the oil.
3 Combine almonds, tomatoes and remaining oil in small serving bowl.
4 Slice avocado thickly into small bowl; sprinkle with lemon juice.
5 Flake trout into bite-sized pieces.
6 Arrange courgette mixture, nut mixture, avocado, trout, salmon and caperberries on large platter; serve with soured cream dip, lemon wedges and bagel crisps.
per serving 54.8g fat; 3624kJ (867 cal)
TIP Hot-smoked trout is available at most supermarkets, sold in filleted portions of various sizes; we used two 150g portions for this recipe.

duck in crisp wonton cups

rice paper rolls with prawns

prawn and crab wontons

chinese dumplings with soy vinegar sauce

duck in crisp wonton cups

preparation time 20 minutes
cooking time 20 minutes (plus cooling time)
makes 24

6 uncooked small crabs (2kg)
24 wonton wrappers
cooking-oil spray
1 chinese barbecued duck
1 tablespoon hoisin sauce
1 tablespoon soy sauce
2 tablespoons coarsely chopped fresh coriander
2 spring onions, chopped coarsely
2 spring onions, extra, sliced thinly

1 Preheat oven to moderate (180°C/160°C fan-assisted). Grease 24 mini (1½-tablespoons/30ml) muffin trays.
2 Press wonton wrappers into pans to form a cup shape; spray lightly with oil. Bake in moderate oven about 8 minutes until browned lightly. Remove from muffin trays, cool.
3 Remove flesh and skin from duck, slice thinly, discard fat. Place duck on oven tray, cover with foil, heat in moderate oven for 10 minutes.
4 Combine duck with sauces, coriander and chopped onions in medium bowl.
5 Spoon duck mixture into wonton cups, top with sliced onions.
per cup 13.5g fat; 732kJ (175 cal)
TIPS Wonton cups can be made a day ahead; store in an airtight container.
The filling can be prepared several hours ahead. Assemble close to serving.
Chinese barbecued duck is available from Asian grocery stores.

rice paper rolls with prawns

preparation time 30 minutes
cooking time 5 minutes (plus cooling time)
makes 12

500g cooked medium prawns
1 cup (80g) finely shredded chinese cabbage
½ cup (120g) coarsely grated carrot
2 tablespoons coarsely chopped fresh mint
2 tablespoons coarsely chopped fresh coriander
12 small round dried rice paper wrappers (16cm)

DIPPING SAUCE
⅓ cup (75g) caster sugar
¼ cup (60ml) white vinegar
¼ cup (60ml) water
2 teaspoons fish sauce
2 fresh red thai chillies, sliced thinly
1 tablespoon chopped fresh coriander

1 Shell and devein prawns. Combine cabbage, carrot, mint and coriander in large bowl.
2 Place one sheet of rice paper in medium bowl of warm water until just softened. Remove from water; place on board. Place a tablespoon of the cabbage mixture in centre of rice paper; top with two prawns. Roll wrapper to enclose filling, folding in the ends. Repeat with remaining ingredients. Cover rolls with a damp towel to prevent rice paper from drying out.
3 Serve rolls with dipping sauce.

DIPPING SAUCE
Place sugar, vinegar and the water in small saucepan; stir over medium heat until sugar dissolves. Bring to a boil; remove from heat. Stir in sauce and chilli; cool. Stir in coriander.
per roll 0.3g fat; 220kJ (53 cal)
TIP This recipe can be made 3 hours ahead.

prawn and crab wontons

preparation time 1 hour
cooking time 30 minutes
makes 80

500g uncooked prawns
500g crab meat
1 teaspoon grated fresh ginger
1 clove garlic, crushed
4 spring onions, chopped finely
1 tablespoon soy sauce
1 tablespoon sweet chilli sauce
80 wonton wrappers
1 tablespoon cornflour
1 tablespoon water
groundnut oil, for deep-frying

DIPPING SAUCE
2 teaspoons soy sauce
2 tablespoons sweet chilli sauce
1 teaspoon dry sherry
1 spring onion, chopped finely

1 Shell and devein prawns; chop prawn meat finely.
2 Combine prawn meat in medium bowl with crab, ginger, garlic, onion and sauces.
3 Place a heaped teaspoon of prawn mixture in centre of each wrapper. Brush edges with blended cornflour and water; pinch edges together to seal. Repeat with remaining wrappers, prawn mixture and cornflour paste.
4 Heat oil in large deep-frying pan; deep-fry wontons, in batches, until browned and cooked through. Drain on absorbent paper; serve with dipping sauce.

DIPPING SAUCE
Combine ingredients in small bowl.
per wonton 0.9g fat; 348kJ (83 cal)
TIP Canned crabmeat can be used; drain well. Frozen wontons can be deep-fried as is; freeze eight-wonton portions so you can take only as many as you need.

chinese dumplings with soy vinegar sauce

preparation time 40 minutes (plus refrigeration time)
cooking time 15 minutes
makes 40

300g minced pork
2 tablespoons kecap manis
1 teaspoon sugar
1 tablespoon sake
1 egg, beaten lightly
2 teaspoons sesame oil
3 cups (240g) finely shredded chinese cabbage
4 spring onions, sliced thinly
40 dumpling or gow gee wrappers
1 tablespoon vegetable oil

SOY VINEGAR SAUCE
½ cup (125ml) light soy sauce
¼ cup (60ml) red vinegar
2 tablespoons white vinegar
2 tablespoons sweet chilli sauce

1 Combine pork, kecap manis, sugar, sake, egg, sesame oil, cabbage and onion in medium bowl; refrigerate 1 hour.
2 Place a heaped teaspoon of the pork mixture in centre of one wrapper; brush wrapper along one side of pork mixture with a little water. Pleat damp side of wrapper only; pinch both sides of wrapper together to seal. Repeat with remaining pork mixture and wrappers.
3 Cover base of large frying pan with water; bring to a boil. Add dumplings, in batches; reduce heat. Simmer, covered, 3 minutes; using slotted spoon, remove dumplings from pan. Drain and dry pan.
4 Heat vegetable oil in same pan; cook dumplings, in batches, unpleated side and base only, until golden brown.
5 Serve hot with soy vinegar sauce.

SOY VINEGAR SAUCE
Combine ingredients in small bowl.
per dumpling 1.4g fat; 139kJ (31 cal)
per tablespoon sauce 0.1g fat; 35kJ (8 cal)
TIP Dumpling filling can be prepared 4 hours ahead and refrigerated, covered.

deep-fried prawn balls

preparation time 25 minutes (plus refrigeration time)
cooking time 10 minutes
serves 4

1kg cooked large prawns
5 spring onions, chopped finely
2 cloves garlic, crushed
4 fresh small red thai chillies, chopped finely
1cm piece fresh ginger (5g), grated finely
1 tablespoon cornflour
2 teaspoons fish sauce
¼ cup coarsely chopped fresh coriander
¼ cup (25g) packaged breadcrumbs
½ cup (35g) stale breadcrumbs
vegetable oil, for deep-frying
⅓ cup (80ml) sweet chilli sauce
1 lime (60g), cut into wedges

1 Shell and devein prawns; cut in half. Blend or process prawns, pulsing, until chopped coarsely. Place in large bowl with onion, garlic, chilli, ginger, cornflour, fish sauce and coriander; mix well.
2 Using hands, roll rounded tablespoons of prawn mixture into balls. Roll prawn balls in combined breadcrumbs; place, in single layer, on cling-film-lined tray. Cover, refrigerate 30 minutes.
3 Heat oil in wok; deep-fry prawn balls, in batches, until browned lightly. Serve with sweet chilli sauce and lime wedges.
per serving 10.7g fat; 1175kJ (281 cal)
TIPS Dip your fingers in cold water when shaping the prawn balls to prevent the mixture from sticking to them. Placing prawn balls on a clin-film-lined tray and refrigerating them for at least half an hour before frying will firm them and help ensure they don't fall apart during cooking.
Prawn balls can be shaped a day ahead and kept, covered, in the refrigerator.

lamb kofta with spiced yogurt

preparation time 30 minutes (plus refrigeration time)
cooking time 20 minutes
makes 40

¼ cup (40g) bulghur wheat
500g minced lamb
1 egg, beaten lightly
1 medium brown onion (150g), chopped finely
¼ cup (40g) pine nuts, chopped finely
2 tablespoons finely chopped fresh mint
2 tablespoons finely chopped fresh flat-leaf parsley
vegetable oil, for shallow-frying

SPICED YOGURT
2 small red thai chillies, chopped finely
1 tablespoon finely chopped fresh mint
1 tablespoon finely chopped fresh flat-leaf parsley
1 tablespoon finely chopped fresh coriander
1 clove garlic, crushed
½ teaspoon ground cumin
500g thick plain yogurt

1 Cover bulghur wheat with cold water in small bowl; stand 10 minutes. Drain; pat dry with absorbent paper to remove as much water as possible.
2 Using one hand, combine bulghur wheat in large bowl with lamb, egg, onion, nuts and herbs. Roll rounded teaspoons of the lamb mixture into kofta balls. Place on tray, cover; refrigerate 30 minutes.
3 Heat oil in large frying pan; shallow-fry kofta, in batches, until browned all over and cooked through. Drain on absorbent paper.
4 Meanwhile, combine ingredients for spiced yogurt in medium bowl.
5 Serve kofta hot with spiced yogurt.
per kofta 3.1g fat; 180kJ (43 cal)
TIP Uncooked kofta and spiced yogurt can be made a day ahead. Cover separately; refrigerate until required.

spring rolls

preparation time 1 hour (plus standing time)
cooking time 25 minutes (plus cooling time)
makes 40

1 medium red pepper (200g)
1 medium carrot (120g)
1 tablespoon groundnut oil
700g chicken breast fillets
1 tablespoon grated fresh ginger
2 cloves garlic, crushed
4 spring onions, chopped finely
100g bean thread noodles
1 tablespoon chopped fresh vietnamese mint
500g pak choy, shredded finely
¼ cup (60ml) sweet chilli sauce
1 tablespoon soy sauce
40 spring roll wrappers
groundnut oil, for deep-frying

DIPPING SAUCE
⅓ cup (80ml) sweet chilli sauce
2 tablespoons lime juice
3 spring onions, chopped finely

1 Halve pepper; discard seeds and membrane. Slice pepper and carrot into paper-thin strips.
2 Heat half of the oil in medium saucepan; cook chicken, in batches, until browned and cooked through. Cool 10 minutes; shred finely.
3 Heat remaining oil in same pan; cook ginger, garlic and onion, stirring, about 2 minutes or until onion is soft.
4 Meanwhile, place noodles in large heatproof bowl. Cover with boiling water; stand 2 minutes. Drain noodles; chop coarsely.
5 Combine pepper, carrot, chicken, onion mixture and noodles in large bowl with mint, pak choy and sauces.
6 Place a rounded tablespoon of the mixture across edge of one wrapper; roll to enclose filling, folding in ends. Place on tray, seam-side down. Repeat with remaining mixture and wrappers, placing on tray in single layer.
7 Just before serving, heat oil in wok or large deep-frying pan; deep-fry spring rolls, in batches, until golden brown and cooked through. Drain on absorbent paper; serve with dipping sauce.

DIPPING SAUCE
Combine ingredients in small bowl.
per roll 4.3g fat; 307kJ (73 cal)
TIPS Freeze spring rolls, in single layer, between sheets of cling film. This makes it easier to remove and defrost small quantities at a time.
Frozen spring rolls can be deep-fried.
Use finely chopped fresh red thai chillies mixed with brown vinegar to make an alternative dipping sauce with more kick.

prawn and avocado cocktail

preparation time 15 minutes
serves 2

400g large cooked prawns
lettuce leaves
½ medium avocado (125g), chopped coarsely
lemon wedges
4 chives, trimmed

COCKTAIL SAUCE
½ cup (150g) mayonnaise
2½ tablespoons tomato sauce
¼ teaspoon worcestershire sauce
¼ teaspoon chilli sauce

1 Pinch heads from bodies of prawns. Peel shell away from centre of body, leaving tails intact.
2 Remove back veins by pulling veins from head end towards tail end.
3 Line serving dishes with lettuce leaves. Place prawns and avocado into dishes; spoon cocktail sauce over prawn mixture. Serve with lemon wedges and chives.

COCKTAIL SAUCE
Combine mayonnaise and sauces in small bowl; mix well.
per serving 40g fat; 2348kJ (561 cal)
TIP The cocktail sauce can be prepared 2 days ahead and refrigerated, covered.

chilli scallops

preparation time 15 minutes
cooking time 15 minutes
serves 4

1 tablespoon groundnut oil
32 small scallops
4 cloves garlic, sliced thinly
50g fresh ginger, peeled, sliced thinly
2 fresh red thai chillies, deseeded, chopped finely
3 spring onions, sliced thinly
⅓ cup (80ml) sweet chilli sauce
1 teaspoon fish sauce
2 teaspoons brown sugar
½ cup (125ml) chicken stock
¼ cup loosely packed, chopped fresh coriander

1 Heat half of the oil in wok or large frying pan; stir-fry scallops, in batches, until just changed in colour.
2 Heat remaining oil in wok; stir-fry garlic, ginger, chilli and onion until onion is soft.
3 Stir in combined sauces, sugar and stock; bring to a boil. Return scallops to wok; stir until heated through. Serve scallops sprinkled with coriander.
per serving 6.1g fat; 585kJ (140 cal)
TIPS We used scallops with roe attached but the roe can be left out if you prefer. If you buy scallops in their shell, don't discard the shell, they are great (washed and dried) to use as serving 'dishes'.
You will need a piece of ginger about 5cm long for this recipe.

baked mussels

preparation time 20 minutes (plus marinating time)
cooking time 10 minutes
serves 4

24 small black mussels (500g)
¾ cup (180ml) water
¼ cup (60ml) olive oil
1 clove garlic, crushed
2 tablespoons finely chopped fresh parsley
½ cup (35g) stale breadcrumbs
1 medium tomato (130g), deseeded, chopped finely

1 Scrub mussels, remove beards. Heat the water in large saucepan. Cook mussels in the water, covered, over high heat about 3 minutes or until shells open. Drain; discard liquid.
2 Loosen mussels; remove from shell. Discard half of each shell; reserve half. Combine mussel meat, oil, garlic, parsley and breadcrumbs in small bowl; mix well. Cover; refrigerate 30 minutes.
3 Place one mussel in each half shell; place on oven tray. Combine tomato with remaining breadcrumb mixture; spoon over mussels. Bake in hot oven about 5 minutes or until breadcrumbs are browned lightly.
per serving 14.5g fat; 738kJ (176 cal)

deep-fried whitebait

preparation time 10 minutes
cooking time 15 minutes
serves 4

1 cup (150g) plain flour
¼ cup chopped fresh coriander
1 teaspoon garlic salt
500g whitebait
vegetable oil, for deep-frying
SPICED YOGURT DIP
10g butter
½ teaspoon ground cumin
½ teaspoon ground coriander
¾ cup (200g) yogurt
½ cucumber (130g), chopped finely
1 clove garlic, crushed
1 tablespoon lemon juice

1 Combine flour, coriander and garlic salt in large bowl. Add whitebait, in batches; toss until coated in mixture.
2 Heat oil in medium saucepan. Deep-fry whitebait, in batches, until browned and cooked through; drain on absorbent paper.
3 Serve with spiced yogurt dip.

SPICED YOGURT DIP
Heat butter in small saucepan. Cook cumin and coriander, stirring, until fragrant; cool. Combine yogurt, cucumber, garlic and juice in small bowl; stir in spice mixture.
per serving 28.6g fat; 2083kJ (498 cal)

prosciutto-wrapped haloumi

preparation time 5 minutes
cooking time 8 minutes
serves 4

120g piece haloumi cheese
8 slices prosciutto
2 tablespoons chopped fresh flat-leaf parsley
1 teaspoon lemon juice

1 Cut cheese into eight fingers. Wrap each finger in a slice of prosciutto, securing ends with toothpicks. Cook on heated oiled grill plate (or grill or barbecue) about 8 minutes or until browned all over.
2 Serve sprinkled with parsley and juice.
per serving 7.6g fat; 531kJ (127 cal)

vodka-cured gravlax

preparation time 10 minutes (plus refrigeration time)
makes 24

1 tablespoon sea salt
1 teaspoon ground black pepper
1 tablespoon white sugar
1 tablespoon vodka
300g salmon fillet, skin on
24 melba toasts

SOURED CREAM SAUCE
⅓ cup (80g) soured cream
2 teaspoons drained baby capers, rinsed
2 teaspoons lemon juice
2 teaspoons finely chopped drained gherkins
½ small red onion (50g), chopped finely

1 Combine salt, pepper, sugar and vodka in small bowl.
2 Remove bones from fish; place fish, skin-side down, on piece of cling film. Spread vodka mixture over flesh side of fish; enclose securely in cling film. Refrigerate overnight, turning parcel several times.
3 Combine ingredients for soured cream sauce in a small bowl.
4 Slice fish thinly; spread sauce on toasts, top with fish.
per piece 2.4g fat; 230kJ (55 cal)

empanadas

preparation time 40 minutes
cooking time 45 minutes
serves 8

400g can tomatoes
1 tablespoon olive oil
1 medium brown onion (150g), chopped finely
1 clove garlic, crushed
1 teaspoon freshly ground black pepper
½ teaspoon ground cinnamon
½ teaspoon ground cloves
600g minced beef
¼ cup (40g) raisins, chopped coarsely
1 tablespoon cider vinegar
¼ cup (35g) toasted slivered almonds
2 x 800g packets ready-rolled flaky pastry
1 egg, beaten lightly
vegetable oil, for deep-frying

1 Blend or process undrained tomatoes until smooth; reserve.
2 Heat olive oil in large heavy-based saucepan; cook onion, garlic and spices, stirring, until onion is soft. Add beef; cook, stirring, until changed in colour. Drain away excess fat from pan. Stir in reserved tomato, raisins and vinegar; simmer, uncovered, about 20 minutes or until filling mixture thickens. Stir in nuts.
3 Cut 9cm rounds from each pastry sheet (you will get 32 rounds). Place a level tablespoon of the beef mixture in centre of each round; brush edge lightly with egg. Fold pastry over to enclose filling; press edges together to seal.
4 Heat vegetable oil in large deep-frying pan. Deep-fry empanadas until crisp and browned lightly; drain on absorbent paper. Serve immediately with a dollop of soured cream or bottled salsa, if desired.
per serving 26g fat; 1664kJ (398 cal)
TIP For a lower-fat version, empanadas can be baked, uncovered, in a preheated hot oven about 25 minutes or until browned.

potato pizzettas

preparation time 15 minutes (plus standing time)
cooking time 30 minutes
makes 24

1.2kg old potatoes
80g butter, melted
⅓ cup (80g) bottled pesto
2 small cooked chicken breast fillets, sliced thinly
6 button mushrooms (60g), sliced thinly
1 cup (100g) grated mozzarella cheese
½ cup (40g) grated parmesan cheese
¼ cup small fresh basil leaves

1 Preheat oven to hot. Peel potatoes; grate coarsely into medium bowl. Cover potato with cold water; stand 5 minutes. Drain potato well; squeeze to remove excess moisture. Place potato onto clean tea towel; pat dry.
2 Combine potato and butter in cleaned medium bowl; mix well.
3 Using 6.5cm round cutter as a guide, firmly press 1 level tablespoon of the potato mixture into cutter on baking parchment-covered oven tray. Repeat with remaining mixture, allowing about 2cm between discs.
4 Bake in hot oven 20 minutes. Turn; bake further 5 minutes or until discs are browned lightly.
5 Spread potato discs with pesto; top with chicken and mushroom. Sprinkle with combined cheeses; bake in hot oven about 5 minutes or until cheese melts.
6 Top with basil leaves to serve.
per pizzetta 6.9g fat; 488kJ (116 cal)
TIP Bases can be made 3 hours ahead. Topping is best added just before serving.

baked mushrooms

preparation time 15 minutes
cooking time 10 minutes
makes 4

9 medium flat mushrooms (900g)
60g butter, melted
3 bacon rashers (210g), chopped finely
4 spring onions, chopped finely
2 cloves garlic, crushed
2 tablespoons stale breadcrumbs
1 tablespoon cream
2 teaspoons fresh oregano, chopped coarsely
2 tablespoons grated parmesan cheese

1 Gently remove stalks from eight of the mushrooms. Finely chop stalks and remaining mushroom.
2 Brush mushroom caps all over with butter. Place on lightly greased oven trays.
3 Cook bacon and onion in small non-stick frying pan until bacon is crisp. Add chopped mushroom, garlic and breadcrumbs. Cook, stirring, until well combined. Remove from heat; stir in cream, oregano and cheese. Divide bacon mixture between mushroom caps.
4 Bake in moderately hot oven about 10 minutes or until hot.
per serving 17.4g fat; 990kJ (236 cal)
TIP Cap mushrooms can be substituted for the flat mushrooms. Cook 5 minutes; cool slightly before serving.

potato terrine

preparation time 1 hour
cooking time 2 hours and 15 minutes
(plus standing time)
serves 8

2 large potatoes (600g)
1 medium red pepper (200g)
1 large aubergine (500g)
cooking-oil spray
1 large leek (500g)
⅓ cup (80ml) olive oil
3 cloves garlic, crushed
2 tablespoons finely chopped fresh thyme
1 teaspoon ground black pepper
10 slices (150g) prosciutto
250g mozzarella, sliced
1 cup loosely packed fresh basil leaves

SAFFRON VINAIGRETTE
⅓ cup (80ml) olive oil
2 tablespoons lemon juice
pinch saffron threads

1 Preheat oven to moderate (180°C/160°C fan-assisted). Grease 14cm x 21cm loaf tin.
2 Cut potatoes into 2mm slices. Add potato to large saucepan of boiling water; cook about 4 minutes or until potatoes are just beginning to soften; drain.
3 Quarter pepper, remove seeds and membranes. Roast under preheated grill, skin-side up, until skin blisters and blackens. Cover pepper pieces in plastic or paper 5 minutes; peel away skin.
4 Cut aubergine lengthways into 5mm slices; spray slices, both sides, with oil. Cook aubergine, in large frying pan, until browned both sides; drain on absorbent paper.
5 Cut white part of leek into 7cm lengths; cut lengths in half. Boil, steam or microwave leek until tender. Drain, rinse under cold water; drain.
6 Combine oil, garlic, thyme and pepper in small bowl.
7 Cover base and long sides of pan with prosciutto, allowing prosciutto to overhang edges. Place half of the potato, overlapping, over base, brush with herb oil mixture; top with half of the cheese, brush with herb oil mixture. Layer pepper, aubergine, basil and leek, brushing each layer with herb oil mixture. Top leek layer with remaining cheese then remaining potato, brushing with herb oil mixture between layers; press down firmly. Cover terrine with prosciutto slices.
8 Cover terrine with foil, place on oven tray. Cook 1 hour; uncover, cook further 40 minutes. Remove from oven, pour off any liquid. Cool 5 minutes; cover top of terrine with cling film, weight with two large heavy cans for 1 hour.
9 Combine ingredients for saffron vinaigrette in jar; shake well. Serve with sliced terrine.
per serving 27.1g fat; 1476kJ (353 cal)
TIPS Terrine is best made a day ahead; keep, covered, in refrigerator.

grilled feta

preparation time 5 minutes
cooking time 5 minutes
serves 6

300g feta cheese, halved
2 tablespoons olive oil
1 teaspoon chilli flakes
1 teaspoon dried oregano leaves

1 Place feta on large sheet of foil; place on oven tray.
2 Combine oil, chilli and oregano in small bowl; drizzle over cheese. Grill about 5 minutes or until browned lightly. Stand 5 minutes; slice thickly.
per serving 17.8g fat; 817kJ (195 cal)

ciabatta with olive and herb paste

preparation time 20 minutes
cooking time 10 minutes (plus cooling time)
serves 6

1 loaf ciabatta
2 tablespoons olive oil

OLIVE AND HERB PASTE
250g pitted green olives
½ small white onion (40g), chopped
freshly ground black pepper
1 clove garlic, crushed
¼ cup (60ml) extra virgin olive oil
1 tablespoon coarsely chopped fresh
    flat-leaf parsley
1 teaspoon coarsely chopped fresh oregano
1 teaspoon lime juice

1 Preheat oven to moderately hot.
2 Cut bread into 1cm slices. Place bread in single layer on oven trays; brush with oil. Bake in moderately hot oven about 5 minutes on each side or until browned lightly and crisp; cool.
3 Serve ciabatta with olive and herb paste.

OLIVE AND HERB PASTE
Process olives, onion, pepper and garlic into a coarse paste. Gradually add oil while motor is operating; stir in herbs and juice.
per serving 19.4g fat; 1845kJ (441 cal)
TIP Recipe can be prepared a day ahead and refrigerated, covered separately.

chile con queso

butterbean dip with pitta crisps

turkish spinach dip

guacamole

chile con queso

preparation time 10 minutes
cooking time 10 minutes
makes 2 cups

2 teaspoons vegetable oil
½ small green pepper (75g), chopped finely
½ small brown onion (40g), chopped finely
1 tablespoon drained bottled jalapeño chillies, chopped finely
1 clove garlic, crushed
½ x 400g can undrained chopped peeled tomatoes
250g packet cream cheese, softened

1 Heat oil in medium saucepan; cook pepper, onion, chilli and garlic, stirring, until onion softens. Add tomato; cook, stirring, 2 minutes.
2 Remove from heat. Add cheese; whisk until cheese melts and dip is smooth.
3 Serve warm with crispy corn chips, if desired.
per tablespoon 3.9g fat; 171kJ (41 cal)

butterbean dip with pitta crisps

preparation time 10 minutes
cooking time 8 minutes
makes 1 cup

1 clove garlic, crushed
½ cup lightly packed fresh flat-leaf parsley leaves
400g can butterbeans, rinsed, drained
1 teaspoon ground cumin
⅓ cup (80ml) olive oil
6 pitta bread (400g), cut into sixths

1 Preheat oven to moderately hot (200°C/180°C fan-assisted).
2 Blend or process garlic, parsley, beans and cumin until combined. With motor operating, add the oil in a thin stream until mixture is smooth.
3 Place pitta pieces on lightly greased oven trays; bake in moderately hot oven 8 minutes or until browned lightly.
4 Serve dip with pitta crisps.
per tablespoon 5.5g fat; 493kJ (118 cal)
TIPS This recipe can be made a day ahead.
Store pitta crisps in an airtight container.

turkish spinach dip

preparation time 10 minutes
cooking time 10 minutes (plus cooling and
*   refrigeration time)*
makes 2 cups

1 tablespoon olive oil
1 small brown onion (80g), chopped finely
1 clove garlic, crushed
1 teaspoon ground cumin
½ teaspoon curry powder
¼ teaspoon ground turmeric
100g trimmed spinach leaves, shredded finely
500g thick Greek-style plain yogurt

1 Heat oil in medium frying pan; cook onion and garlic, stirring, until onion softens. Add spices; cook, stirring, until fragrant. Add spinach; cook, stirring, until spinach wilts. Transfer mixture to serving bowl; cool.
2 Stir yogurt through mixture, cover; refrigerate 1 hour.
3 Serve cold with toasted turkish bread, if desired.
per tablespoon 2.2g fat; 142kJ (34 cal)
TIPS You need a bunch of spinach weighing 300g for this recipe.
Dip can be made a day ahead. Cover; refrigerate until required.

guacamole

preparation time 10 minutes
makes 2½ cups

3 medium avocados (750g), peeled, chopped
½ small red onion (50g), chopped finely
1 large plum tomato (90g), deseeded, chopped
    finely
1 tablespoon lime juice
¼ cup coarsely chopped fresh coriander

1 Mash avocado in medium bowl; stir in remaining ingredients.
per tablespoon 4g fat; 159kJ (38 cal)

spicy tomato salsa

preparation time 10 minutes
cooking time 15 minutes (plus cooling time)
serves 4

4 medium tomatoes (760g), chopped finely
2 cloves garlic, crushed
1 small brown onion (80g), sliced thinly
1 teaspoon cajun seasoning
2 teaspoons no-added-salt tomato paste

1 Combine tomato with remaining ingredients in small saucepan.
2 Cook, stirring, about 15 minutes or until onion is soft and sauce has thickened; cool.
per serving 0.4g fat; 153kJ (37 cal)
TIP Salsa can be made 3 days ahead and refrigerated, covered.

baba ghanoush

preparation time 10 minutes (plus refrigeration time)
cooking time 35 minutes (plus cooling time)
serves 4

2 small aubergines (460g)
⅓ cup (95g) low-fat plain yogurt
1 tablespoon lemon juice
2 cloves garlic, crushed
1 teaspoon tahini
1 teaspoon ground cumin
½ teaspoon sesame oil
2 tablespoons chopped fresh coriander

1 Preheat oven to moderately hot.
2 Halve aubergines lengthways; place on oven tray. Bake in moderately hot oven about 35 minutes or until tender.
3 Cool; remove and discard skin. Blend or process aubergine with remaining ingredients until smooth. Cover; refrigerate 30 minutes.
per serving 2.2g fat; 218kJ (52 cal)
TIP Baba ghanoush can be made 3 days ahead and refrigerated, covered.

quick beetroot dip

preparation time 10 minutes
serves 4

225g can sliced beetroot, drained well
¼ cup (70g) low-fat plain yogurt
1 teaspoon ground coriander
2 teaspoons ground cumin

1 Blend or process ingredients until well combined.
per serving 0.6g fat; 137kJ (33 cal)
TIP Dip can be made 3 days ahead and refrigerated, covered.

seafood

Hot and spicy fish cutlets,
prawn and fennel risotto, and
smoked salmon and caviar salad
are all perfect to serve as a
casual lunch party or a lovely
light evening meal.

salt and pepper prawns

mustard-seed chilli prawns

crystal prawns

prawns with chilli, coriander and lime butter

salt and pepper prawns

preparation time 20 minutes
cooking time 5 minutes
serves 6

18 uncooked large prawns (1.2kg)
2 teaspoons sea salt
¼ teaspoon five-spice powder
½ teaspoon freshly ground black pepper

1 Shell and devein prawns leaving tails intact. Thread each of the prawns onto a skewer lengthways.
2 Combine remaining ingredients in small bowl.
3 Cook prawn skewers on heated oiled barbecue (or grill or grill plate) over high heat until browned both sides and just cooked through. Sprinkle with half the salt mixture during cooking.
4 Serve prawn skewers with remaining salt mixture.
per serving 0.5g fat; 309kJ (74 cal)
TIPS You will need to soak the skewers in water for up to one hour before using to prevent them scorching and splintering.
Prawns can be peeled and skewered up to six hours ahead. Barbecue just before serving.

mustard-seed chilli prawns

preparation time 20 minutes
cooking time 7 minutes
serves 4

1kg uncooked large prawns
¼ teaspoon ground turmeric
2 fresh small red thai chillies, chopped finely
2 tablespoons vegetable oil
2 teaspoons black mustard seeds
2 cloves garlic, crushed
2 tablespoons finely chopped fresh coriander

1 Shell and devein prawns, leaving tails intact. Cut along backs of prawns, taking care not to cut all the way through; flatten prawns slightly.
2 Rub turmeric and chilli into prawns in medium bowl.
3 Heat oil in large frying pan; cook mustard seeds and garlic, stirring, until seeds start to pop. Add prawns; cook, stirring, until prawns just change colour. Stir in coriander.
per serving 10g fat; 811kJ (194 cal)
TIP If you like hot dishes, don't seed the chillies before chopping, as removing the seeds and membranes lessens the heat level.

crystal prawns

preparation time 15 minutes (plus standing time)
cooking time 10 minutes
serves 8

1 medium carrot (120g)
1 trimmed stick celery (75g)
2 spring onions
24 uncooked king prawns (1kg)
1 tablespoon dry sherry
1 tablespoon lemon juice
1 tablespoon groundnut oil
¼ cup (60ml) soy sauce

1 Cut carrot, celery and onions into long thin strips. Place vegetables in small bowl of iced water. Stand about 10 minutes or until they begin to curl; drain.
2 Shell prawns, leaving tails intact. To butterfly prawns, cut halfway through the back of each prawn. Remove vein; press flat.
3 Place prawns, sherry and juice in small bowl. Toss until combined; stand 10 minutes.
4 Heat oil in wok or large frying pan; cook prawns, in batches, until changed in colour. Serve prawns with vegetables and soy sauce.

per serving 2.7g fat; 364kJ (87 cal)
TIPS Prawns can be butterflied 3 hours ahead. They are best when cooked just before serving. Crystal prawns are so called because they look transparent if they are cooked properly.

prawns with chilli, coriander and lime butter

preparation time 10 minutes
cooking time 5 minutes
serves 4

16 large uncooked king prawns
100g butter, melted
2 fresh red thai chillies, seeded, chopped finely
2 tablespoons lime juice
2 tablespoons finely chopped fresh coriander
50g mixed salad leaves

1 Shell prawns, leaving tails intact. To butterfly prawns, cut halfway through the back of each prawn. Remove veins; press flat.
2 Cook prawns on heated oiled grill pan or in heavy-based frying pan until changed in colour and just cooked through.
3 Meanwhile, combine butter, chilli, juice and coriander in medium bowl.
4 Serve salad leaves with prawns, drizzled with hot butter mixture.

per serving 21.2g fat; 1153kJ (275 cal)

garlic prawns and pak choy with herbed rice

preparation time 20 minutes
cooking time 15 minutes
serves 6

36 medium uncooked prawns (1kg)
6 cloves garlic, crushed
2 teaspoons finely chopped fresh coriander
3 fresh red thai chillies, deseeded, chopped finely
⅓ cup (80ml) lime juice
1 teaspoon sugar
1 tablespoon groundnut oil
1kg baby pak choy, quartered lengthways
6 spring onions, sliced thinly
1 tablespoon sweet chilli sauce

HERBED RICE
2 cups (400g) jasmine rice
2 tablespoons chopped fresh coriander
1 tablespoon chopped fresh mint
1 tablespoon chopped fresh flat-leaf parsley
1 teaspoon finely grated lime rind

1 Shell and devein prawns, leaving tails intact.
2 Combine prawns in large bowl with garlic, coriander, chilli, juice and sugar.
3 Heat half of the oil in wok or large non-stick frying pan; stir-fry prawns, in batches, until just changed in colour.
4 Heat remaining oil with pan liquids in wok; stir-fry pak choy, onion and sauce, in batches, until just tender. Combine pak choy mixture and prawns in wok; stir-fry until hot. Serve prawns on herbed rice.

HERBED RICE
Cook rice, uncovered, in large saucepan of boiling water until tender; drain. Return rice to pan; combine with remaining ingredients.
per serving 4.5g fat; 1602kJ (383 cal)

prawn and fennel risotto

preparation time 30 minutes
cooking time 45 minutes
serves 4

600g uncooked small prawns
1 litre (4 cups) chicken or fish stock
2 cups (500ml) water
pinch of saffron threads
¼ cup (60ml) olive oil
1 small fennel bulb (200g), sliced thinly
1 medium brown onion (150g), chopped finely
2 cloves garlic, crushed
2 cups (400g) arborio rice
½ cup (125ml) dry white wine
¼ teaspoon dried chilli flakes, optional
30g butter
2 tablespoons chopped fennel tips

1 Shell and devein prawns leaving tails intact. Place stock, the water and saffron in large saucepan. Bring to a boil, reduce to a simmer; cover.
2 Meanwhile, heat oil in large saucepan; add fennel, cook, stirring, until fennel is tender. Remove fennel from pan with slotted spoon. Add prawns to same pan; cook, stirring, until prawns just change colour. Remove from pan with slotted spoon. Add onion and garlic to same pan; cook, stirring, until onion is soft.
3 Add rice to pan, stir about 1 minute or until rice is well coated. Add wine to pan, bring to a boil; simmer, uncovered, until most of the wine has evaporated.
4 Stir in ½ cup (125ml) hot stock; cook, stirring, over medium heat until liquid is absorbed. Continue adding stock in ½-cup batches, stirring until absorbed after each addition. Cooking time should be about 25 minutes, or until rice is just tender.
5 Return fennel to pan with prawns and chilli; cook, stirring, until hot. Stir in butter and fennel tips.
per serving 21.9g fat; 2738kJ (655 cal)
TIPS This recipe is best made just before serving. When preparing the fennel, reserve the tips to use in the recipe.

tuna mornay

preparation time 10 minutes
cooking time 25 minutes
serves 2

30g butter
1 medium brown onion (150g), chopped finely
1 trimmed stick celery (75g), chopped finely
1 tablespoon plain flour
¾ cup (180ml) milk
½ cup (125ml) cream
⅓ cup (40g) grated cheddar cheese
130g can corn kernels, drained
185g can tuna, drained
½ cup (35g) stale breadcrumbs
¼ cup (30g) grated cheddar cheese, extra

1 Melt butter in medium saucepan; cook onion and celery, stirring constantly over medium heat, about 3 minutes or until onion is soft. Add flour; cook, stirring constantly, 1 minute or until mixture is bubbly. Gradually stir in combined milk and cream; stir constantly over high heat until mixture boils and thickens.
2 Remove from heat; add cheese, corn and tuna. Stir gently until cheese is melted. Spoon mixture into two 2-cup (500ml) ovenproof dishes. Sprinkle with combined breadcrumbs and extra cheese. Bake in moderate oven about 15 minutes or until heated through completely.
per serving 58.2g fat; 3480kJ (831 cal)
TIP Tuna mornay can be prepared up to the stage of baking a day ahead and refrigerated, covered. Milk can be used instead of the cream; we added cream for a little extra richness.

grilled oysters

preparation time 5 minutes
cooking time 10 minutes
serves 4

40g butter, melted
⅓ cup (45g) finely chopped shaved ham
2 tablespoons finely chopped fresh flat-leaf parsley
12 fresh oysters in half-shells

1 Combine butter, ham and parsley in small bowl. Divide mixture evenly over oysters. Place oysters in single layer on oven tray; cook under hot grill about 10 minutes or until ham is crisp.
per serving 9.7g fat; 496kJ (119 cal)

char-grilled swordfish with roasted mediterranean vegetables

preparation time 20 minutes
cooking time 25 minutes
serves 4

1 medium red pepper (200g), sliced thickly
1 medium yellow pepper (200g), sliced thickly
1 medium aubergine (300g), sliced thickly
2 large courgettes (300g), sliced thickly
½ cup (125ml) olive oil
250g cherry tomatoes
¼ cup (60ml) balsamic vinegar
1 clove garlic, crushed
2 teaspoons sugar
4 x 220g swordfish steaks
¼ cup coarsely chopped fresh basil

1 Preheat oven to hot.
2 Combine peppers, aubergine and courgettes with 2 tablespoons of the oil in large baking dish; roast, uncovered, in hot oven 15 minutes. Add tomatoes; roast, uncovered, about 5 minutes or until vegetables are just tender.
3 Meanwhile, combine remaining oil, vinegar, garlic and sugar in screw-top jar; shake well. Brush a third of the dressing over fish; cook fish, in batches, on heated oiled grill plate (or grill or barbecue) until browned both sides and cooked as desired.
4 Combine vegetables in large bowl with basil and remaining dressing; toss gently to combine. Divide vegetables among serving plates; top with fish.
per serving 35.2g fat; 2300kJ (549 cal)

pan-fried fish with tartare sauce

preparation time 15 minutes
cooking time 5 minutes
serves 2

2 boneless white fish fillets (320g)
coarse cooking salt
1 tablespoon plain flour
2 tablespoons vegetable oil

TARTARE SAUCE
½ cup (150g) mayonnaise
1 large gherkin, chopped finely
1 tablespoon drained capers, chopped finely
2 teaspoons finely chopped fresh flat-leaf parsley
½ teaspoon lemon juice
¼ teaspoon worcestershire sauce

1 Remove skin by placing fillets, skin-side down, onto chopping board. Dip fingers into a little salt; this makes it easier for you to hold the fish. Hold skin at tail firmly. Using sharp knife held at an angle, use a 'press and push' action to carefully separate flesh from skin.
2 Dust fillets lightly with flour. Heat oil in large shallow heavy-based frying pan; cook fish, skinned-side up, over medium heat until fillets are browned lightly underneath. Use fish slice to turn fillets over carefully; continue to cook over medium heat until fish flakes easily when tested using fork.
3 Serve immediately with tartare sauce and pan-fried potato slices, if desired.

TARTARE SAUCE
Place mayonnaise in small bowl. Add other ingredients; mix well.
per serving 46.1g fat; 2671kJ (638 cal)
TIP Sauce can be prepared 2 days ahead and refrigerated, covered.

baked fish cutlets

preparation time 10 minutes
cooking time 25 minutes
serves 2

2 x 200g white fish cutlets
30g butter
2 tablespoons lime or lemon juice
black pepper
2 spring onions, sliced thinly
1 tablespoon thinly sliced fresh ginger
1 red thai chilli, sliced thinly
2 teaspoons finely grated lime rind

1 Place each piece of fish on large piece of foil; pleat ends of foil to partially enclose fish.
2 Divide butter between fish parcels; top fish with juice and pepper.
3 Pleat foil firmly over fish to enclose. Place fish parcels on oven tray; bake in moderate oven about 20 minutes or until fish flakes easily when tested using fork.
4 Meanwhile, combine onion, ginger, chilli and rind in small bowl.
5 Top fish with onion mixture. Close fish parcels; bake 5 minutes.
per serving 16.7g fat; 1334kJ (319 cal)

steamed coconut fish

preparation time 10 minutes
cooking time 25 minutes
serves 4

2 cups chopped fresh coriander
2 fresh red thai chillies, chopped coarsely
2 cloves garlic, quartered
20g fresh ginger, peeled, chopped coarsely
1 tablespoon cumin seeds
⅔ cup (50g) shredded coconut
1 tablespoon groundnut oil
4 medium whole snapper (1.8kg)

1 Blend or process coriander, chilli, garlic, ginger and seeds until chopped finely.
2 Combine coriander mixture with coconut and oil in small bowl; mix well.
3 Score each fish three times both sides; place fish on large sheet of foil. Press coconut mixture onto fish; fold foil over to enclose fish.
4 Place fish in large bamboo steamer; steam fish, covered, over wok or large saucepan of simmering water about 25 minutes or until cooked through. Serve with lemon wedges, steamed long-grain white rice and stir-fried pak choy, if desired.
per serving 15.8g fat; 1237kJ (296 cal)
TIPS Prick the foil with a skewer to allow steam to escape.
Score fish by making shallow cuts in a criss-cross pattern, to allow the herbs and spices to penetrate the flesh and enhance flavour.
We used snapper in this recipe, but you can use any whole white-fleshed fish, such as bream or flathead. You will need a piece of ginger about 3cm long for this recipe.

smoked salmon and caviar salad

preparation time 15 minutes
cooking time 30 minutes
serves 4

1.2kg salad potatoes
1 tablespoon olive oil
500g fresh asparagus, trimmed
400g finely sliced smoked salmon
100g mixed salad leaves
25g red caviar

AVOCADO PUREE
1 small avocado (200g)
¼ cup (60g) soured cream
1 tablespoon chopped fresh dill
2 tablespoons lime juice

1 Boil, steam or microwave potatoes until just tender; drain. Preheat oven to very hot.
2 Halve potatoes; place, cut-side up, on lightly oiled oven tray. Drizzle with oil; bake, uncovered, in very hot oven about 15 minutes or until crisp and brown, turning occasionally.
3 Boil, steam or microwave asparagus until just tender; drain, cut spears in half crossways.
4 Cut salmon slices into strips.
5 Divide avocado puree among serving plates; top with potato, salad leaves, asparagus, salmon and caviar.

AVOCADO PUREE
Halve avocado; discard stone. Scoop out flesh and chop coarsely; blend or process avocado with remaining ingredients until smooth.
per serving 24.2g fat; 2216kJ (530 cal)

fish with garlic and chilli

preparation time 5 minutes
cooking time 8 minutes
serves 4

¼ cup (60ml) olive oil
4 white fish fillets with skin on (800g)
1 clove garlic, crushed
1½ tablespoons sherry vinegar
1 teaspoon dried chilli flakes
2 tablespoons chopped fresh flat-leaf parsley

1 Heat 1 tablespoon of the oil in large non-stick frying pan. Cook fish, flesh-side down, until well browned. Turn fish; cook until browned and just cooked through.
2 Meanwhile, place remaining oil, garlic, vinegar, chilli and parsley in small saucepan; stir over low heat until just warm – do not overheat. Spoon oil mixture over fish. Serve with lemon wedges and steamed courgettes and beans, if desired.
per serving 18.2g fat; 1376kJ (329 cal)
TIP Sherry vinegar is available in some supermarkets; if unavailable, substitute red or white wine vinegar.

baked fish with ginger and soy

preparation time 10 minutes
cooking time 25 minutes
serves 4

800g whole snapper
1 tablespoon finely grated fresh ginger
1 tablespoon groundnut oil
¼ cup (60ml) chinese rice wine
¼ cup (60ml) light soy sauce
½ teaspoon sugar
3 spring onions, sliced thinly

1 Cut three deep slits in each side of fish; place in oiled baking dish.
2 Rub ginger into fish; drizzle with combined oil, wine, soy sauce and sugar. Bake, covered, in moderately hot oven about 25 minutes or until fish is cooked. Serve fish drizzled with some of the pan juices and topped with onion.
per serving 5.8g fat; 590kJ (141 cal)

hot and spicy fish cutlets

preparation time 10 minutes (plus marinating time)
cooking time 10 minutes
serves 4

4 white fish cutlets (1kg)
MARINADE
1 tablespoon paprika
2 teaspoons ground ginger
1 teaspoon curry powder
¼ teaspoon chilli powder
¼ cup (60ml) brown vinegar
¼ cup (60ml) tomato paste
1 cup (250ml) dry white wine
2 cloves garlic, crushed

1 Combine fish and marinade in large bowl. Cover; refrigerate 3 hours or overnight.
2 Remove fish from marinade; discard marinade.
3 Cook fish on heated oiled grill plate (or grill or barbecue) until cooked as desired; remove from pan. Serve with couscous and lemon, if desired.

MARINADE
Combine ingredients in medium bowl; mix well.
per serving 5g fat; 1134kJ (271 cal)
TIP Fish is best marinated a day ahead and refrigerated, covered; uncooked marinated fish is suitable to freeze.

herbed and spiced sashimi with ginger cabbage salad

preparation time 45 minutes
cooking time 5 minutes
serves 4

2 tablespoons sesame seeds
1 tablespoon black sesame seeds
2 teaspoons coriander seeds
1 teaspoon sea salt
½ teaspoon cracked black pepper
2 tablespoons finely chopped fresh chives
300g piece sashimi tuna
300g piece sashimi salmon
200g green beans, trimmed, sliced thinly
6 trimmed radishes (90g)
3 cups (240g) finely shredded chinese cabbage
6 spring onions, sliced thinly
1½ cups (150g) mung bean sprouts
1 cup firmly packed fresh coriander leaves

GINGER DRESSING
2cm piece fresh ginger (10g), grated
2 tablespoons rice vinegar
2 tablespoons vegetable oil
2 teaspoons sesame oil
1 tablespoon mirin
1 tablespoon soy sauce

1 Dry-fry seeds in heated small frying pan, stirring, until fragrant; cool. Using mortar and pestle, crush seeds; combine in large bowl with salt, pepper and chives.
2 Cut each piece of fish into three 5cm-thick pieces. Roll each piece in seed mixture; wrap tightly, individually, in cling film. Refrigerate until required.
3 Make ginger dressing.
4 Boil, steam or microwave beans until just tender; drain. Rinse beans under cold water; drain. Slice radishes thinly; cut slices into matchstick-sized pieces.
5 Combine beans and radish in large bowl with cabbage, onion, sprouts, coriander leaves and half of the dressing.
6 Unwrap fish; slice thinly. Divide fish and salad among serving plates; drizzle fish with remaining dressing.

GINGER DRESSING
Combine ingredients in screw-top jar; shake well.
per serving 26.8g fat; 1731kJ (414 cal)
TIPS Salmon and tuna sold as sashimi have to meet stringent guidelines regarding their handling and treatment after leaving the water; however, it is best to seek local advice from knowledgeable authorities before eating any raw fish.
You need half a medium chinese cabbage for this recipe.

mussels with beer

preparation time 20 minutes
cooking time 15 minutes
serves 4

1kg large mussels
1 tablespoon olive oil
2 cloves garlic, crushed
1 large red onion (300g), sliced thinly
2 fresh long red chillies, sliced thinly
1½ cups (375ml) beer
2 tablespoons sweet chilli sauce
1 cup coarsely chopped fresh flat-leaf parsley

GARLIC BREAD
1 loaf ciabatta bread (430g)
50g butter, melted
2 cloves garlic, crushed
2 tablespoons finely chopped fresh flat-leaf parsley

1 Scrub mussels; remove beards.
2 Make garlic bread.
3 Meanwhile, heat oil on heated barbecue flat plate (or grill plate or large frying pan); cook garlic, onion and chilli, stirring, until onion softens. Add mussels and combined beer and sauce; cook, covered, about 5 minutes or until mussels open (discard any that do not). Remove from heat; stir in parsley.
4 Serve mussels with garlic bread.

GARLIC BREAD
Halve bread horizontally; cut each half into four pieces, brush with combined butter, garlic and parsley. Cook bread on heated oiled grill plate (or grill or barbecue), uncovered, until browned both sides.
per serving 19.7g fat; 2129kJ (509 cal)

soy and chilli squid

preparation time 20 minutes (plus refrigeration time)
cooking time 10 minutes (plus cooling time)
serves 6

500g squid hoods
12cm piece fresh ginger (60g), sliced thinly
6 spring onions, sliced thinly
2 fresh medium red chillies, sliced thinly
⅓ cup (80ml) groundnut oil
½ cup (125ml) light soy sauce
¼ cup (60ml) kecap manis
1 tablespoon sesame oil

1 Cut squid down centre to open out, score inside in diagonal pattern; cut into 5cm squares. Set aside in small bowl.
2 Combine ginger, half the onion and one of the chillies in small heatproof bowl. Heat groundnut oil in small saucepan until moderately hot; carefully pour hot oil over ingredients in bowl. Slowly add sauce, kecap manis and sesame oil, whisking constantly; cool.
3 Pour two-thirds of the soy mixture over squid; cover, refrigerate 3 hours or overnight. Cover and refrigerate remaining soy mixture.
4 Drain marinade from squid. Cook squid, in batches, on heated, oiled barbecue plate (or grill or frying pan) until cooked through.
5 Toss squid with remaining onion and remaining chilli; serve with the remaining soy mixture.
per serving 16.3g fat; 911kJ (218 cal)
TIP This recipe can be prepared a day ahead. Cook just before serving.

paella

preparation time 20 minutes (plus standing time)
cooking time 1 hour 10 minutes
serves 8

1kg clams
1 tablespoon coarse cooking salt
1kg uncooked medium prawns
1kg small mussels
⅓ cup (80ml) olive oil
1.5 litres (6 cups) chicken or fish stock
1 large pinch saffron threads
4 chicken thigh fillets (440g), chopped coarsely
400g chorizo sausage, sliced thickly
2 large red onions (600g), chopped finely
2 medium red peppers (400g), chopped finely
4 cloves garlic, crushed
1 tablespoon smoked paprika
4 medium tomatoes (600g), peeled, deseeded, chopped finely
3 cups (600g) short-grain rice
2 cups (240g) frozen peas
¼ cup finely chopped fresh flat-leaf parsley

1 Rinse clams under cold water, place in large bowl with salt, cover with cold water, stand 2 hours. Drain then rinse.

2 Shell and devein prawns, leaving tails intact. Reserve shells. Scrub mussels and remove beards.

3 Heat 1 tablespoon of the oil in large saucepan; add prawn shells, cook, stirring, until browned. Add stock, bring to a boil; simmer, uncovered, 20 minutes. Strain through fine sieve into jug or bowl; add saffron to the liquid.

4 Heat another 1 tablespoon of the oil in 45cm paella pan or large non-stick frying pan, add chicken; cook until browned all over, remove from pan. Add chorizo to same pan, cook until browned all over; drain on absorbent paper.

5 Heat remaining oil in paella pan, add onion, pepper, garlic, paprika and tomatoes; cook, stirring, until soft. Add rice; stir to coat in mixture.

6 Add chicken, chorizo and stock to pan; stir until just combined. Do not stir again. Bring mixture to a boil then simmer, uncovered, about 15 minutes or until the rice is almost tender.

7 Sprinkle peas over rice; place clams, prawns and mussels evenly over surface of paella. Cover pan with large sheets of foil; simmer about 5 minutes or until mussels and clams have opened (discard any that do not) and prawns are just cooked through. Sprinkle with parsley, serve immediately.

per serving 30.4g fat; 3206kJ (767 cal)

TIPS The traditional paella pan is shallow and wide.
If you don't have a large enough pan, use two smaller frying pans; the mixture is about 4cm deep.
A good-quality marinara mix could replace the seafood.

salmon cutlets with green apple salad

preparation time 20 minutes
cooking time 10 minutes (plus cooling time)
serves 4

½ teaspoon sea salt
4 salmon cutlets (1kg)
2 medium green apples (300g), sliced thinly
2 spring onions, sliced thinly
1 medium red onion (170g), sliced thinly
1½ cups loosely packed fresh mint leaves
¾ cup loosely packed fresh coriander leaves
½ cup (125ml) lemon juice
¾ cup (120g) roasted unsalted cashews

PALM SUGAR DRESSING
⅓ cup (90g) grated palm sugar
2 tablespoons fish sauce
2cm piece fresh ginger (10g), grated

1 Combine ingredients for palm sugar dressing in small saucepan; bring to a boil. Remove from heat; strain. Cool to room temperature.
2 Sprinkle salt evenly over fish. Cook fish on heated oiled grill plate (or grill or barbecue) until browned and cooked as desired.
3 Combine apple, onions, mint, coriander and juice in large bowl; pour over half of the palm sugar dressing, toss to combine. Divide fish among serving plates; top with salad then cashews. Drizzle with remaining dressing.
per serving 29.5g fat; 2157kJ (516 cal)
TIPS You can also use ocean trout fillets in this recipe. Cooking times will change slightly for each different kind and thickness of fish you select. Salmon and ocean trout are at their best if slightly underdone.
Don't slice the apples until you are ready to toss the salad with the dressing because the flesh will brown when exposed to air.

slow-roasted salmon with asian greens

preparation time 15 minutes
cooking time 40 minutes
serves 4

750g piece salmon fillet, boned, with skin on
1 fresh kaffir lime, quartered
1 tablespoon finely shredded kaffir lime leaves
1 tablespoon groundnut oil
250g fresh asparagus, trimmed, chopped coarsely
150g mangetout
150g baby pak choy, chopped coarsely
150g chinese cabbage, chopped coarsely

CHILLI SAUCE
½ cup (110g) caster sugar
¼ cup (60ml) lime juice
¼ cup (60ml) water
2 fresh red thai chillies, seeded, chopped finely
¼ cup firmly packed fresh coriander

1 Preheat oven to very low.
2 Cook fish and lime on heated oiled grill plate (or grill or barbecue) until both are lightly coloured all over. Place fish and lime in large oiled baking dish; sprinkle with lime leaves. Bake, covered tightly, in very low oven about 30 minutes or until cooked as desired.
3 Heat oil in wok or large frying pan; stir-fry asparagus and mangetout until just tender. Add pak choy and chinese cabbage with half of the chilli sauce; stir-fry until leaves are just wilted.
4 Serve vegetables with fish, drizzled with remaining chilli sauce.

CHILLI SAUCE
Combine sugar, juice and the water in small saucepan; stir over heat, without boiling, until sugar dissolves. Simmer, uncovered, without stirring, 3 minutes; cool slightly. Stir in chilli and coriander.
per serving 16.3g fat; 1686kJ (403 cal)

chicken
and poultry

One of the most versatile of ingredients, chicken is perfectly suited to casual eating. Noodle wedges with smoked chicken, green chicken curry, or honey chilli chicken – whatever flavours you prefer, the result will be delicious every time.

honey soy wings

lime marmalade wings

tandoori wings

deep-south wings

honey soy chicken wings

preparation time 10 minutes
cooking time 30 minutes
makes 32

16 small chicken wings (1.3kg)
⅓ cup (120g) honey
½ cup (125ml) salt-reduced soy sauce
3 cloves garlic, crushed
4cm piece fresh ginger (20g), grated finely

1 Preheat oven to hot (220°C/200°C fan-assisted).
2 Cut wings into three pieces at joints; discard tips. Combine chicken with remaining ingredients in large bowl; toss chicken to coat in soy mixture.
3 Place chicken, in single layer, in large shallow baking dish; brush any remaining soy mixture over chicken. Bake, uncovered, in hot oven, turning occasionally, about 30 minutes or until chicken is browned and cooked through. Serve with lemon wedges, if desired.
per wing 1.4g fat; 205kJ (49 cal)
TIP Wing tips can be used to make chicken stock.

lime marmalade chicken wings

preparation time 20 minutes (plus refrigeration time)
cooking time 30 minutes
makes 32

16 small chicken wings (1.3 kg)
¾ cup (250g) lime marmalade, warmed
½ cup (125ml) light soy sauce
⅓ cup (80ml) barbecue sauce
¼ cup (60ml) dry white wine
1 clove garlic, crushed
1 tablespoon lime juice

1 Preheat oven to hot (220°C/200°C fan-assisted).
2 Cut wings into three pieces at joints; discard tips. Combine marmalade, sauces, wine and garlic in large bowl, add chicken; toss chicken to coat in marinade. Cover; refrigerate 3 hours or overnight.
3 Place chicken, in single layer, in large shallow baking dish; brush any remaining marinade over chicken. Bake, uncovered, in hot oven, turning occasionally, about 30 minutes or until chicken is browned and cooked through. Serve hot, drizzled with lime juice.
per wing 1.4g fat; 259kJ (62 cal)

tandoori chicken wings

preparation time 10 minutes (plus refrigeration time)
cooking time 30 minutes
makes 32

16 small chicken wings (1.3kg)
½ cup (150g) tandoori paste
½ cup (140g) plain yogurt
1 medium brown onion (150g), grated

1 Preheat oven to hot (220°C/200°C fan-assisted).
2 Cut wings into three pieces at joints; discard tips. Combine remaining ingredients in large bowl, add chicken; toss chicken to coat in mixture. Cover; refrigerate 3 hours or overnight.
3 Place chicken, in single layer, on oiled wire rack set inside large shallow baking dish. Roast, uncovered, in hot oven, about 30 minutes or until chicken is well browned and cooked through. Serve with lime wedges, if desired.
per wing 3g fat; 234kJ (56 cal)

deep-south chicken wings

preparation time 10 minutes (plus refrigeration time)
cooking time 30 minutes
makes 32

16 small chicken wings (1.3kg)
¼ cup (60ml) tomato sauce
¼ cup (60ml) worcestershire sauce
¼ cup (55g) brown sugar
1 tablespoon american mustard

DIPPING SAUCE
1 tablespoon american mustard
2 tablespoons tomato sauce
1 tablespoon worcestershire sauce
2 tablespoons brown sugar

1 Preheat oven to hot (220°C/200°C fan-assisted).
2 Cut wings into three pieces at joints; discard tips. Combine chicken with remaining ingredients in large bowl. Cover; refrigerate 3 hours or overnight.
3 Place chicken, in single layer, on oiled wire rack set inside large shallow baking dish; brush remaining marinade over chicken. Roast, uncovered, in hot oven, about 30 minutes or until chicken is cooked through.

DIPPING SAUCE
Combine ingredients in small bowl; cook, covered, in microwave oven on high (100%) for 1 minute. Serve with chicken wings.
per wing 1.4g fat; 213kJ (51 cal)

pepper-roasted garlic and lemon chicken

preparation time 35 minutes
cooking time 1 hour 50 minutes
serves 4

2 bulbs garlic
2kg chicken
cooking-oil spray
2 teaspoons salt
2 tablespoons cracked black pepper
1 medium lemon (140g), cut into 8 wedges
1 cup (250ml) water
3 medium globe artichokes (600g)
2 tablespoons lemon juice
2 medium red onions (340g), quartered
3 baby fennel bulbs (390g), trimmed, halved
2 medium leeks (700g), halved lengthways then
   quartered
250g cherry tomatoes
⅓ cup (80ml) dry white wine
¼ cup (60ml) lemon juice, extra

1 Preheat oven to moderately hot (200°C/180°C fan-assisted).
2 Separate cloves from garlic bulb, leaving skin intact. Wash chicken under cold water; pat dry inside and out with absorbent paper. Coat chicken with cooking-oil spray; press combined salt and pepper onto skin and inside cavity. Place garlic and lemon inside cavity; tie legs together with kitchen string. Place chicken on small wire rack in large flameproof baking dish, pour the water in baking dish; roast, uncovered, in moderately hot oven 50 minutes.
3 Meanwhile, discard outer leaves from artichokes; cut tips from remaining leaves. Trim then peel stalks. Quarter artichokes lengthways; using teaspoon remove chokes. Cover artichoke with cold water in medium bowl, stir in the 2 tablespoons of lemon juice; soak artichoke until ready to cook.
4 Add drained artichoke, onion, fennel and leek to dish with chicken; coat with cooking-oil spray. Roast, uncovered, in moderately hot oven about 40 minutes or until vegetables are just tender.
5 Add tomatoes to dish; roast, uncovered, in a moderately hot oven about 20 minutes or until tomatoes soften and chicken is cooked through. Place chicken on serving dish and vegetables in large bowl; cover to keep warm.
6 Stir wine and extra juice into dish with pan juices; bring to a boil. Boil 2 minutes then strain sauce over vegetables; toss gently to combine.
7 Discard garlic and lemon from cavity; serve chicken with vegetables.
per serving 35.7g fat; 2771kJ (663 cal)

chicken cacciatore

preparation time 30 minutes (plus standing time)
cooking time 1 hour 20 minutes
serves 4

2 tablespoons olive oil
1.5kg chicken pieces
1 medium brown onion (150g), chopped finely
1 clove garlic, crushed
½ cup (125ml) dry white wine
1½ tablespoons vinegar
½ cup (125ml) chicken stock
400g can tomatoes
1 tablespoon tomato paste
1 teaspoon finely chopped fresh basil
1 teaspoon sugar
3 anchovy fillets, chopped finely
¼ cup (60ml) milk
½ cup (60g) pitted black olives, halved
2 tablespoons chopped fresh flat-leaf parsley

1 Preheat oven to moderate.
2 Heat oil in large frying pan; cook chicken until browned all over. Place chicken in ovenproof dish.
3 Pour off most pan juices, leaving about 1 tablespoon in pan. Add onion and garlic to pan; cook until onion is soft. Add wine and vinegar; bring to a boil. Boil until reduced by half. Add stock; stir over high heat 2 minutes. Push tomatoes with their liquid through sieve; add to pan with paste, basil and sugar. Cook further 1 minute.
4 Pour tomato mixture over chicken pieces. Cover; cook in moderate oven 1 hour.
5 Soak anchovy in milk 5 minutes; drain on absorbent paper. Arrange chicken pieces in serving dish; keep warm. Pour pan juices into medium saucepan. Bring to a boil; boil 1 minute. Add anchovy, olive and half of the parsley to pan; cook 1 minute. Pour sauce over chicken pieces. Sprinkle with remaining parsley.
per serving 42.2g fat; 2571kJ (615 cal)

moroccan chicken with couscous

preparation time 10 minutes
cooking time 10 minutes
serves 4

4 single chicken breast fillets (680g)
⅓ cup (80ml) moroccan marinade
2 cups (500ml) vegetable stock
2 cups (400g) couscous
20g butter
1 small red onion (100g), sliced thinly
2 fresh small red thai chillies, deseeded, chopped finely
½ cup (110g) coarsely chopped pitted prunes
⅓ cup (45g) slivered almonds, toasted
½ cup coarsely chopped fresh mint
¼ cup (50g) finely chopped preserved lemon

1 Toss chicken in large bowl with marinade; stand 10 minutes. Cook chicken, in batches, on heated, oiled grill plate (or grill or barbecue) until browned lightly and cooked through. Stand 5 minutes; slice chicken thickly.
2 Meanwhile, bring stock to a boil in medium saucepan. Remove from heat; stir in couscous and butter. Cover; stand 5 minutes or until liquid is absorbed, fluffing couscous with fork occasionally. Stir in remaining ingredients. Serve chicken on couscous.
per serving 16.2g fat; 3097kJ (741 cal)
TIPS Preserved lemons are available from specialty shops and delicatessens. Rinse well under cold water, discard flesh, then finely chop the rind.
Moroccan marinade is a bottled blend of garlic, peppers, chilli, lemon and various spices, and can be found in most supermarkets.

honey chilli chicken

preparation time 10 minutes
cooking time 25 minutes
serves 4

vegetable oil, for deep-frying
100g bean thread vermicelli
1 teaspoon chilli oil
3 teaspoons groundnut oil
2 medium brown onions (300g), sliced thinly
4 cloves garlic, crushed
1 tablespoon grated fresh ginger
1kg chicken thigh fillets, halved
½ cup (180g) honey
2 tablespoons sweet chilli sauce
500g tender stem broccoli, chopped coarsely
¼ cup coarsely chopped fresh garlic chives

1 Heat vegetable oil in wok or large frying pan. Deep-fry noodles, in batches, until puffed and white; drain on absorbent paper.
2 Heat chilli oil and groundnut oil in wok or large frying pan; stir-fry onion, garlic and ginger until fragrant. Add chicken, honey and sauce; stir-fry until chicken is browned and cooked through. Add broccoli and chives; stir-fry until broccoli is just tender. Serve over noodles.
per serving 27.7g fat; 2681kJ (641 cal)

pesto chicken with salsa

preparation time 15 minutes (plus marinating
  and cooling times)
cooking time 25 minutes
serves 4

1kg chicken breast mini fillets
¾ cup (195g) sun-dried tomato pesto

SALSA
4 medium tomatoes (760g)
6 spring onions, sliced thinly
1 medium red onion (170g), chopped finely
2 tablespoons lemon juice
1 tablespoon olive oil
½ teaspoon freshly ground black pepper

1 Trim chicken. Combine chicken and pesto in large bowl. Cover; marinate in refrigerator 3 hours or overnight.
2 Preheat oven to hot. Place chicken on wire rack over baking dish; cook, uncovered, in hot oven about 25 minutes or until chicken is cooked and tender. Cool 5 minutes; refrigerate until cold. Slice chicken and serve with salsa.

SALSA
Remove seeds from tomatoes; chop tomatoes finely. Combine tomato with remaining ingredients in medium bowl.
per serving 26g fat; 2142kJ (512 cal)
TIP We used vine-ripened tomatoes in our salsa, however any variety of tomato can be used.

thai chicken stir-fry

preparation time 20 minutes (plus marinating time)
cooking time 20 minutes
serves 8

1 teaspoon sesame oil
½ cup (125ml) light soy sauce
¼ cup (90g) honey
¼ cup (60ml) lime juice
3 fresh red thai chillies, deseeded, sliced thinly
2 teaspoons cornflour
850g chicken breast fillets, sliced thinly
2 tablespoons groundnut oil
3 cloves garlic, crushed
2 large red onions (600g), sliced thinly
240g fresh baby corn
2 teaspoons finely grated lime rind
3 cups (240g) beansprouts
2 cups loosely packed fresh thai basil leaves
1 cup loosely packed fresh coriander leaves

1 Combine sesame oil, sauce, honey, juice, chilli and cornflour in large bowl. Add chicken; toss to coat in marinade. Cover; refrigerate 3 hours or overnight.
2 Drain chicken over medium bowl; reserve marinade.
3 Heat half of the groundnut oil in wok or large non-stick frying pan; stir-fry chicken, in batches, until browned all over. Heat remaining groundnut oil in wok; stir-fry garlic, onion and corn until just tender. Return chicken to wok with reserved marinade and rind; stir-fry until sauce boils and chicken is cooked through.
4 Remove from heat; add sprouts, basil and coriander. Toss with chicken and vegetables until combined. Serve with steamed jasmine rice and wedges of fresh lime, if desired.
per serving 11.5g fat; 1219kJ (292 cal)
TIP Grate rind from lime before juicing it.

stir-fried chicken with pepper

preparation time 10 minutes
cooking time 15 minutes
serves 4

2 tablespoons sesame oil
500g chicken thigh fillets, sliced thinly
2 teaspoons sambal oelek
190g can sliced water chestnuts, drained
227g can bamboo shoot strips, drained
1 large red pepper (350g), sliced thinly
⅓ cup (80ml) kecap manis
500g tender stem broccoli, chopped coarsely
2 cups (160g) beansprouts

1 Heat half of the oil in wok; stir-fry chicken, in batches, until browned lightly.
2 Heat remaining oil in same wok; stir-fry sambal, chestnuts, bamboo and pepper.
3 Return chicken to wok with kecap manis and broccoli; stir-fry until broccoli is just wilted and chicken is cooked through. Remove from heat; stir in beansprouts.
per serving 18.9g fat; 1338kJ (320 cal)
TIP Chinese broccoli, also known as gai lum or gai larn, can be found in Asian-food stores.

chicken parmesan with basil sauce

preparation time 25 minutes
cooking time 35 minutes
serves 4

1 cup (70g) stale breadcrumbs
⅓ cup (25g) coarsely grated parmesan
1 tablespoon finely chopped fresh flat-leaf parsley
3 bacon rashers (210g), chopped finely
80g butter, melted
2 cloves garlic, crushed
1 teaspoon worcestershire sauce
½ teaspoon mustard powder
4 single chicken breast fillets (800g)

BASIL SAUCE
⅓ cup (80ml) olive oil
¼ cup (60ml) white vinegar
1 clove garlic
1 cup firmly packed fresh basil leaves
⅓ cup (80ml) cream
1 egg yolk

1 Preheat oven to moderate (180°C/160°C fan-assisted).
2 Combine breadcrumbs, cheese and parsley in large bowl.
3 Cook bacon in large non-stick frying pan until crisp; drain on absorbent paper. Add bacon to breadcrumb mixture.
4 Combine butter, garlic, sauce and mustard in shallow dish.
5 Dip chicken into butter mixture; place chicken, in single layer, in shallow ovenproof dish. Press crumb mixture on top of chicken.
6 Cook, uncovered, about 25 minutes or until chicken is cooked through.
7 Meanwhile, make basil sauce.
8 Serve chicken with basil sauce, and a green salad, if desired.

BASIL SAUCE
Blend oil, vinegar, garlic, basil and cream until smooth. Pour sauce into small saucepan, add egg yolk; whisk over low heat, without boiling, until sauce thickens slightly.
per serving 54.5g fat; 3210kJ (768 cal)

green chicken curry

preparation time 25 minutes
cooking time 15 minutes
serves 4

750g chicken thigh fillets, sliced thinly
200g green beans, chopped coarsely
1 cup (250ml) coconut cream

GREEN CURRY PASTE
3 fresh green thai chillies, chopped finely
3 spring onions, chopped finely
2 cloves garlic, crushed
¼ cup finely chopped fresh lemongrass
¼ cup chopped fresh coriander
2 tablespoons groundnut oil
2 tablespoons water
1 teaspoon shrimp paste
½ teaspoon ground cumin
¼ teaspoon ground turmeric

1 Cook green curry paste in large heated saucepan, stirring, about 3 minutes or until fragrant.
2 Add chicken and beans to pan; cook, stirring, about 5 minutes or until chicken is tender. Stir in coconut cream; simmer, uncovered, about 3 minutes or until slightly thickened. Top with sliced spring onion, if desired.

GREEN CURRY PASTE
Blend or process ingredients until smooth.
per serving 30.4g fat; 1898kJ (454 cal)
TIP Curry is best made just before serving. Paste can be made a week ahead and refrigerated, covered.

noodle wedges with smoked chicken

preparation time 35 minutes (plus standing
* and refrigeration times)*
cooking time 15 minutes
serves 4

250g thin fresh egg noodles
1 tablespoon polenta
2 tablespoons olive oil
150g mangetout
150g green beans
4 spring onions
400g coarsely shredded smoked chicken

LIME AND CHILLI DRESSING
½ cup (125ml) groundnut oil
⅓ cup (80ml) lime juice
1 tablespoon sweet chilli sauce
1 tablespoon hoisin sauce

1 Place noodles in large heatproof bowl; cover with boiling water. Stand 3 minutes; drain.
2 Sprinkle polenta over base of oiled deep 19cm-square cake tin. Press cooled noodles firmly into tin. Cover; refrigerate 3 hours or overnight.
3 Turn noodle cake onto board; cut into quarters. Heat oil in large frying pan; cook noodle squares, in batches, until browned lightly both sides. Drain on absorbent paper; cut each square into two triangles.
4 Slice mangetout diagonally; cut beans into 5cm lengths. Boil, steam or microwave mangetout and beans, separately, until just tender; drain. Cut onions into long thin strips.
5 Toss mangetout, beans and onion in large bowl with chicken. Divide noodle wedges among plates. Top with chicken salad; drizzle with dressing.

LIME AND CHILLI DRESSING
Combine ingredients in screw-top jar; shake well.
per serving 48.8g fat; 3347kJ (801 cal)
TIPS Dressing can be made a day ahead and refrigerated, covered.
A purchased barbecue chicken can be substituted for the smoked chicken.

cajun chicken with tomato salsa

preparation time 20 minutes
cooking time 15 minutes
serves 4

750g chicken breast fillets, sliced thinly
¼ cup (18g) cajun seasoning
2 teaspoons grated lime rind
2 trimmed corn cobs (500g)
2 tablespoons olive oil
1 small red onion (100g), cut into thin wedges

TOMATO SALSA
2 small plum tomatoes (120g), chopped finely
2 spring onions, sliced thinly
2 teaspoons lime juice
2 teaspoons balsamic vinegar

1 Combine chicken, seasoning and rind in large bowl; mix well. Cut kernels from corn.
2 Heat half of the oil in wok or large frying pan; stir-fry chicken mixture, in batches, until cooked through.
3 Heat remaining oil in wok; stir-fry corn and onion until onion is soft.
4 Return chicken to wok; stir-fry until hot.
5 Serve chicken mixture topped with tomato salsa.

TOMATO SALSA
Combine ingredients in small bowl; mix well.
per serving 21.2g fat; 1877kJ (449 cal)
TIP Recipe best made just before serving; serve with soured cream, if desired.

chicken and green beans

preparation time 5 minutes
cooking time 15 minutes
serves 4

700g green beans
1 tablespoon groundnut oil
880g chicken thigh fillets, chopped coarsely
2 medium white onions (300g), sliced thickly
3 cloves garlic, crushed
1 teaspoon five-spice powder
½ cup (125ml) oyster sauce
2 tablespoons light soy sauce
½ cup (75g) cashews, toasted
½ cup loosely packed thai basil leaves

1 Cut green beans into 5cm lengths.
2 Heat half of the oil in wok or large frying pan; stir-fry chicken, in batches, until browned all over and cooked through.
3 Heat remaining oil in wok; stir-fry onion, garlic and five-spice until onion softens. Add beans; stir-fry until beans are tender. Return chicken to wok with sauces and nuts; stir-fry until sauce boils and thickens slightly. Just before serving, stir in basil. Serve with noodles, if desired.
per serving 30.7g fat; 2353kJ (563 cal)
TIP Sweet basil can be substituted for the thai basil, if unavailable.

braised poussins with peas and lettuce

preparation time 30 minutes
cooking time 1 hour
serves 6

3 poussins (1.5kg)
1 medium leek (350g)
2 bay leaves
1 sprig fresh thyme
1 sprig fresh rosemary
4 stalks fresh flat-leaf parsley
50g butter
2 cloves garlic, crushed
1 large brown onion (200g), chopped finely
8 bacon rashers (560g), rind removed, chopped
   coarsely
¼ cup (35g) plain flour
1½ cups (375ml) dry white wine
3 cups (750ml) chicken stock
1.5kg potatoes, chopped coarsely
¾ cup (180ml) milk
50g butter, extra
4 cups frozen peas (480g)
1 large butter lettuce, shredded finely
½ cup coarsely chopped fresh mint

1 Cut along both sides of poussins' backbones; discard backbones. Cut poussins in half between breasts; rinse halves under cold water, pat dry.

2 Cut leek in half crossways; chop white bottom half finely, reserve. Using kitchen string, tie green top half of leek, bay leaves, thyme, rosemary and parsley into a bundle.

3 Heat butter in large saucepan; cook poussins, in batches, until browned lightly both sides. Cook reserved chopped leek, garlic, onion and bacon in same pan, stirring, about 10 minutes or until onion softens. Add flour; cook, stirring, 2 minutes. Gradually add wine and stock; bring to a boil, stirring constantly, until mixture boils and thickens. Return poussins to pan with herb bundle, reduce heat; simmer, covered, 30 minutes.

4 Meanwhile, boil, steam or microwave potato until tender; drain. Mash potato with warmed milk and extra butter in large bowl until smooth. Cover to keep warm.

5 Discard herb bundle. Add peas, lettuce and mint to pan; simmer, uncovered, about 5 minutes or until peas are just tender.

6 Divide mashed potato among serving plates; top with poussin mixture.

per serving 37.8g fat; 3131kJ (749 cal)
TIP Chicken pieces, quails or pigeons can be used rather than poussins, if desired.

nam jim chicken

preparation time 20 minutes
cooking time 20 minutes
serves 4

8 chicken thigh fillets (880g)
1 teaspoon ground cumin
1 teaspoon ground coriander
2 tablespoons grated palm sugar
1 cup loosely packed fresh thai basil leaves
1 cup loosely packed fresh coriander leaves
3 cups (240g) beansprouts
3 long green chillies, chopped coarsely
2 cloves garlic, quartered
10cm stick (20g) fresh lemongrass, sliced thinly
3 spring onions, chopped coarsely
1 coriander root, chopped coarsely
¼ cup (60ml) lime juice
1 tablespoon fish sauce
2 tablespoons grated palm sugar, extra

1 Combine chicken in large bowl with ground spices and sugar. Cook chicken in large oiled frying pan until cooked through. Serve on combined herbs and beansprouts.
2 Meanwhile, blend or process remaining ingredients until smooth; spoon over chicken.
per serving 16g fat; 1580kJ (378 cal)

spiced chicken drumsticks with baba ghanoush

preparation time 20 minutes
cooking time 50 minutes
serves 4

2 teaspoons ground allspice
1 teaspoon ground black pepper
1 teaspoon ground cumin
2 tablespoons olive oil
8 chicken drumsticks (1.2kg)
4 large pitta breads

BABA GHANOUSH
2 medium aubergines (600g)
1 clove garlic, crushed
1 tablespoon tahini
¼ cup (60ml) lemon juice
2 tablespoons olive oil

1 Preheat oven to moderately hot (200°C/180°C fan-assisted).
2 Make baba ghanoush.
3 Meanwhile, combine spices and oil in large bowl, add drumsticks; turn to coat in mixture.
4 Place drumsticks on wire rack over dish. Roast, uncovered, about 50 minutes or until chicken is cooked through, turning occasionally.
5 Serve drumsticks with baba ghanoush and bread, and lemon wedges and fresh parsley, if desired.

BABA GHANOUSH
Pierce aubergines all over with fork; place on oiled oven tray. Roast, uncovered, about 40 minutes or until aubergine is soft, turning occasionally. Stand 10 minutes. Peel aubergines, discard skin; drain aubergine in colander 10 minutes then blend or process with garlic, tahini, juice and oil.
per serving 44.4g fat; 3164kJ (757 cal)

stir-fried noodles, chicken and pak choy

preparation time 10 minutes
cooking time 20 minutes
serves 4

250g dried thin rice noodles
1 tablespoon groundnut oil
3 eggs, beaten lightly
1 medium brown onion (150g), chopped finely
2 cloves garlic, crushed
2 tablespoons grated fresh ginger
500g minced chicken
500g baby pak choy, chopped coarsely
¼ cup (60ml) light soy sauce
½ cup chopped fresh coriander
3 cups (240g) beansprouts

1 Place noodles in large heatproof bowl; cover with boiling water. Stand until just tender; drain.
2 Brush heated wok or large frying pan with a little of the oil. Add half of the egg; swirl to cover base of wok. Cook, covered, about 3 minutes or until cooked through. Remove omelette from wok; repeat with remaining egg. Roll omelettes tightly; slice thinly.
3 Heat remaining oil in wok; stir-fry onion, garlic and ginger until onion softens. Add chicken; stir-fry until chicken is cooked through.
4 Add pak choy, sauce and coriander; stir-fry until pak choy is just tender. Stir in noodles and beansprouts; serve immediately, topped with omelette.
per serving 19.8g fat; 2149kJ (514 cal)
TIPS Create a vegetarian version of this dish by substituting fried tofu for the chicken.
You can substitute chinese cabbage, chinese broccoli or trimmed, thinly sliced pak choy for the baby pak choy.

curried chicken pies

preparation time 50 minutes
cooking time 1 hour 45 minutes (plus standing time)
serves 6

1.6kg chicken
90g butter
1 small leek (200g), chopped finely
1 medium white onion (150g), chopped finely
1 medium red pepper (200g), chopped finely
2 trimmed celery stalks (200g), chopped finely
3 teaspoons curry powder
¼ teaspoon chilli powder
¼ cup (35g) plain flour
⅓ cup (80g) soured cream
½ cup finely chopped fresh flat-leaf parsley
2 sheets ready-rolled puff pastry
1 egg, beaten lightly

1 Place chicken in large pan, add enough water to just cover chicken; bring to a boil, reduce heat, simmer, uncovered, 1 hour. Remove from heat; when cool enough to handle, remove from stock. Reserve 1¾ cups (430ml) of the stock for this recipe.
2 Preheat oven to moderately hot (200°C/180°C fan-assisted).
3 Remove skin and bones from chicken; chop chicken flesh roughly.
4 Heat butter in large frying pan, add leek, onion, pepper and celery; cook, stirring, until soft.
5 Add curry powder and chilli powder; cook, stirring, until fragrant. Stir in flour. Add reserved stock, stir over heat until mixture boils and thickens; reduce heat, simmer 1 minute, remove from heat.
6 Add soured cream, chicken and parsley to vegetable mixture. Spoon mixture into six 1¼-cup (310ml) ovenproof dishes.
7 Cut pastry into six rounds large enough to cover top of each dish. Lightly brush pastry with egg. Place pies on oven tray.
8 Bake pies 10 minutes; reduce temperature to moderate (180°C/160°C fan-assisted), bake further 15 minutes or until pastry is golden brown.
per serving 52.8g fat; 3001kJ (718 cal)

chicken, mushroom and fennel pies

preparation time 20 minutes
cooking time 30 minutes
serves 4

1 tablespoon olive oil
2 cloves garlic, crushed
1 medium leek (350g), sliced thinly
1 small fennel bulb (200g), sliced thinly
200g button mushrooms, quartered
½ cup (125ml) dry white wine
4 chicken breast fillets (800g), chopped coarsely
300ml cream
1 tablespoon dijon mustard
¼ cup coarsely chopped fresh flat-leaf parsley
1 sheet puff pastry, cut into quarters
1 egg, beaten lightly
1 tablespoon fennel seeds

1 Preheat oven to moderately hot (200°C/180°C fan-assisted).
2 Heat oil in large saucepan; cook garlic, leek, fennel and mushrooms, stirring, until vegetables soften.
3 Stir in wine; bring to a boil. Reduce heat; simmer, uncovered, 3 minutes. Add chicken and cream; bring to a boil. Reduce heat; simmer, uncovered, about 10 minutes or until chicken is cooked through and sauce thickened slightly. Stir in mustard and parsley.
4 Meanwhile, place pastry quarters onto oven tray, brush pastry with egg then sprinkle with seeds; bake in oven about 10 minutes or until golden brown.
5 Divide chicken mixture among small serving bowls, top each with pastry; serve with a rocket salad.
per serving 52.8g fat; 3340kJ (799 cal)

turkey steaks with mustard cream sauce on bacon mash

preparation time 15 minutes
cooking time 30 minutes
serves 4

8 turkey steaks (880g)
2 shallots (50g), chopped finely
1 clove garlic, crushed
½ cup (125ml) dry white wine
½ cup (125ml) cream
2 teaspoons wholegrain mustard

BACON MASH
1kg medium potatoes, chopped coarsely
2 bacon rashers (140g), rind removed, chopped coarsely
20g butter
¼ cup (60ml) cream
1 tablespoon coarsely chopped fresh chives

1 Make chive and bacon mash.
2 Melt half of the butter in large frying pan; cook steaks, in batches, until browned both sides.
3 Melt remaining butter in same pan; cook shallot and garlic, stirring, until soft. Add wine; bring to a boil. Reduce heat; simmer, uncovered, about 5 minutes or until almost evaporated. Stir in cream and mustard then return steaks to pan; bring to a boil. Reduce heat; simmer, covered, about 10 minutes or until steaks are cooked through.
4 Serve steaks with chive and bacon mash, drizzled with sauce.

BACON MASH
Boil, steam or microwave potato until tender; drain. Cook bacon in small frying pan; drain on absorbent paper. Mash potato in large bowl with butter and cream until smooth. Stir in bacon and chives.
per serving 37.4g fat; 2918kJ (698 cal)

slow-roasted duck with sour cherry, apple and walnut salad

preparation time 40 minutes
cooking time 2 hours
serves 4

680g jar morello cherries
½ cup (125ml) chicken stock
½ cup (125ml) port
1 cinnamon stick
3 whole cloves
1 clove garlic, crushed
4 duck leg joints (1.2kg), excess fat removed
2 small green apples (260g)
1 cup (100g) toasted walnuts, chopped coarsely
3 spring onions, sliced thinly
1 cup firmly packed fresh flat-leaf parsley leaves
2 tablespoons olive oil
1 tablespoon lemon juice

1 Preheat oven to moderately low (160°C/140°C fan-assisted).
2 Strain cherries over small bowl. Combine cherry juice with stock, port, cinnamon, cloves and garlic in large baking dish. Place duck on metal rack over baking dish; cover tightly with oiled foil. Roast, covered, in moderately low oven about 2 hours or until duck is tender. Strain cherry sauce into large jug; skim away fat.
3 Cut apples into thin slices; cut slices into matchstick-sized pieces. Place apple and pitted cherries in large bowl with nuts, onion, parsley, oil and lemon juice; toss gently. Serve duck with salad and cherry sauce.
per serving 81.2g fat; 3963kJ (948 cal)
TIP Do not slice apples until you're ready to assemble the salad as they will discolour.

chicken schnitzel with mixed bean salad

preparation time 25 minuteS
cooking time 20 minutes
serves 4

300g green beans
200g yellow beans
4 medium tomatoes (600g), deseeded, sliced thickly
2 tablespoons olive oil
1 tablespoon red wine vinegar
2 teaspoons wholegrain mustard
2 tablespoons coarsely chopped fresh tarragon
2 tablespoons coarsely chopped fresh chervil
2 teaspoons drained green peppercorns, crushed
4 chicken breast fillets (800g)
¼ cup (35g) plain flour
2 eggs, beaten lightly
1 tablespoon milk
2 teaspoons finely grated lemon rind
½ cup (85g) polenta
½ cup (50g) packaged breadcrumbs
vegetable oil, for shallow-frying

1 Boil, steam or microwave beans until tender. Rinse under cold water; drain. Place beans in large bowl with tomato, olive oil, vinegar, mustard, herbs and peppercorns; toss gently to combine. Cover; refrigerate until required.

2 Using meat mallet, gently pound chicken, one piece at a time, between sheets of cling film until 1cm thick.

3 Whisk flour, egg, milk and rind together in shallow bowl; combine polenta and breadcrumbs in a second shallow bowl. Coat chicken pieces, first in egg mixture then in breadcrumb mixture.

4 Heat vegetable oil in large frying pan; shallow-fry chicken, in batches, until browned and cooked through. Drain on absorbent paper.

5 Serve schnitzel, sliced, with bean salad.

per serving 35.4g fat; 2897kJ (693 cal)

spanish chicken casserole

preparation time 10 minutes
cooking time 1 hour 25 minutes
serves 4

1 tablespoon olive oil
4 chicken drumsticks (600g)
4 chicken thigh cutlets (800g)
1 large brown onion (200g), chopped finely
4 medium potatoes (800g), quartered
½ cup (80g) toasted pine nuts
½ cup (80g) toasted blanched almonds
3 cups (750ml) chicken stock
1 cup (250ml) dry white wine
⅓ cup (80ml) lemon juice
4 cloves garlic, crushed
2 tablespoons fresh thyme leaves
½ cup coarsely chopped fresh flat-leaf parsley
500g fine green beans, trimmed

1 Preheat oven to moderate (180°C/160°C fan-assisted).
2 Heat oil in large flameproof casserole dish; cook chicken, in batches, until browned.
3 Cook onion in same dish, stirring, until soft. Return chicken to dish with potato, nuts, stock, wine, juice, garlic, thyme and half of the parsley; bring to a boil. Cover; cook in oven about 1 hour or until chicken is cooked through.
4 Meanwhile, boil, steam or microwave beans until tender; drain.
5 Serve chicken with beans; sprinkle with remaining parsley.
per serving 61.4g fat; 4050kJ (969 cal)

pot roast with mustard cream sauce

preparation time 25 minutes
cooking time 1 hour 50 minutes
serves 4

1.6kg chicken
1 tablespoon olive oil
12 shallots (300g), halved
20 baby carrots (400g), trimmed
3 small parsnips (360g), chopped coarsely
1 cup (250ml) dry white wine
2 cups (500ml) chicken stock
2 dried bay leaves
200g chestnut mushrooms
2 tablespoons cream
2 tablespoons wholegrain mustard

1 Preheat oven to moderately hot (200°C/180°C fan-assisted).
2 Wash chicken under cold water; pat dry inside and out with absorbent paper.
3 Heat oil in large flameproof casserole dish; cook chicken until browned all over. Remove chicken. Cook shallots, carrots and parsnips in same dish, stirring, about 5 minutes or until vegetables are browned lightly.
4 Return chicken to dish with wine, stock and bay leaves; bring to a boil. Cook, covered, in oven 30 minutes. Uncover; cook about 30 minutes or until chicken is cooked through. Add mushrooms; cook, uncovered, about 10 minutes or until mushrooms are tender.
5 Remove chicken and vegetables from dish; cover to keep warm. Add cream and mustard to dish; bring to a boil. Boil, uncovered, about 5 minutes or until sauce thickens slightly.
6 Serve chicken with vegetables and mustard cream sauce.
per serving 42.2g fat; 2859kJ (684 cal)

chicken parmigiana-style

preparation time 10 minutes
cooking time 20 minutes
serves 4

2 chicken breast fillets (400g)
2 tablespoons plain flour
1 egg
1 tablespoon milk
1 cup (70g) stale breadcrumbs
¼ cup (60ml) vegetable oil
⅓ cup (85g) bottled tomato pasta sauce, warmed
4 slices ham (185g)
100g gruyère, grated coarsely

1 Preheat grill.
2 Split chicken fillets in half horizontally. Toss chicken in flour; shake away excess. Dip chicken pieces, one at a time, in combined egg and milk, then in breadcrumbs.
3 Heat oil in large frying pan; shallow-fry chicken, in batches, until browned and cooked through. Drain on absorbent paper.
4 Place chicken on oven tray; divide pasta sauce, then ham and finally cheese over chicken. Place under grill until cheese melts.
5 Serve with a parmesan and baby rocket salad, if desired.
per serving 28.6g fat; 2103kJ (503 cal)

southern fried chicken with buttermilk mash and gravy

preparation time 15 minutes (plus refrigeration time)
cooking time 40 minutes
serves 4

20 chicken drumsticks (1.4kg)
1 cup (250ml) buttermilk
1 cup (150g) plain flour
¼ cup cajun seasoning
½ cup (125ml) vegetable oil
40g butter
5 medium potatoes (1kg), chopped coarsely
¾ cup (180ml) buttermilk, warmed, extra
40g butter, extra
250g green beans, trimmed, cut into 4cm lengths
2 cups (500ml) chicken stock

1 Combine drumsticks and buttermilk in large bowl. Cover; refrigerate 3 hours or overnight. Drain; discard buttermilk.
2 Combine flour and seasoning in large bowl; add chicken pieces, toss to coat in mixture. Cover; refrigerate about 30 minutes or until flour forms a paste.
3 Preheat oven to very hot (240°C/220°C fan-assisted).
4 Heat oil and butter in large deep frying pan; shake excess paste from drumsticks back into bowl. Cook drumsticks, in batches, over medium heat until browned and crisp. Place drumsticks on wire rack over large baking dish; cook, covered, in oven 15 minutes. Uncover; cook about 10 minutes or until drumsticks are cooked through and crisp.
5 Meanwhile, boil, steam or microwave potato until tender; drain. Mash in large bowl with extra buttermilk and extra butter until smooth. Cover to keep warm.
6 Boil, steam or microwave beans until tender; drain.
7 To make gravy, add excess paste to pan; cook, stirring, until mixture bubbles. Gradually stir in stock; cook, stirring, until gravy boils and thickens. Strain gravy into large jug.
8 Serve drumsticks with mash, beans and gravy.
per serving 69.7g fat; 4585kJ (1097 cal)

chicken breast stuffed with smoked salmon and goat's cheese

preparation time 25 minutes
cooking time 1 hour 15 minutes
serves 4

4 medium potatoes (800g), sliced thinly
¼ cup coarsely chopped fresh flat-leaf parsley
2 cloves garlic, crushed
1 tablespoon olive oil
⅔ cup (160ml) milk, warmed
2 tablespoons finely chopped fresh chives
100g soft goat's cheese
4 chicken breast fillets (800g)
4 slices smoked salmon (120g)
50g baby spinach leaves

SPINACH SALAD
100g baby spinach leaves
1 tablespoon olive oil
2 tablespoons lemon juice
1 clove garlic, crushed

1 Preheat oven to moderately hot (200°C/180°C fan-assisted).
2 Combine potato, parsley, garlic and oil in medium bowl. Layer potato mixture in 2.5-litre (10-cup) ceramic baking dish; pour over milk. Roast, uncovered, about 40 minutes or until potato is just tender.
3 Meanwhile, combine chives and cheese in small bowl. Cut fillets in half horizontally almost all the way through; open out each fillet. Spread each fillet with a quarter of the cheese mixture; top with one slice of salmon and a quarter of the spinach. Roll each fillet tightly to enclose filling; secure with toothpicks.
4 Cook chicken in large oiled frying pan, uncovered, until browned.
5 Place chicken on cooked potato; roast, uncovered, in oven about 15 minutes or until chicken is cooked through. Stand 5 minutes; remove toothpicks, slice chicken thickly.
6 Meanwhile, place ingredients for spinach salad in medium bowl; toss gently to combine.
7 Serve chicken with potato and salad.
per serving 21g fat; 2316kJ (554 cal)

jambalaya

preparation time 10 minutes
cooking time 1 hour
serves 4

1 chorizo sausage (170g), sliced thickly
4 chicken drumsticks (600g)
4 chicken thigh cutlets (800g)
2 medium brown onions (300g), chopped finely
1½ cups (300g) white long-grain rice
¼ teaspoon cayenne pepper
2 teaspoons fresh thyme leaves
2 dried bay leaves
4 cloves garlic, crushed
3 trimmed celery stalks (300g), sliced thickly
3 cups (750ml) chicken stock
400g can crushed tomatoes
1 cup (120g) frozen peas

1 Cook chorizo in large saucepan, stirring, until browned all over; remove from pan.
2 Cook chicken, in batches, in same pan, until browned all over.
3 Cook onion in same pan, stirring, until onion softens. Add rice, cayenne, thyme, bay leaves, garlic, celery, stock, undrained tomatoes, chorizo and chicken; bring to a boil. Reduce heat; simmer, uncovered, about 15 minutes or until rice is tender and chicken is cooked through.
4 Add peas; cook, uncovered, about 5 minutes or until peas are tender.
per serving 44.9g fat; 3942kJ (943 cal)

chicken fricassee

preparation time 20 minutes
cooking time 1 hour 10 minutes
serves 4

40g butter
8 shallots (200g), peeled
20 baby carrots (400g), halved
1kg chicken thigh fillets, cut into thirds
2 tablespoons plain flour
½ cup (125ml) dry white wine
1½ cups (375g) chicken stock
2 tablespoons dijon mustard
2 large sweet potatoes (1kg), chopped coarsely
20g butter, extra
½ cup (125ml) cream
2 egg yolks
¼ cup (60ml) cream, extra
1 tablespoon lemon juice
2 tablespoons coarsely chopped fresh tarragon

1 Heat butter in large heavy-based saucepan; cook shallots and carrots, over low heat, stirring occasionally, about 5 minutes or until browned lightly, remove from pan. Cook chicken, in batches, in same pan, over low heat, until browned lightly.
2 Add flour; cook, stirring, until mixture bubbles and thickens. Gradually stir in combined wine, stock and mustard. Return chicken to pan with shallots and carrots; bring to a boil. Reduce heat; simmer, covered, about 45 minutes or until chicken is cooked through.
3 Meanwhile, boil, steam or microwave sweet potatoes until tender; drain. Mash sweet potatoes with extra butter and cream in large bowl until smooth. Cover to keep warm.
4 Combine egg yolks, extra cream, juice and tarragon in medium jug. Remove fricassee from heat. Gradually add cream mixture, stirring constantly.
5 Serve fricassee with mash.
per serving 54.1g fat; 3825kJ (915 cal)

Tandoori lamb cutlets, beef and vegetables with herb pesto, osso buco, and spicy pork ribs are a few of the creative lamb, beef, veal and pork recipes for you to try.

meat

roast pork with pears and parsnips

pork ribs with chorizo and smoked paprika

spicy pork ribs

asian-spiced roasted pork belly

roast pork with pears and parsnips

preparation time 15 minutes
cooking time 55 minutes
serves 6

6-cutlet pork rib roast (1kg), french-trimmed,
   rind scored, tied
2 teaspoons olive oil
1 tablespoon sea salt
2 small red onions (200g), quartered
2 medium parsnips (500g), quartered
3 small hard pears (540g), cored, quartered
4 cloves garlic, unpeeled
¼ cup (55g) brown sugar
2 tablespoons olive oil, extra

1 Preheat oven to very hot (240°C/220°C fan-assisted).
2 Rub pork rind with oil and salt. Place pork on wire rack in baking dish.
3 In separate baking dish, gently combine remaining ingredients.
4 Bake pork and pear mixture in very hot oven about 25 minutes or until pork rind blisters; reduce temperature to moderate (180°C/160°C fan-assisted). Cook in moderate oven further 25 minutes or until pork is cooked through. Turn or shake pear mixture occasionally.
5 Remove pork and vegetables from oven, cover with foil; stand pork about 10 minutes before cutting.
6 Serve pork with pear mixture.
per serving 22.8g fat; 1810kJ (433 cal)
TIPS This recipe is best made close to serving.
Ask your butcher to score the rind of the pork for you.

pork ribs with chorizo and smoked paprika

preparation time 15 minutes
 cooking time 2 hours
serves 4

1.5kg American-style pork ribs
4 cloves garlic, crushed
2 teaspoons smoked paprika
1 tablespoon olive oil
200g chorizo, sliced thinly
1 tablespoon olive oil, extra
1 medium red onion (170g), chopped coarsely
1 medium red pepper (200g), chopped coarsely
1 tablespoon brown sugar
800g can chopped tomatoes
1 cup (250ml) chicken stock

1 Cut between bones of pork to separate into individual ribs. Combine garlic, paprika and olive oil in small bowl; rub over pork ribs.
2 Preheat oven to moderately low (160°C/140°C fan-assisted).
3 Cook chorizo in heated large flameproof baking dish, stirring, until browned lightly. Remove from dish with slotted spoon; drain on absorbent paper.
4 Cook ribs, in same dish, in batches, until well browned all over. Drain ribs on absorbent paper.
5 Add extra olive oil, onion and red pepper to same dish; cook, stirring, until onion is soft. Return ribs and chorizo to dish; add sugar, undrained tomatoes and stock, bring to a boil.
6 Cover dish tightly with foil, bake in moderately low oven 1 hour. Remove foil, bake further 30 minutes or until ribs are tender
per serving 38.5g fat; 2516kJ (602 cal)
TIP This recipe can be made a day ahead.

spicy pork ribs

preparation time 10 minutes
cooking time 20 minutes
serves 4

1.5kg trimmed pork spare rib slabs
¾ cup (180ml) light soy sauce
1 egg, beaten lightly
¼ cup (35g) plain flour
2 tablespoons vegetable oil
½ cup (125ml) rice wine
½ cup (100g) firmly packed brown sugar
¼ cup (50g) yellow mustard seeds
⅓ cup loosely packed, chopped fresh coriander
3 cloves garlic, crushed
1 tablespoon grated fresh ginger
3 teaspoons dried chilli flakes
1 teaspoon five-spice powder
½ teaspoon cayenne pepper

1 Cut pork into individual-rib pieces.
2 Place ribs in large saucepan. Cover with water; bring to a boil. Reduce heat; simmer, uncovered, about 10 minutes or until ribs are almost cooked through. Drain; pat dry with absorbent paper.
3 Blend ¼ cup (60ml) of the soy sauce with the egg and flour in large bowl. Add ribs; stir to coat in soy mixture.
4 Heat oil in wok or large frying pan; stir-fry ribs, in batches, until browned all over.
5 Cook remaining soy sauce and remaining ingredients in wok, stirring, until sugar dissolves. Return ribs to wok; stir-fry until heated through. Serve with steamed rice and individual finger bowls filled with water and a few slices of lemon, if desired.
per serving 17.7g fat; 2066kJ (494 cal)
TIPS Spicy spare ribs can be made a day ahead and refrigerated, covered, or frozen for up to 3 months.
To serve, reheat in the microwave oven or wok.
Ask your butcher to cut the pork ribs 'American-style' so that as much fat as possible has been removed, leaving only tender, flavoursome meat.

asian-spiced roasted pork belly

preparation time 10 minutes (plus refrigeration time)
cooking time 1 hour 25 minutes
serves 6

1kg pork belly, skin on, boned
½ cup (125ml) chinese cooking wine
¼ cup (60ml) soy sauce
1 tablespoon tamarind concentrate
2 tablespoons honey
½ teaspoon sesame oil
4cm piece fresh ginger (20g), chopped finely
3 cloves garlic, crushed
2 teaspoons five-spice powder
1 star anise
1 dried long red chilli
1 teaspoon sichuan pepper
3 cups (750ml) water
900g baby pak choy, halved lengthways

1 Place pork in large saucepan of boiling water; return to a boil. Reduce heat; simmer, uncovered, about 40 minutes or until pork is cooked through, drain.
2 Meanwhile, combine wine, sauce, tamarind, honey, oil, ginger, garlic, five-spice, star anise, chilli, pepper and the water in large bowl, add pork; toss pork to coat in marinade. Cover; refrigerate 3 hours or overnight.
3 Preheat oven to hot (220°C/200°C fan-assisted).
4 Place pork, skin-side up, on wire rack in large shallow baking dish; reserve marinade. Pour enough water into baking dish to come halfway up side of dish. Roast pork, uncovered, in hot oven about 30 minutes or until browned.
5 Meanwhile, strain marinade into small saucepan; bring to a boil. Boil, uncovered, about 20 minutes or until sauce reduces to about 1 cup.
6 Boil, steam or microwave pak choy until just tender; drain. Serve pork with sauce and pak choy.
per serving 37.9g fat; 2165kJ (518 cal)
TIP Serve with steamed jasmine rice, if desired.

chilli pork with oyster sauce

preparation time 156 minutes
cooking time 10 minutes
serves 4

1 tablespoon groundnut oil
450g pork fillets, sliced thinly
1 clove garlic, crushed
1 medium white onion (150g), sliced thinly
1 large red pepper (350g), sliced thinly
1 small green courgette (90g), sliced thinly
1 small yellow courgette (90g), sliced thinly
¼ cup (60ml) oyster sauce
1 tablespoon mild sweet chilli sauce
1 tablespoon chopped fresh coriander

1 Heat oil in wok or large frying pan. Stir-fry pork, in batches, until browned.
2 Stir-fry garlic and onion until onion is just soft.
3 Add pepper and courgettes; stir-fry.
4 Return pork to wok. Add sauces; stir-fry until hot. Serve sprinkled with coriander.
per serving 7.6g fat; 907kJ (217 cal)

pork fillet with apple and leek

preparation time 10 minutes (plus standing time)
cooking time 15 minutes
serves 4

800g pork fillets
¾ cup (180ml) chicken stock
2 medium leeks (700g), sliced thickly
1 clove garlic, crushed
2 tablespoons brown sugar
2 tablespoons red wine vinegar
2 medium apples (300g)
10g butter
1 tablespoon brown sugar, extra
400g baby carrots, trimmed, halved
8 medium patty-pan squash (100g), quartered
250g asparagus, trimmed, chopped coarsely

1 Preheat oven to very hot.
2 Place pork, in single layer, in large baking dish; bake, uncovered, in very hot oven about 25 minutes or until pork is browned and cooked as desired. Cover; stand 5 minutes before slicing thickly.
3 Meanwhile, heat half of the stock in medium frying pan; cook leek and garlic, stirring, until leek softens and browns slightly. Add sugar and vinegar; cook, stirring, about 5 minutes or until leek caramelises. Add remaining stock; bring to a boil. Reduce heat; simmer, uncovered, about 5 minutes or until liquid reduces by half. Place leek mixture in medium bowl; cover to keep warm.
4 Peel, core and halve apples; cut into thick slices.
5 Melt butter in same pan as used for leek mixture; cook apple and extra sugar, stirring, until apple is browned and tender.
6 Boil, steam or microwave carrot, squash and asparagus, separately, until just tender; drain.
7 Serve pork, topped with caramelised apple and sweet and sour leek, on top of the mixed vegetables.
per serving 7.5g fat; 1624kJ (389 cal)
TIP You can make the sweet and sour leek 3 hours ahead; reheat before serving.

wiener schnitzel with lemon spaetzle

preparation time 20 minutes (plus refrigeration time)
cooking time 20 minutes
serves 4

½ cup (75g) plain flour
3 eggs, beaten lightly
2 tablespoons milk
2 cups (140g) stale breadcrumbs
¾ cup (75g) packaged breadcrumbs
1/2 cup (40g) finely grated parmesan cheese
8 veal schnitzels (800g)
vegetable oil, for shallow-frying

LEMON SPAETZLE
2 cups (300g) plain flour
4 eggs, beaten lightly
½ cup (125ml) water
2 teaspoons finely grated lemon rind
40g butter, chopped

1 Whisk flour, egg and milk in medium shallow bowl; combine breadcrumbs and cheese in another medium shallow bowl. Coat schnitzels, one at a time, in flour mixture then in breadcrumb mixture. Place, in single layer, on tray. Cover; refrigerate 15 minutes.
2 Make lemon spaetzle.
3 Heat oil in large frying pan; cook schnitzels, in batches, until browned both sides and cooked through.
4 Serve schnitzel with lemon spaetzle.

LEMON SPAETZLE
Place flour in large bowl, make well in centre. Gradually add egg and the water, stirring, until batter is smooth. Stir in rind. Pour half of the batter into metal colander set over large saucepan of boiling water; using wooden spoon, push batter through holes of colander, remove colander. When water returns to a boil, boil, uncovered, about 2 minutes or until spaetzle float to the surface. Use slotted spoon to remove spaetzle; drain, place in large bowl. Add half of the butter; toss spaetzle gently until butter melts. Keep warm; repeat with remaining batter and butter.
per serving 58.1g fat; 5245kJ (1253 cal)
TIP Spaetzle, served throughout Germany, Austria, Switzerland and the French region of Alsace, are tiny noodle-like dumplings made by pushing a batter through the holes of a colander or strainer into a pan of boiling water or stock. The cooked spaetzle are generally tossed in a frying pan with melted butter, herbs or gravy then served as a side dish, or added to soups or stews in place of pasta or potatoes.

saltimbocca with risotto milanese

preparation time 10 minutes
cooking time 25 minutes
serves 4

8 veal steaks (680g)
4 slices prosciutto (60g), halved crossways
8 fresh sage leaves
½ cup (50g) finely grated pecorino cheese
40g butter
1 cup (250ml) dry white wine
1 tablespoon coarsely chopped fresh sage

RISOTTO MILANESE
1½ cups (375ml) water
2 cups (500ml) chicken stock
½ cup (125ml) dry white wine
¼ teaspoon saffron threads
20g butter
1 large brown onion (200g), chopped finely
2 cups (400g) arborio rice
¼ cup (20g) finely grated parmesan cheese

1 Place steaks on board. Place one piece prosciutto, one sage leaf and ⅛ of the cheese on each steak; fold in half to secure filling, secure with a toothpick or small skewer.

2 Make risotto milanese.

3 Melt half of the butter in medium non-stick frying pan; cook saltimbocca, in batches, about 5 minutes or until browned both sides and cooked through. Cover to keep warm.

4 Pour wine into same frying pan; bring to a boil. Boil, uncovered, until wine reduces by half. Stir in remaining butter then chopped sage.

5 Divide risotto milanese and saltimbocca among serving plates; drizzle saltimbocca with sauce and accompany with steamed green beans, if desired.

RISOTTO MILANESE
Place the water, stock, wine and saffron in medium saucepan; bring to a boil. Reduce heat; simmer, covered. Heat butter in another medium saucepan; cook onion, stirring, until softened. Add rice; stir to coat rice in onion mixture. Stir in ½ cup of the simmering stock mixture; cook, stirring, over low heat, until liquid is absorbed. Continue adding stock mixture, in ½-cup batches, stirring until absorbed after each addition. Total cooking time should be about 35 minutes or until rice is just tender. Stir cheese gently into risotto.

per serving 23.3g fat; 3429kJ (819 cal)
TIP Saltimbocca is a classic Italian veal dish that literally means 'jump in the mouth' – just the sensation the wonderful flavours will produce with your first bite. Tinged with the taste and colour of saffron, a Milanese is the classic risotto generally served with saltimbocca.

calves liver and onions

preparation time 10 minutes
cooking time 25 minutes
serves 6

2 cups (500ml) water
2 cups (500ml) milk
1 cup (170g) polenta
½ cup (40g) finely grated parmesan cheese
½ cup (125ml) cream
¼ cup coarsely chopped fresh flat-leaf parsley
40g butter
2 tablespoons olive oil
3 medium brown onions (450g), sliced thinly
2 teaspoons cornflour
¾ cup (180ml) beef stock
2 teaspoons dijon mustard
500g calves liver, sliced thinly
½ teaspoon balsamic vinegar

1 Combine the water and milk in large saucepan; bring to a boil. Add polenta in a slow, steady stream, stirring constantlly. Reduce heat; simmer, stirring occasionally, about 20 minutes or until polenta thickens. Stir in cheese, cream and parsley. Cover to keep warm.
2 Meanwhile, heat butter and half of the oil in large frying pan; cook onion, stirring, until onion softens. Stir in blended cornflour, stock and mustard; cook, stirring, until sauce boils and thickens.
3 Heat remaining oil in large frying pan; cook liver quickly over high heat until browned both sides and cooked as desired.
4 Stir vinegar into sauce just before serving with polenta and liver; accompany with a balsamic-dressed mixed green salad, if desired.
per serving 47.2g fat; 3171kJ (757 cal)
TIP The calves liver should be sliced into paper-thin scallops then quickly seared – overcooking will toughen its delicate texture.

osso buco

preparation time 20 minutes
cooking time 1 hour 45 minutes
serves 4

¼ cup (35g) plain flour
8 pieces veal shin or osso buco (1kg)
2 tablespoons olive oil
3 large plum tomatoes (270g), peeled, chopped
   coarsely
½ cup (125ml) dry white wine
2 cloves garlic, crushed
2 cups (500ml) chicken stock

GREMOLATA
¼ cup finely chopped fresh flat-leaf parsley
2 teaspoons finely chopped lemon rind
2 cloves garlic, chopped finely

1 Preheat oven to moderately low.
2 Place flour in plastic bag. Add one piece of veal at a time, gently shaking bag to coat veal all over. Remove veal from bag, shaking off excess flour; repeat with remaining veal pieces.
3 Heat oil in large flameproof casserole dish over high heat. Cook veal, in batches, until browned on all over.
4 Return veal to dish, fitting pieces upright and tightly together in a single layer. Add tomato, wine, garlic and stock; if necessary, add enough water so that the liquid just covers the surface of the veal. Bring to a boil; place a round piece of baking parchment, cut to the same diameter as the dish, on top of veal. Cover dish with a tight-fitting lid; cook in moderately low oven 1½ hours.
5 After 1 hour, check liquid content in dish; if it looks too thin, remove dish from oven. Simmer, uncovered, on top of stove until mixture reduces and thickens slightly. Return covered pan to oven; cook osso buco 30 minutes. Serve osso buco with polenta (see recipe above) and sprinkled with gremolata.

GREMOLATA
Combine ingredients in small bowl; cover tightly with cling film. Refrigerate until required.
per serving 14.6g fat; 2710kJ (648 cal)

mustard-crusted rack of veal with sweet potato mash

preparation time 25 minutes
cooking time 35 minutes
serves 4

2 tablespoons wholegrain mustard
3 spring onions, chopped finely
2 cloves garlic, crushed
1 tablespoon finely chopped fresh rosemary
2 tablespoons olive oil
1kg veal rack (8 cutlets), trimmed
2 small sweet potatoes (500g), chopped coarsely
20g butter
⅓ cup (80ml) cream
1 large brown onion (200g), sliced thinly
400g mushrooms, sliced thinly
1 tablespoon plain flour
¼ cup (60ml) dry white wine
¾ cup (180ml) chicken stock
¼ cup coarsely chopped fresh flat-leaf parsley

1 Preheat oven to moderately hot.

2 Combine mustard, spring onion, half of the garlic, rosemary and half of the oil in small jug. Place veal on wire rack over large shallow flameproof baking dish; coat veal all over with mustard mixture. Roast, uncovered, in moderately hot oven, about 30 minutes or until browned all over and cooked as desired. Cover to keep warm.

3 Meanwhile, boil, steam or microwave sweet potatoes until tender; drain. Mash sweet potatoes in large bowl with butter and half of the cream until smooth.

4 Heat remaining oil in same flameproof dish; cook brown onion and remaining garlic, stirring, until onion softens. Add mushrooms; cook, stirring, about 5 minutes or until just tender. Add flour; cook, stirring, until mixture thickens and bubbles. Gradually stir in wine and stock; stir until sauce boils and thickens. Add remaining cream and parsley; stir until heated well through.

5 Serve veal with sweet potatoes mash and the mushroom sauce.

per serving 26.2g fat; 2302kJ (550 cal)

savoury-glazed meatloaf

beef roulade

wonton lasagne stacks

hamburger with a twist

savoury-glazed meatloaf

preparation time 15 minutes
cooking time 1 hour 15 minutes
serves 4

750g minced beef
1 cup (70g) stale breadcrumbs
1 medium brown onion (150g), chopped finely
1 egg
1 tablespoon worcestershire sauce
2 tablespoons tomato sauce
185g can evaporated milk
2 teaspoons mustard powder
1 tablespoon brown sugar
½ teaspoon mustard powder, extra
¼ cup (60ml) tomato sauce, extra

1 Preheat oven to moderate (180°C/160°C fan-assisted). Grease 14cm x 21cm loaf tin.
2 Combine beef, breadcrumbs, onion, egg, sauces, milk and mustard in medium bowl; press mixture into tin. Turn tin upside down onto a foil-lined oven tray. Leave tin in place. Cook 15 minutes.
3 Meanwhile, combine sugar, extra mustard and extra sauce in small bowl.
4 Remove loaf from oven; remove tin. Brush loaf well with glaze, return loaf to oven; cook 1 hour or until well browned and cooked through. Serve with rocket leaves and balsamic dressing, if desired.
per serving 19.9g fat; 1986kJ (475 cal)

beef roulade

preparation time 20 minutes (plus refrigeration time)
cooking time 55 minutes
serves 4

500g lean minced beef
1 small brown onion (80g), chopped finely
2 cloves garlic, crushed
1 egg
1 tablespoon tomato paste
1 tablespoon coarsely chopped fresh basil
2 cups (140g) stale breadcrumbs
40g baby spinach leaves
6 slices prosciutto (90g)
9 cherry tomatoes (150g)

TOMATO AND MUSTARD SAUCE
½ cup (125ml) tomato sauce
2 tablespoons barbecue sauce
2 tablespoons dijon mustard
¼ cup (60ml) water

1 Grease 25cm x 30cm swiss roll tin; line with baking parchment, extending paper 5cm over the edge of both long sides.
2 Using hands, combine minced beef, onion, garlic, egg, paste, basil and breadcrumbs in large bowl; press mixture into prepared tin, top with spinach leaves then prosciutto.
3 Place cherry tomatoes along one long side. Starting with this side, lift paper and roll, holding filling in place as you roll away from you, pressing roll gently but tightly around filling. Discard paper, wrap roll in foil; refrigerate 20 minutes. Preheat oven to hot.
4 Make tomato and mustard sauce.
5 Place roulade, still wrapped in foil, on oven tray; bake in hot oven 40 minutes. Unwrap roulade; bake on oven tray in hot oven about 15 minutes or until browned. Serve roulade, sliced, with tomato and mustard sauce, and accompanied by creamy polenta, if desired.

TOMATO AND MUSTARD SAUCE
Combine ingredients in small saucepan; cook, stirring, until heated through.
per serving 13g fat; 1804kJ (431 cal)

wonton lasagne stacks

preparation time 20 minutes
cooking time 1 hour
serves 4

600g minced beef
2 tablespoons tomato paste
2 spring onions, chopped finely
2 eggs, beaten lightly
250g ricotta cheese
2 tablespoons finely shredded fresh basil
12 wonton wrappers
½ cup (55g) grated pizza cheese
700g bottled tomato pasta sauce

1 Preheat oven to moderate.
2 Using hands, combine minced beef, paste, onion and half of the egg in medium bowl; roll mince mixture into eight patties.
3 Combine ricotta, basil and remaining egg in separate medium bowl.
4 Place four wrappers, in single layer, in shallow 2-litre (8 cup) square baking dish; top each wrapper with one patty. Divide half of the ricotta mixture among patties; sprinkle with half of the pizza cheese. Top each stack with one of the remaining wrappers; repeat layering with remaining patties, ricotta mixture and cheese, finishing with remaining wrappers.
5 Pour sauce over lasagne stacks; cook, uncovered, in moderate oven, about 50 minutes or until stacks are cooked through and set. Serve with crusty Italian bread and a mixed green salad dressed in a white wine vinaigrette, if desired.
per serving 29.3g fat; 2231kJ (533 cal)

hamburger with a twist

preparation time 15 minutes
cooking time 10 minutes
serves 4

80g gorgonzola cheese, crumbled
¼ cup (60g) soured cream
400g minced beef
120g sausagemeat
1 small brown onion (80g), chopped finely
1 tablespoon barbecue sauce
2 teaspoons worcestershire sauce
½ cup (75g) drained sun-dried tomatoes in oil,
   chopped finely
4 hamburger buns
50g baby rocket leaves
170g marinated artichoke hearts, drained, quartered

1 Blend or process half of the cheese with the cream until smooth. Stir in remaining cheese.
2 Using hands, combine minced beef, sausagemeat, onion, sauces and tomato in medium bowl; shape mixture into four hamburger patties.
3 Cook patties in large lightly oiled heated frying pan until browned both sides and cooked through.
4 Meanwhile, halve buns; toast, cut-side up. Sandwich rocket, patties, gorgonzola cream and artichoke in toasted buns.
per serving 30.8g fat; 2954kJ (706 cal)

beef burgers with cabbage mash

preparation time 25 minutes
cooking time 20 minutes
serves 4

2 bacon rashers (140g), rind removed,
　chopped finely
1 small brown onion (80g), chopped finely
1 clove garlic, crushed
1 fresh red thai chilli, deseeded, chopped finely
1 tablespoon worcestershire sauce
1 cup (70g) stale breadcrumbs
1 egg
¼ cup coarsely chopped fresh flat-leaf parsley
500g minced beef
2 tablespoons barbecue sauce
1 tablespoon vegetable oil
1 tablespoon dijon mustard
2 cups (500ml) beef stock
1 tablespoon cornflour
2 tablespoons water

CABBAGE MASH
1kg potatoes, quartered
¼ cup (60ml) cream
30g butter, chopped
200g finely shredded savoy cabbage
1 small white onion (80g), chopped finely

1 Cook potato for cabbage mash.
2 Cook bacon, onion, garlic and chilli in medium frying pan, stirring until onion softens. Remove from heat.
3 Using hands, combine worcestershire sauce, breadcrumbs, egg, parsley, minced beef and half of the barbecue sauce with bacon mixture in large bowl; shape mixture into eight rissoles.
4 Heat oil in same pan; cook burgers, in batches, until browned both sides and cooked through. Cover to keep warm.
5 Place mustard, stock and remaining barbecue sauce in same pan; bring to a boil. Stir in blended cornflour and water; cook, stirring, until gravy boils and thickens slightly.
6 Finish cabbage mash. Serve burgers, topped with gravy, with cabbage mash.

CABBAGE MASH
Boil, steam or microwave potato until tender; drain. Mash potato with cream and butter until smooth; stir in cabbage and onion.
per serving 35.9g fat; 3038kJ (726 cal)
TIP Burgers can be prepared a day ahead and kept, covered, under refrigeration.

beef stew with red wine and mushrooms

preparation time 10 minutes
cooking time 2 hours 50 minutes
serves 4

2 tablespoons olive oil
1.5kg braising steak, cut into 2cm cubes
1 large brown onion (200g), sliced thickly
2 cloves garlic, crushed
250g mushrooms, quartered
2 trimmed sticks celery (150g), sliced thickly
2 x 425g cans crushed tomatoes
½ cup (125ml) dry red wine
1½ cups (375ml) beef stock
2 medium potatoes (400g), quartered
2 large carrots (360g), sliced thickly
2 teaspoons coarsely chopped fresh thyme
200g green beans, trimmed
200g yellow beans, trimmed

1 Heat half of the oil in large heavy-based pan; cook steak, in batches, over high heat until browned all over.
2 Heat remaining oil in same pan; cook onion and garlic, stirring, until onion softens. Add mushrooms and celery; cook, stirring, 3 minutes. Return steak to pan with undrained tomatoes, wine and stock; bring to a boil. Reduce heat; simmer, covered, 2 hours.
3 Add potato and carrot; simmer, covered, about 30 minutes or until steak is tender. Stir in thyme.
4 Meanwhile, boil, steam or microwave beans until just tender; drain.
5 Serve stew with beans and, if desired, a warmed loaf of ciabatta.
per serving 35.2g fat; 3458kJ (826 cal)
TIP Rump or round steak are also suitable for this recipe.

roast beef with yorkshire puddings

preparation time 40 minutes (plus refrigeration time)
cooking time 1 hour 45 minutes
serves 8

2kg corner piece beef topside roast
2 cups (500ml) dry red wine
2 bay leaves
6 black peppercorns
¼ cup (70g) wholegrain mustard
4 cloves garlic, sliced
4 sprigs fresh thyme
1 medium brown onion (150g), chopped coarsely
2 medium carrots (240g), chopped coarsely
1 large leek (500g), chopped coarsely
2 trimmed sticks celery (150g), chopped coarsely
1 tablespoon olive oil
2 tablespoons plain flour
1¼ cups (375ml) beef stock

YORKSHIRE PUDDINGS
1 cup (150g) plain flour
½ teaspoon salt
2 eggs, beaten lightly
½ cup (125ml) milk
½ cup (125ml) water

1 Combine beef, wine, bay leaves, peppercorns, mustard, garlic, thyme and onion in large bowl, cover; refrigerate 3 hours or overnight.
2 Preheat oven to moderate. Drain beef; reserve 1 cup (250ml) of the marinade. Combine carrot, leek and celery in large baking dish, place beef on top; brush beef with oil. Bake, uncovered, in moderate oven about 1½ hours or until beef is cooked as desired.
3 Remove beef from dish, wrap in foil; stand for 20 minutes before serving.
5 Remove and discard vegetables with slotted spoon. Pour pan juices into jug, stand 5 minutes then pour off excess oil; reserve 1½ tablespoons of the oil for yorkshire puddings and 2 tablespoons of pan juices for gravy.
6 Heat reserved pan juices in same baking dish, add flour; cook, stirring, until bubbling. Gradually add reserved marinade and stock; cook, stirring, until gravy boils and thickens. Strain gravy into heatproof jug. Serve beef with gravy and yorkshire puddings.

YORKSHIRE PUDDINGS
Sift flour and salt into bowl, make well in centre; add combined egg, milk and water. Using wooden spoon, gradually stir in flour until batter is smooth. Cover; let stand 30 minutes. Divide reserved oil among 12-hole (2 tablespoon/40ml) patty tray; heat in hot oven 2 minutes. Divide batter among tray holes; bake about 15 minutes or until puddings are golden.
per serving 15.6g fat; 2131kJ (509 cal)

chilli marinated beef in coconut curry sauce

preparation time 20 minutes (plus marinating time)
cooking time 2 hours
serves 6

1.5kg beef braising steak, chopped coarsely
40g ghee
2 medium red peppers (400g), chopped finely
2 medium brown onions (300g), chopped finely
½ cup (125ml) beef stock
½ cup (125ml) coconut milk
1 cinnamon stick
5 dried curry leaves
⅓ cup chopped fresh coriander

MARINADE
⅓ cup (80ml) white vinegar
2 fresh red thai chillies, sliced thinly
2 tablespoons tomato paste
1 tablespoon chopped fresh coriander
2 cloves garlic, crushed
3 cardamom pods, crushed
2 teaspoons cumin seeds
1 teaspoon ground turmeric

1 Combine beef and marinade in large bowl; mix well. Cover; refrigerate 3 hours or overnight.
2 Heat half of the ghee in large saucepan; cook beef, in batches, stirring, until browned.
3 Heat remaining ghee in same pan; cook pepper and onion, stirring, until onion is soft.
4 Return beef to pan; add stock, coconut milk, cinnamon and curry leaves. Simmer, covered, 1 hour, stirring occasionally.
5 Remove cover; simmer about 30 minutes or until beef is tender. Discard cinnamon stick; stir in coriander.
6 Serve with steamed or boiled rice, if desired.

MARINADE
Combine ingredients in large bowl; mix well.
per serving 23g fat; 1853kJ (443 cal)
TIP Recipe can be made a day ahead and refrigerated, covered; suitable to freeze.

beef curry with dhal

preparation time 15 minutes (plus refrigeration time)
cooking time 2 hours 30 minutes
serves 8

1 tablespoon groundnut oil
2 medium brown onions (300g), chopped coarsely
2 cloves garlic, crushed
1 fresh red thai chilli, chopped finely
1 tablespoon grated fresh ginger
2 teaspoons garam masala
2 tablespoons ground cumin
2 tablespoons ground coriander
2 teaspoons hot paprika
4 cardamom pods, bruised
3 cinnamon sticks, broken
2 cups (500ml) water
2kg beef braising steak, cut into 2cm pieces
3 cups (750ml) beef stock
½ cup (125ml) coconut milk
⅓ cup chopped fresh coriander
3 cups (600g) red lentils

1 Heat oil in large heavy-base saucepan; cook onion, garlic, chilli and ginger, stirring, until onion is soft. Stir in spices; cook, stirring, until fragrant.
2 Gradually stir ¼ cup (60ml) of the water into onion mixture until it forms a paste; cook, stirring, 2 minutes. Add beef; stir to coat in paste.
3 Add the remaining water and stock; bring to a boil. Reduce heat; simmer, covered, stirring occasionally, about 1½ hours or until beef is tender. Refrigerate overnight, to allow flavours to develop.
4 Add coconut milk; simmer, uncovered, about 30 minutes or until thickened slightly. Discard cardamom pods and cinnamon sticks. Stir in coriander.
5 Meanwhile, cook lentils in medium saucepan of boiling water, uncovered, about 10 minutes or until tender; drain. Serve lentils with curry.
per serving 20.1g fat; 2516kJ (602 cal)

beef vindaloo with raita and spicy dhal

preparation time 40 minutes (plus refrigeration time)
cooking time 2 hours
serves 4

2 teaspoons cumin seeds
2 teaspoons garam masala
4 cardamom pods, bruised
4cm piece fresh ginger (20g), grated finely
6 cloves garlic, crushed
8 fresh small red thai chillies, chopped finely
2 tablespoons white vinegar
1 tablespoon tamarind concentrate
1.5kg beef braising steak, diced into 3cm pieces
2 tablespoons ghee
2 large brown onions (400g), chopped finely
1 cinnamon stick
6 cloves
2 teaspoons plain flour
3 cups (750ml) beef stock

SPICY DHAL
2 tablespoons vegetable oil
2 cloves garlic, crushed
1cm piece fresh ginger (5g), grated finely
1 medium brown onion (150g), chopped finely
3 teaspoons chilli powder
2 teaspoons white sugar
2 teaspoons garam masala
2 teaspoons ground turmeric
½ teaspoon ground coriander
1 tablespoon ground cumin
1 cup (200g) red lentils
400g can crushed tomatoes
1 trimmed celery stalk (100g), sliced thinly
2 tablespoons lemon juice
2½ cups (625ml) vegetable stock
⅓ cup (80ml) cream
2 tablespoons coarsely chopped fresh coriander

RAITA
½ cucumber (130g), grated coarsely, drained
1 small brown onion (80g), chopped finely
400g plain yogurt
¼ teaspoon chilli powder
1 teaspoon toasted black mustard seeds
1 tablespoon coarsely chopped fresh coriander
1 tablespoon coarsely chopped fresh mint

1 Dry-fry cumin, garam masala and cardamom in large heated frying pan; stir over low heat until fragrant. Combine roasted spices with ginger, garlic, chilli, vinegar and tamarind in large bowl, add beef; toss beef to coat in marinade. Cover; refrigerate 1 hour or overnight.
2 Melt ghee in large frying pan; cook onion, cinnamon and cloves, stirring, until onion is browned lightly. Add beef mixture; cook, stirring, until beef is browned all over. Stir in flour; cook, stirring, 2 minutes. Gradually add stock; bring to a boil, stirring. Reduce heat; simmer, uncovered, 1 hour.
3 Meanwhile, make spicy dahl and raita.
4 Serve vindaloo with spicy dhal, raita and, if desired, a bowl of crisp pappadums.

SPICY DHAL
Heat oil in large heavy-based saucepan; cook garlic, ginger and onion, stirring, until onion softens. Add chilli, sugar, garam masala, turmeric, coriander and cumin; cook, stirring, until fragrant. Add lentils, undrained tomatoes, celery, juice and stock; bring to a boil. Reduce heat; simmer, covered, about 30 minutes or until lentils are tender. Blend or process dhal mixture, in batches, until pureed; return to pan. Add cream and coriander; cook, stirring, until heated through.

RAITA
Combine ingredients in medium bowl.
per serving 49.8g fat; 4318kJ (1033 cal)
TIPS Both the vindaloo curry and the spicy dhal are best made a day ahead to allow their flavours to develop fully.

Mango chutney and cold lager are ideal accompaniments to this dish

satay beef with noodles

preparation time 10 minutes
cooking time 15 minutes
serves 4

2 tablespoons groundnut oil
500g beef strips
450g fresh wide rice noodles
3 cloves garlic, crushed
2 teaspoons grated fresh ginger
6 spring onions, cut into 2cm pieces
1 small red pepper (150g), sliced thinly
2 cups (160g) beansprouts
¼ cup (75g) satay sauce
2 tablespoons fish sauce

1 Heat half of the oil in wok or large frying pan; stir-fry beef, in batches, until browned all over.
2 Place noodles in large heatproof bowl; cover with boiling water, separate with fork, drain.
3 Heat remaining oil in wok; stir-fry garlic and ginger until fragrant. Add onion and pepper; stir-fry until vegetables are just soft. Return beef to wok with noodles, sprouts and sauces; stir-fry until heated through.
per serving 22g fat; 1913kJ (457 cal)
TIP Beef strips can be prepared from blade, fillet, rib-eye, rump, sirloin or topside steak.

beef and rice noodle stir-fry

preparation time 15 minutes
cooking time 20 minutes
serves 4

500g fresh rice noodles
2 tablespoons groundnut oil
500g beef fillets, sliced thinly
1 clove garlic, crushed
1 tablespoon grated fresh ginger
1 tablespoon finely chopped fresh lemongrass
1 fresh red thai chilli, deseeded, chopped finely
1 tablespoon chopped fresh mint
1 large carrot (180g), halved lengthways, sliced thinly
200g fresh baby corn, halved lengthways
200g tender stem broccoli, chopped coarsely
1 tablespoon brown sugar
2 teaspoons cornflour
¼ cup (60ml) rice wine
¼ cup (60ml) oyster sauce
2 tablespoons light soy sauce

1 Rinse noodles under hot water; drain. Transfer to large bowl; separate noodles with fork.
2 Heat half of the oil in wok or large frying pan; stir-fry beef, in batches, until browned all over.
3 Heat remaining oil in wok; stir-fry garlic, ginger, lemongrass, chilli and mint until fragrant. Add carrot and corn; stir-fry until carrot is just tender.
4 Return beef to wok with broccoli, sugar and blended cornflour, wine and sauces; stir-fry until broccoli just wilts and sauce boils and thickens slightly. Add noodles; stir-fry until hot.
per serving 16.5g fat; 2011kJ (481 cal)
TIP Fresh rice noodles must be rinsed under hot water to remove starch and excess oil before using. You can substitute egg noodles for the rice noodles.

beef kebabs with roasted potato salad

preparation time 25 minutes
cooking time 30 minutes
serves 4

1kg salad potatoes
1 tablespoon olive oil
250g minced beef
1 clove garlic, crushed
¼ teaspoon cayenne pepper
1 egg white, beaten lightly
2 tablespoons packaged breadcrumbs
400g rump steak, cut into 2cm cubes
1 teaspoon hot paprika
⅓ cup (95g) plain yogurt
1 tablespoon coarsely chopped fresh coriander

LEMON GARLIC DRESSING
¼ cup (60ml) lemon juice
2 cloves garlic, crushed
⅓ cup (80ml) olive oil
2 teaspoons dijon mustard
1 tablespoon coarsely chopped fresh coriander

1 Preheat oven to moderately hot.
2 Scrub unpeeled potatoes, dry with absorbent paper; quarter lengthways. Place potatoes, in single layer, in medium baking dish; drizzle with oil. Roast, uncovered, in moderately hot oven about 30 minutes or until tender.
3 Meanwhile, using hands, combine minced beef, garlic, pepper, egg white and breadcrumbs in medium bowl; shape mixture into eight sausages. Thread one sausage onto each of eight skewers, cover; refrigerate 15 minutes.
4 Thread steak onto eight remaining skewers; sprinkle with paprika. Cook steak and minced beef skewers, in batches, on heated oiled grill plate (or grill or barbecue) until browned all over and cooked as desired.
5 Make lemon garlic dressing, pour over potatoes in large serving bowl; toss to combine. Combine yogurt and coriander in small bowl.
6 Serve potato salad with kebabs; serve yogurt mixture separately.

LEMON GARLIC DRESSING
Combine ingredients in screw-top jar; shake well.
per serving 38.7g fat; 2843kJ (679 cal)
TIP Soak 16 small bamboo skewers in cold water for at least 1 hour before use, to prevent them from scorching and splintering.

beef and vegetables with herb pesto

preparation time 25 minutes
cooking time 15 minutes
serves 4

1 tablespoon olive oil
400g beef steak, sliced thinly
1 clove garlic, crushed
20 baby carrots, halved lengthways
1 medium red pepper (200g), chopped coarsely
1 medium yellow pepper (200g), chopped coarsely
200g sugar snap peas
½ cup (125ml) beef stock
HERB PESTO
1½ cups firmly packed fresh basil leaves
¼ cup firmly packed fresh oregano leaves
⅓ cup (25g) grated parmesan cheese
¼ cup (60ml) olive oil
¼ cup (60ml) cream
1 clove garlic, crushed
1 tablespoon balsamic vinegar
2 teaspoons water

1 Heat oil in wok or large frying pan. Stir-fry beef and garlic, in batches, until beef is browned.
2 Stir-fry carrot and pepper.
3 Return beef mixture to wok with peas and stock; stir until hot.
4 Serve stir-fry topped with warm herb pesto.

HERB PESTO
Blend or process herbs, cheese, oil, cream, garlic, vinegar and the water until combined. Transfer mixture to small saucepan; stir over low heat, without boiling, until heated through.
per serving 31.9g fat; 1893kJ (453 cal)

steak and chips

preparation time 10 minutes (plus standing time)
cooking time 30 minutes
serves 4

1kg potatoes
vegetable oil, for deep-frying
1 tablespoon olive oil
1kg piece beef fillet, cut into 4 steaks
¾ cup (180ml) dry white wine
250g crème fraîche
1 tablespoon wholegrain mustard

1 Cut potatoes into 5mm slices, then each slice into thin 5mm chips. Place chips in large bowl of cold water; stand 30 minutes. Drain; pat chips dry with absorbent paper.
2 Heat vegetable oil in large saucepan; deep-fry chips, in batches, about 5 minutes or until browned lightly. Drain chips on absorbent paper; cover to keep warm.
3 Meanwhile, heat olive oil in large frying pan; cook steaks, in batches, until browned both sides and cooked as desired. Cover to keep warm.
4 Place wine in same frying pan; bring to a boil, stirring. Reduce heat; simmer, uncovered, 1 minute. Whisk in crème fraîche and mustard; simmer, uncovered, about 2 minutes or until sauce thickens slightly. Serve sauce with steak and chips.
per serving 60.5g fat; 4055kJ (969 cal)
TIP We used beef fillet from the rump, but rib-eye, boneless sirloin or eye fillet steaks are all suitable.

beef souvlaki with greek salad

preparation time 30 minutes (plus marinating time)
cooking time 15 minutes
serves 4

750g rump steak, cut into 2cm cubes
1 large brown onion (200g), cut into wedges
¼ cup (60ml) olive oil
¼ cup (60ml) lemon juice
1 tablespoon dried rigani

GREEK SALAD
4 medium plum tomatoes (300g), chopped coarsely
1 cucumber (260g), chopped coarsely
1 small red onion (100g), sliced thinly
1 large green pepper (350g), chopped coarsely
½ cup (80g) pitted kalamata olives
150g feta cheese, chopped coarsely
1 tablespoon olive oil
1 tablespoon lemon juice
2 teaspoons fresh oregano leaves

1 Thread steak and onion alternately on skewers; place souvlaki, in single layer, in large shallow dish. Combine oil, juice and rigani in jug; pour over souvlaki. Cover; refrigerate 3 hours or overnight.
2 Make greek salad.
3 Cook souvlaki, in batches, on heated oiled grill plate (or grill or barbecue) until browned all over and cooked as desired. Serve souvlaki and greek salad with tzatziki (yogurt and cucumber salad), if desired.

GREEK SALAD
Combine tomato, cucumber, onion, pepper, olives and cheese in large bowl. Place remaining ingredients in screw-top jar; shake well. Pour dressing over salad in bowl; toss gently to combine.
per serving 40.8g fat; 2627kJ (627 cal)
TIPS Souvlaki is a Greek speciality: delectably tender meat skewers which have been marinated in a herb, lemon and olive oil mixture.
Rigani (Greek oregano) is a stronger, sharper version of the herb we usually associate with Italian cooking, and is available from good delicatessens and Mediterranean food stores.
You can also use a piece of scotch fillet for this recipe. Soak 8 bamboo skewers in water for at least 1 hour before use to prevent scorching and splintering.

teriyaki steak

preparation time 10 minutes (plus marinating time)
cooking time 10 minutes
serves 4

750g piece rump steak, sliced thinly
¼ cup (60ml) rice vinegar
¼ cup (60ml) kecap manis
1 tablespoon brown sugar
¼ cup (60ml) lime juice
1 clove garlic, crushed
2 small fresh red chillies, deseeded, chopped finely
1 teaspoon sesame oil
1 tablespoon groundnut oil
1 large carrot (180g), cut into matchsticks
200g cabbage, shredded finely
¼ cup (50g) japanese pickled cucumber

1 Combine steak, vinegar, kecap manis, sugar, juice, garlic, chilli and sesame oil in large bowl, cover; refrigerate 3 hours or overnight. Drain steak; reserve marinade.
2 Heat groundnut oil in wok or large frying pan; stir-fry steak, in batches, until browned all over. Cover steak to keep warm.
3 Pour reserved marinade into wok; bring to a boil. Boil, uncovered, until sauce reduces by a third. Divide combined carrot and cabbage among serving plates; top with steak, drizzle with sauce. Serve with pickles and, if desired, steamed koshihikari rice.
per serving 18.6g fat; 1636kJ (391 cal)
TIPS Japanese pickled cucumber has a sour taste and is available, packaged in brine, from most Asian food stores.
You can also use scotch fillet in this recipe if you like.

pepper steak with scalloped potatoes

preparation time 15 minutes
cooking time 55 minutes
serves 6

6 beef fillet steaks (600g)
2 teaspoons freshly ground black pepper
1 clove garlic, crushed
1 tablespoon cornflour
1 cup (250ml) beef stock

SCALLOPED POTATOES
2 medium brown onions (300g), sliced thinly
2 cloves garlic, crushed
5 medium potatoes (1kg), sliced thinly
½ cup (120g) light soured cream
½ cup (125ml) chicken stock
1 cup (125g) coarsely grated low-fat cheddar cheese

1 Prepare scalloped potatoes.
2 Coat beef all over with pepper; cook, in batches, in large heated lightly oiled non-stick frying pan until browned both sides and cooked as desired. Cover beef to keep warm.
3 Cook garlic in same pan, stirring, until fragrant. Blend cornflour with stock in small jug; add to pan. Stir over heat until sauce mixture boils and thickens slightly. Drizzle steaks with sauce; serve with scalloped potatoes.

SCALLOPED POTATOES
Preheat oven to moderate. Heat large lightly oiled non-stick frying pan. Cook onion and garlic, stirring, until onion softens. Layer onion mixture and potato in shallow 2.5-litre (10-cup) baking dish, finishing with potato layer. Pour combined soured cream and stock over potato mixture; sprinkle with cheese. Bake, covered, in moderate oven 45 minutes. Uncover; bake further 10 minutes or until tender and browned lightly on top.
per serving 10.5g fat; 1124kJ (269 cal)

moroccan beef with citrus couscous

preparation time 15 minutes (plus standing time)
cooking time 20 minutes
serves 4

2 cloves garlic, crushed
1 teaspoon ground ginger
1 tablespoon ground cumin
2 teaspoons ground coriander
500g piece beef fillet
1 tablespoon harissa
1 cup (250ml) beef stock
200g pitted green olives, crushed slightly
½ cup coarsely chopped fresh coriander

CITRUS COUSCOUS
2 medium oranges (480g)
1 cup (250ml) water
1 cup (250ml) orange juice
2 cups (400g) couscous
¼ cup (35g) toasted slivered almonds
1 tablespoon thinly sliced preserved lemon
1 small red onion (100g), sliced thinly
500g radishes, trimmed, sliced thinly

1 Combine garlic and spices in medium bowl; reserve about a third of the spice mixture. Add beef to bowl with remaining two-thirds of the spice mixture; toss to coat beef all over. Cook beef on heated oiled grill plate (or grill or barbecue) until charred lightly both sides and cooked as desired. Cover; stand 10 minutes.

2 Make citrus couscous.

3 Meanwhile, cook harissa and remaining spice mixture in dry heated small non-stick frying pan until fragrant. Add stock; bring to a boil. Reduce heat; simmer, uncovered, about 3 minutes or until harissa dressing reduces by half. Remove from heat; stir in olives and coriander. Serve sliced beef on citrus couscous, drizzle with warm harissa dressing.

CITRUS COUSCOUS
Remove skin and white pith from oranges; cut in half, slice thinly. Place the water and juice in medium saucepan; bring to a boil. Remove from heat; stir in couscous. Cover; stand about 5 minutes or until liquid is absorbed, fluffing with fork occasionally. Add orange and remaining ingredients; toss gently to combine.

per serving 15.5g fat; 3114kJ (744 cal)
TIPS Harissa is a paste made from dried red chillies, garlic, oil and caraway seeds, and is a staple of Moroccan cooking.
Preserved lemons, a prominent ingredient in North African cooking, are lemons which have been bottled in salt and oil for several months; their flavour is subtle and perfumed. Rinse the lemons well then remove and discard flesh, using the rind only.
Rump steak can be substituted for the beef fillet.

slow-roasted leg of lamb with artichokes and lemon

preparation time 30 minutes
cooking time 4 hours
serves 4

½ cup coarsely chopped fresh flat-leaf parsley
½ cup (75g) pitted kalamata olives, quartered
4 drained anchovy fillets
4 cloves garlic, quartered
2 teaspoons finely grated lemon rind
2 tablespoons lemon juice
2 tablespoons capers, rinsed, drained
2 tablespoons olive oil
2kg leg of lamb
800g jerusalem artichokes (800g), halved
   lengthways
2 small red onions (200g), cut into wedges
2 medium lemons (280g), cut into wedges
12 cloves garlic, unpeeled

1 Preheat oven to low (140ºC/120ºC fan-assisted).
2 Blend or process parsley, olives, anchovies, quartered garlic, rind, juice, capers and 1 tablespoon of the oil until mixture is chopped coarsely.
3 Using sharp knife, pierce lamb down to the bone at 3cm intervals along the length of the leg. Spread olive mixture all over lamb, pressing into cuts.
4 Combine artichokes in large shallow baking dish with onion, lemon, unpeeled garlic and remaining oil.
5 Place lamb on artichoke mixture; cover tightly with foil. Roast in low oven 4 hours. Serve lamb with vegetable mixture.
per serving 30.4g fat; 2888kJ (691 cal)
TIP After they're peeled, keep jerusalem artichokes submerged in acidulated water to keep them from discolouring.

Looking like a knobbly parsnip, the jerusalem artichoke is a crisp tuber with the texture of a fresh water chestnut and its own unique earthy taste

roast lamb with garlic and vegetables

preparation time 25 minutes
cooking time 1 hour 25 minutes
serves 4

1.5kg easy carve leg of lamb
1 tablespoon fresh rosemary leaves
2 cloves garlic, sliced thinly
2 bulbs garlic, halved horizontally, extra
4 small parsnips (480g)
2 tablespoons olive oil
500g asparagus
12 small tomatoes on the vine
¼ cup (60ml) red wine
1 tablespoon balsamic vinegar
1 cup (250ml) beef stock

1 Preheat oven to moderate (180°C/160°C fan-assisted).
2 Using the point of a sharp knife, pierce the lamb about 12 times all over, gently twisting to make a small hole. Press rosemary and sliced garlic evenly into the holes. Place lamb on a rack in baking dish.
3 Roast lamb in moderate oven about 1 hour 10 minutes or until lamb is cooked as desired.
4 Meanwhile, place extra garlic and parsnips in separate baking dish, drizzle with half of the olive oil; bake with lamb 40 minutes. Add asparagus, tomatoes and remaining oil, bake further 10 minutes or until vegetables are tender.
5 Remove lamb from dish; cover lamb, stand 10 minutes. Drain fat from dish; place baking dish over medium heat. Add wine; bring to a boil. Add balsamic vinegar, stock and any juices collected from lamb; cook, stirring, until sauce boils and reduces to 1 cup. Serve lamb with vegetables and sauce.
per serving 31.9g fat; 3077kJ (736 cal)
TIP The lamb can be prepared several hours ahead. Recipe is best cooked close to serving.

slow-cooked lamb shoulder

preparation time 15 minutes
cooking time 4 hours 15 minutes
serves 4

2 tablespoons olive oil
1.2kg shoulder of lamb
2 medium brown onions (300g), chopped coarsely
2 medium carrots (240g), chopped coarsely
2 trimmed sticks celery (150g), chopped coarsely
1 tablespoon sugar
½ cup (125ml) dry red wine
½ cup (125ml) lamb stock
10 sprigs fresh oregano

1 Preheat oven to low.
2 Heat oil in large flameproof baking dish. Cook lamb, uncovered, over high heat until browned all over; remove lamb from dish. Cook vegetables in same dish, stirring, until browned lightly. Add sugar; cook, stirring, 1 minute. Add wine and stock. Bring to a boil; remove from heat.
3 Place half of the oregano on vegetables; place lamb on top, then place remaining oregano on lamb. Bake, covered tightly, in low oven 1½ hours. Turn lamb; bake, covered, another 1½ hours. Turn again; bake, covered, further 1 hour.
4 Carefully remove lamb from dish; wrap in foil. Strain pan contents, discarding vegetables, oregano and as much fat as possible. Serve lamb with strained hot juice.
per serving 26.4g fat; 2340kJ (559 cal)
TIP Beef stock can be substituted for lamb stock, and rosemary can be substituted for oregano.

leg of lamb with roasted vegetables and cauliflower cheese

preparation time 30 minutes
cooking time 1 hour 10 minutes
serves 6

2kg lamb leg
3 sprigs fresh rosemary, chopped coarsely
½ teaspoon sweet paprika
1kg potatoes, chopped coarsely
500g butternut squash, chopped coarsely
3 small brown onions (240g), halved
2 tablespoons olive oil
2 tablespoons plain flour
1 cup (250ml) chicken stock
¼ cup (60ml) dry red wine

CAULIFLOWER CHEESE
1 small cauliflower (1kg), cut into florets
50g butter
¼ cup (35g) plain flour
2 cups (500ml) milk
¾ cup (90g) coarsely grated cheddar cheese

1 Preheat oven to moderately hot (200°C/180°C fan-assisted).
2 Place lamb in large lightly oiled baking dish; using sharp knife, score skin at 2cm intervals, sprinkle with rosemary and paprika. Roast lamb, uncovered, in moderately hot oven 15 minutes.
3 Reduce heat to moderate (180°C/160°C fan-assisted); roast lamb, uncovered, about 45 minutes or until cooked as desired.
4 Meanwhile, place potato, squash and onion, in single layer, in large shallow baking dish; drizzle with oil. Roast, uncovered, in moderate oven for last 45 minutes of lamb cooking time.
5 Make cauliflower cheese.
6 Remove lamb and vegetables from oven; cover to keep warm. Strain pan juices from lamb into medium jug. Return ¼ cup of the pan juices to flameproof dish over medium heat, add flour; cook, stirring, about 5 minutes or until mixture bubbles and browns. Gradually add stock and wine; cook over high heat, stirring, until gravy boils and thickens.
7 Strain gravy; serve with sliced lamb, roasted vegetables and cauliflower cheese.

CAULIFLOWER CHEESE
Boil, steam or microwave cauliflower until tender; drain. Melt butter in medium saucepan, add flour; cook, stirring, until mixture bubbles and thickens. Gradually add milk; cook, stirring, until mixture boils and thickens. Stir in half of the cheese. Preheat grill. Place cauliflower in 1.5-litre (6-cup) shallow flameproof dish; pour sauce over cauliflower, sprinkle with remaining cheese. Place under preheated grill about 10 minutes or until browned lightly.
per serving 35.6g fat; 3244kJ (776 cal)

stuffed leg of lamb with roasted vegetables

preparation time 30 minutes
cooking time 1 hour 45 minutes
serves 4

40g butter
150g chestnut mushrooms, chopped finely
1 clove garlic, crushed
3 shallots (75g), chopped finely
½ cup (125ml) balsamic vinegar
1.2kg easy carve leg of lamb
1 teaspoon sea salt
2 large parsnips (700g)
2 large carrots (360g)
1 large sweet potato (500g)
2 large potatoes (600g)
2 tablespoons olive oil
½ cup (125ml) beef stock

1 Melt butter in large frying pan; cook mushrooms, garlic and shallot, stirring, until onion softens. Add half of the vinegar; bring to a boil. Reduce heat; simmer, uncovered, about 5 minutes or until liquid has evaporated.
2 Fill lamb cavity with stuffing; rub all over with salt.
3 Preheat oven to moderate (180°C/160°C fan-assisted).
4 Halve parsnips, carrots and sweet potato first crossways, then lengthways; cut pieces into thick slices. Cut potatoes into wedges. Place vegetables, in single layer, in large shallow flameproof baking dish; drizzle with oil. Place lamb on wire rack over vegetables; roast, uncovered, in moderate oven about 1 hour 30 minutes or until lamb is cooked as desired and vegetables are tender. Remove lamb and vegetables from dish, cover lamb; stand 10 minutes.
5 Meanwhile, place dish containing juices over heat; stir in stock and remaining vinegar, bring to a boil. Strain sauce into small jug. Serve vegetables with sliced lamb, drizzled with sauce.
per serving 34.3g fat; 3432kJ (821 cal)

lamb fillets with vegetable crisps and beurre blanc

preparation time 20 minutes
cooking time 35 minutes
serves 4

½ small sweet potato (125g)
1 small parsnip (120g)
1 large beetroot (200g), trimmed
1 tablespoon olive oil
4 lamb fillets (800g)
vegetable oil, for deep-frying

BEURRE BLANC
¼ cup (60ml) dry white wine
1 tablespoon lemon juice
¼ cup (60ml) cream
125g cold butter, chopped

1 Using vegetable peeler, slice sweet potato and parsnip into ribbons. Slice beetroot thinly.
2 Heat olive oil in large frying pan; cook lamb, in batches, about 5 minutes both sides or until cooked as desired. Cover to keep warm.
3 Make beurre blanc.
4 Heat vegetable oil in wok; deep-fry vegetables, in batches, until crisp. Drain on absorbent paper.
5 Cut each piece of lamb into three pieces. Divide half of the sauce among serving plates; top with lamb, remaining sauce and vegetable crisps.

BEURRE BLANC
Combine wine and juice in medium saucepan; bring to a boil. Boil, without stirring, until reduced by two-thirds. Add cream; return to a boil. Whisk in cold butter, piece by piece, whisking between additions. Pour into medium jug; cover to keep warm.
per serving 48.4g fat; 2805kJ (671 cal)

harissa-marinated leg of lamb
with warm couscous salad

*preparation time 40 minutes (plus standing
and refrigeration time)*
cooking time 1 hour 5 minutes
serves 4

1 teaspoon ground cumin
1 teaspoon ground coriander
1 teaspoon caraway seeds
2 cloves garlic, crushed
1 teaspoon salt
1 teaspoon white sugar
⅓ cup (90g) tomato puree
⅓ cup (80ml) olive oil
2kg leg of lamb

WARM COUSCOUS SALAD
2 small sweet potatoes (500g), diced into
   1cm pieces
cooking-oil spray
2 cups (400g) couscous
½ cup (60g) frozen peas, thawed
1 tablespoon finely grated lemon rind
2½ cups (625ml) boiling water
1 small red onion (100g), chopped finely
½ cup finely shredded fresh flat-leaf parsley
¼ cup finely shredded fresh mint
2 tablespoons olive oil
1 tablespoon red wine vinegar

1 Place chilli in small heatproof bowl, cover with boiling water; stand 1 hour. Drain chilli; reserve ¼ cup of the soaking liquid.
2 Dry-fry cumin, coriander and caraway in heated small frying pan until fragrant. Blend or process spices with chilli, reserved liquid, garlic, salt, sugar and tomato puree until mixture is almost smooth. With motor operating, add oil in thin, steady stream; process until harissa forms a smooth paste.
3 Reserve ¼ cup harissa. Using sharp knife, pierce lamb all over; place in large bowl. Rub remaining harissa over lamb, pressing into cuts. Cover; refrigerate 3 hours or overnight.
4 Preheat oven to moderately hot (200°C/180°C fan-assisted).
5 Pour enough water into large shallow baking dish to come about 5mm up the sides; place lamb on wire rack over dish. Roast, uncovered, in moderately hot oven about 1 hour or until cooked as desired. Cover lamb; stand 20 minutes then slice thinly.
6 Meanwhile, make warm couscous salad.
7 Serve lamb with salad.

WARM COUSCOUS SALAD
Place sweet potatoes, in single layer, on oiled oven tray; coat with cooking-oil spray. Roast, uncovered, in moderately hot oven for last 30 minutes of lamb cooking time. Combine couscous, peas, rind and the water in large heatproof bowl; cover, stand about 5 minutes or until water is absorbed, fluffing with fork occasionally. Stir sweet potatoes, onion, herbs and combined olive oil, vinegar and juice into couscous salad just before serving.
per serving 49g fat; 5150kJ (1232 cal)
TIPS Harissa, a traditional spice paste used throughout North Africa,is made from dried red chillies, garlic, olive oil and caraway seeds. It can be used as a rub for meat, an ingredient in sauces and dressings, or eaten on its own as a condiment.

tandoori lamb cutlets

preparation time 20 minutes
cooking time 10 minutes
serves 4

12 lamb cutlets (900g)
½ cup (150g) tandoori paste
¾ cup (200g) plain yogurt

CHUTNEY
1 tablespoon vegetable oil
1 small red onion (100g), chopped finely
2 large tomatoes (500g), chopped finely
1 tablespoon lime juice
1 tablespoon sweet chilli sauce
2 tablespoons chopped fresh coriander

RAITA
½ cucumber (130g), chopped finely
2 tablespoons finely chopped fresh mint
¾ cup (200g) plain yogurt

1 Combine lamb with paste and yogurt in large bowl.
2 Cook lamb on heated oiled grill plate (or grill or barbecue), in batches, until browned both sides and cooked as desired.
3 Serve lamb with separate bowls of chutney and raita. Top with thinly sliced spring onion, if desired.

CHUTNEY
Combine ingredients in small bowl.

RAITA
Combine ingredients in small bowl.
per serving 49.4g fat; 2553kJ (611 cal)
TIP Lamb can be marinated a day ahead and refrigerated, covered.

lamb cutlets with potato and parsnip mash

preparation time 15 minutes (plus marinating time)
cooking time 20 minutes
serves 6

18 french-trimmed lamb cutlets (1.4kg)
4 cloves garlic, crushed
2 teaspoons grated fresh ginger
¼ cup chopped fresh mint
⅓ cup (80ml) balsamic vinegar
2 large potatoes (600g), chopped coarsely
5 medium parsnips (625g), chopped coarsely
½ cup (125ml) buttermilk
1½ cups (375ml) vegetable stock

1 Combine lamb in large bowl with garlic, ginger, mint and half of the vinegar; toss to coat lamb all over. Cover; marinate in refrigerator 3 hours or overnight.
2 Boil, steam or microwave potato and parsnip until tender; drain. Mash potato and parsnip in large bowl with buttermilk until smooth.
3 Meanwhile, heat large lightly oiled non-stick frying pan; cook lamb, in batches, until browned both sides and cooked as desired. Cover to keep warm.
4 Add remaining vinegar and stock to same pan; bring to a boil. Reduce heat; simmer, uncovered, until sauce reduces by two-thirds. Serve lamb with mash; drizzle with strained sauce.
per serving 11.8g fat; 1396kJ (334 cal)

slow-cooked lamb shank and bean ragout

preparation time 30 minutes (plus standing time)
cooking time 2 hours 30 minutes
serves 4

½ cup (100g) dried haricot beans
½ cup (100g) dried borlotti beans
8 french-trimmed lamb shanks (1.6kg)
2 tablespoons plain flour
1 tablespoon olive oil
1 large brown onion (200g), chopped coarsely
1 medium carrot (120g), chopped coarsely
1 trimmed celery stalk (100g), chopped coarsely
1 fresh long red chilli, chopped finely
¼ cup (60ml) balsamic vinegar
425g can crushed tomatoes
8 drained anchovies in oil
½ cup (125ml) dry white wine
1 cup (250ml) water
⅓ cup coarsely chopped fresh flat-leaf parsley

1 Place beans in large bowl, cover with water; stand overnight. Rinse under cold water; drain. Place beans in medium saucepan, cover with boiling water; bring to a boil. Reduce heat; simmer, uncovered, about 15 minutes or until beans are just tender. Drain.
2 Preheat oven to moderate (180°C/160°C fan-assisted).
3 Toss lamb in flour; shake away excess. Heat oil in large flameproof casserole dish; cook lamb, in batches, until browned. Cook onion, carrot, celery and chilli in same dish, stirring, about 5 minutes or until onion softens. Return lamb to dish with beans, vinegar, undrained tomatoes, anchovies, wine and the water; bring to a boil. Cook ragout, covered, in moderate oven 1 hour, stirring occasionally. Uncover; cook in moderate oven about 1 hour or until meat is almost falling off the bone. Stir parsley through ragout just before serving.
per serving 18.1g fat; 2077kJ (497 cal)
TIP Haricot and borlotti beans are high in soluble fibre and low in fat, and best of all, they fill you up without filling you out.

Haricot and borlotti beans are just two members of the legume family. From the humble baked bean to the chickpea, legumes contain healthy components linked with protection against diseases such as cancer, diabetes and heart problems

lamb shanks with madeira and olive sauce

preparation time 15 minutes
cooking time 1 hour 45 minutes
serves 8

1 teaspoon vegetable oil
8 french-trimmed lamb shanks (1.2kg)
4 medium brown onions (600g), chopped finely
8 cloves garlic, peeled
¼ cup (30g) pitted black olives, quartered
2 tablespoons tomato paste
6 medium plum tomatoes (450g), halved
1 cup (250ml) beef stock
½ cup (125ml) madeira
2 teaspoons dried rosemary leaves

1 Preheat oven to moderate.
2 Heat oil in 3-litre (12-cup) flameproof casserole dish. Cook lamb, in batches, until browned all over. Cook onion and garlic in dish, stirring, until onion is soft.
3 Return lamb to dish. Add olive, paste, tomato, stock, madeira and rosemary; cook, uncovered, in moderate oven 1½ hours or until lamb is tender.
per serving 25g fat; 1832kJ (438 cal)
TIP Recipe can be made a day ahead and refrigerated, covered; suitable to freeze.

slow-roasted lamb shanks with tomato and olives

preparation time 15 minutes
cooking time 2 hours 25 minutes
serves 4

8 french-trimmed lamb shanks (2kg)
¼ cup (35g) plain flour
1 tablespoon olive oil
1 clove garlic, crushed
¾ cup (180ml) dry white wine
¾ cup (180ml) salt-reduced beef stock
2 x 400g cans chopped tomatoes
6 anchovy fillets, drained, chopped coarsely
½ teaspoon dried chilli flakes
1 sprig fresh basil
1 cup (150g) pitted kalamata olives
1 tablespoon balsamic vinegar
½ cup loosely packed small fresh basil leaves, extra

1 Preheat oven to moderate (180°C/160°C fan-assisted).
2 Toss lamb in flour; shake away excess flour. Heat oil in 3-litre (12-cup) flameproof casserole or baking dish; cook lamb, in batches, until browned all over.
3 Add garlic and wine to same dish; bring to a boil. Add stock, undrained tomatoes, anchovies, chilli and basil sprig; stir to combine.
4 Return lamb to dish; bring to a boil. Remove from heat. Cover with lid or tightly with foil; cook in moderate oven about 2 hours or until lamb is tender, turning lamb halfway through cooking. Remove lamb from dish; cover to keep warm.
5 Add olives and vinegar to dish; simmer, uncovered, over medium heat about 5 minutes or until thickened slightly. Remove basil sprig.
6 Sprinkle extra basil leaves over lamb and sauce; serve with risoni, if desired.
per serving 25.4g fat; 2178kJ (521 cal)

lamb racks with garlic and sage

preparation time 10 minutes
cooking time 25 minutes
serves 4

3 large red onions (900g)
12 fresh sage leaves
⅓ cup (80ml) olive oil
2 tablespoons coarsely chopped fresh sage
4 cloves garlic, chopped coarsely
4 x 4 french-trimmed lamb cutlet racks (600g)

1 Preheat oven to hot (220°C/200°C fan-assisted).
2 Halve onions, slice into thin wedges; place in large baking dish with sage leaves and half of the oil.
3 Combine remaining oil in small bowl with chopped sage and garlic. Press sage mixture all over lamb; place on onion in dish.
4 Roast, uncovered, in hot oven about 25 minutes or until lamb is browned all over and cooked as desired. Cover lamb racks; stand 10 minutes.
per serving 31.3g fat; 1676kJ (401 cal)
TIP Red onions are sweet and have a less aggressive flavour than their brown and white counterparts.

bacon-wrapped lamb chops with baby potatoes in olive pesto

preparation time 20 minutes
cooking time 20 minutes
serves 4

8 lamb loin chops (800g)
4 bacon rashers (280g), rind removed, halved
  lengthways
⅓ cup (80ml) olive oil
4 medium plum tomatoes (300g), halved
800g baby new potatoes, halved
1 cup firmly packed fresh basil leaves
1 tablespoon lemon juice
¼ cup (60ml) buttermilk
½ cup (60g) pitted green olives
¼ cup (40g) toasted pine nuts

1 Wrap each chop around the outside with one strip of the bacon; securing each with a toothpick.
2 Heat 1 tablespoon of the oil in large frying pan; cook chops, in batches, until browned both sides and cooked as desired. Remove toothpicks, cover chops; stand 5 minutes.
3 Meanwhile, cook tomato in same pan, cut-side down, until soft. Boil, steam or microwave potato until tender; drain.
4 Blend or process remaining oil with basil, juice and buttermilk until mixture forms a smooth paste. Add olives and pine nuts; process pesto until just combined.
5 Place potato and pesto in large bowl; toss gently to combine. Divide potato, chops and tomato among serving plates. Serve with tomato chutney, if desired.
per serving 44g fat; 3001kJ (718 cal)
TIP Always press the trimmed basil leaves firmly into a measuring cup so that the proportion of the herb to the other pesto ingredients is correct: too little basil will give the paste a watery texture and a taste that's more of olive than herb.

cassoulet with herb and rocket salad

preparation time 40 minutes (plus standing time)
cooking time 1 hour 40 minutes
serves 4

1 cup (200g) dried white beans
150g piece streaky bacon, rind removed,
    diced into 1cm pieces
500g thin lamb sausages, sliced thickly
1 medium brown onion (150g), chopped finely
2 trimmed celery stalks (200g), chopped finely
2 cloves garlic, crushed
1 sprig fresh rosemary
2 bay leaves
425g can crushed tomatoes
1½ cups (375ml) chicken stock
2 cups (140g) stale breadcrumbs
⅓ cup coarsely chopped fresh flat-leaf parsley

HERB AND ROCKET SALAD
60g baby rocket leaves
1 cup loosely packed fresh flat-leaf parsley leaves
1 cup loosely packed fresh chervil sprigs
½ cup loosely packed fresh basil leaves
¼ cup (60ml) olive oil
2 tablespoons red wine vinegar
1 teaspoon white sugar

1 Place beans in large bowl, cover with water; soak overnight, drain. Rinse under cold water; drain. Place beans in medium saucepan covered with boiling water; bring to a boil. Reduce heat; simmer, covered, about 15 minutes or until beans are just tender. Drain.

2 Preheat oven to moderately low (160°C/140°C fan-assisted).

3 Cook bacon in large flameproof casserole dish over high heat, pressing down with back of spoon, until browned all over; remove from dish. Cook sausage in same dish until browned all over; remove from dish.

4 Cook onion, celery and garlic in same dish, stirring, about 5 minutes or until soft. Add rosemary, bay leaves, undrained tomatoes, stock, beans, bacon and sausage; bring to a boil. Cover; cook in moderately low oven 30 minutes. Remove from oven; sprinkle with combined breadcrumbs and parsley. Return to oven; cook, covered, 30 minutes. Uncover; cook about 10 minutes or until top browns lightly.

5 Meanwhile, make herb and rocket salad by combining rocket, parsley, chervil and basil in large bowl. Place remaining ingredients in screw-top jar; shake vinaigrette well.

6 Toss salad with vinaigrette just before serving with cassoulet.

per serving 44.3g fat; 3603kJ (862 cal)
TIPS We used dried white haricot beans in this recipe, but cannellini, borlotti or even lima beans can be used if you prefer.

moussaka

preparation time 40 minutes (plus standing time)
cooking time 1 hour 30 minutes
serves 6

2 large aubergines (1kg), sliced thinly
1 tablespoon coarse cooking salt
¼ cup (60ml) olive oil
1 large brown onion (200g), chopped finely
2 cloves garlic, crushed
1kg minced lamb
425g can crushed tomatoes
½ cup (125ml) dry white wine
1 teaspoon ground cinnamon
¼ cup (20g) finely grated parmesan cheese

WHITE SAUCE
80g butter
⅓ cup (50g) plain flour
2 cups (500ml) milk

1 Place aubergine in colander, sprinkle all over with salt; stand 30 minutes. Rinse under cold water; drain. Pat dry with absorbent paper. Heat oil in large frying pan; cook aubergine, in batches, until browned both sides; drain on absorbent paper.
2 Cook onion and garlic in same pan, stirring, until onion softens. Add lamb; cook, stirring, until it changes colour. Stir in undrained tomatoes, wine and cinnamon; bring to a boil. Reduce heat; simmer, uncovered, about 30 minutes or until liquid has evaporated.
3 Preheat oven to moderate (180°C/160°C fan-assisted). Oil shallow 2-litre (8-cup) rectangular baking dish.
4 Make white sauce.
5 Place a third of the aubergine, overlapping slices slightly, in prepared dish; spread half the meat sauce on top. Repeat layering with another third of the aubergine, remaining meat sauce and remaining aubergine. Spread white sauce over top; sprinkle with cheese. Cook, uncovered, in moderate oven about 40 minutes until lightly browned. Cover; stand 10 minutes before serving.

WHITE SAUCE
Melt butter in medium saucepan. Add flour; cook, stirring, until mixture thickens and bubbles. Gradually add milk; stir until mixture boils and thickens.
per serving 36.6g fat; 2420kJ (579 cal)

lamb burgers with beetroot relish and yogurt

preparation time 30 minutes
cooking time 45 minutes
serves 4

500g minced lamb
1 small brown onion (80g), chopped finely
2 cloves garlic, crushed
1 teaspoon ground cumin
1 egg, beaten lightly
1 tablespoon olive oil
¾ cup (210g) greek-style yogurt
½ teaspoon ground cumin, extra
1 tablespoon finely chopped fresh mint
1 long ciabatta loaf
50g baby rocket leaves

BEETROOT RELISH
⅓ cup (80ml) water
4 medium beetroots (700g), grated coarsely
1 small brown onion (80g), chopped finely
½ cup (110g) white sugar
⅔ cup (160ml) apple cider vinegar

1 Make beetroot relish.
2 Meanwhile, using hand, combine lamb, onion, garlic, cumin and egg in medium bowl; shape mixture into four patties.
3 Heat oil in large frying pan; cook patties, uncovered, until browned both sides and cooked as desired. Cover to keep warm.
4 Combine yogurt, extra cumin and mint in small bowl.
5 Cut pide into quarters; halve quarters horizontally. Toast bread pieces, cut-side up. Sandwich rocket, patties, yogurt mixture and relish between bread pieces.

BEETROOT RELISH
Combine the water, beetroot and onion in large non-stick frying pan; cook, covered, about 15 minutes or until beetroot is tender. Stir in sugar and vinegar; cook, covered, stirring occasionally, 20 minutes. Uncover; cook, stirring occasionally, about 10 minutes or until liquid evaporates.
per serving 22g fat; 3173kJ (759 cal)
TIP Beetroot relish will keep, covered and refrigerated, for up to three days.

lamb and apricot tagine
with citrus couscous

preparation time 20 minutes (plus standing time)
cooking time 1 hour
serves 8

1⅔ cups (250g) dried apricots
¾ cup (180ml) orange juice
½ cup (125ml) boiling water
2 tablespoons olive oil
900g lamb steaks, chopped coarsely
2 medium red peppers (400g), chopped coarsely
1 large brown onion (200g), chopped coarsely
2 medium sweet potatoes (800g), chopped coarsely
3 cloves garlic, crushed
1 teaspoon ground cinnamon
2 teaspoons ground cumin
2 teaspoons ground coriander
1 cup (250ml) dry red wine
1 litre (4 cups) chicken stock
2 tablespoons honey
1 cup loosely packed fresh coriander leaves
¾ cup (200g) low-fat plain yogurt

CITRUS COUSCOUS
1 litre (4 cups) water
4 cups (800g) couscous
1 tablespoon finely grated orange rind
2 teaspoons finely grated lemon rind
2 teaspoons finely grated lime rind

1 Combine apricots, juice and the water in small bowl. Cover; allow to stand 45 minutes.
2 Meanwhile, heat half of the oil in large saucepan; cook lamb, in batches, until browned all over.
3 Heat remaining oil in same pan; cook capsicum, onion, sweet potato, garlic and ground spices, stirring, until onion softens and mixture is fragrant. Add wine; bring to a boil. Reduce heat; simmer, uncovered, about 5 minutes or until liquid reduces by half.
4 Return lamb to pan with undrained apricots, stock and honey; bring to a boil. Reduce heat; simmer, covered, about 50 minutes or until lamb is tender. Remove from heat; stir in fresh coriander.
5 Serve lamb and apricot tagine on citrus couscous; drizzle with yogurt.

CITRUS COUSCOUS
Bring the water to a boil in medium saucepan; stir in couscous and rinds. Remove from heat; stand, covered, about 5 minutes or until liquid is absorbed, fluffing with fork occasionally to separate grains.
per serving 12.8g fat; 1837kJ (439 cal)

navarin of lamb

preparation time 30 minutes
cooking time 1 hour 15 minutes
serves 4

2 tablespoons olive oil
8 lamb chump chops (880g)
1 medium brown onion (150g), sliced thinly
3 cloves garlic, crushed
2 tablespoons plain flour
2 cups (500ml) vegetable stock
2 cups (500ml) water
2 x 400g cans diced tomatoes
½ teaspoon black peppercorns
2 bay leaves
1 sprig fresh rosemary
8 baby new potatoes (320g), halved
3 small brown onions (240g), quartered
1 bunch baby turnips (500g), trimmed, peeled, quartered
10 baby carrots (200g), halved lengthways
1 cup (120g) frozen peas
½ cup coarsely chopped fresh flat-leaf parsley

1 Heat oil in large heavy-based saucepan; cook chops, in batches, only until browned.
2 Cook sliced onion in same pan, stirring, until just softened. Add garlic and flour; stir until mixture bubbles and thickens. Gradually add stock and the water; stir until mixture boils and thickens slightly. Return chops to pan with undrained tomatoes, peppercorns, bay leaves and rosemary; bring to a boil. Reduce heat; simmer, covered, 20 minutes.
3 Add potato, quartered onion, turnip and carrot to pan; simmer, covered, 30 minutes, stirring occasionally. Add peas; simmer, uncovered, until peas are just tender. Sprinkle parsley over navarin just before serving.
per serving 37.2g fat; 2721kJ (651 cal)
TIP Rather like a French version of a hot pot, a navarin is an aromatic stew, which, in the spring, is traditionally made with the best of new season vegetables and lamb.

lamb curry with yogurt

preparation time 20 minutes (plus marinating time)
cooking time 1 hour 15 minutes
serves 6

1 medium brown onion (150g), chopped coarsely
1 tablespoon grated fresh ginger
2 cloves garlic, crushed
1 teaspoon coriander seeds
1 teaspoon cumin seeds
½ teaspoon cardamom seeds
2 tablespoons lime juice
2.5kg leg of lamb, boned, chopped coarsely
30g ghee
¼ teaspoon cayenne pepper
2 teaspoons ground turmeric
1 teaspoon garam masala
⅔ cup (190g) plain yogurt
⅔ cup (160ml) cream
1 cup (250ml) water
400g can chickpeas, rinsed, drained
2 medium tomatoes (380g), chopped coarsely
1 tablespoon plain flour
2 tablespoons water, extra
¼ cup chopped fresh flat-leaf parsley

1 Blend or process onion, ginger, garlic, seeds and juice until well combined. Place blended mixture and lamb in medium bowl; stir until lamb is well coated. Cover; marinate in refrigerator 3 hours or overnight.
2 Heat ghee in large saucepan; add cayenne pepper, turmeric and garam masala; stir over medium heat 1 minute.
3 Stir in yogurt, then lamb; stir over high heat until lamb is well browned. Stir in combined cream and water; bring to a boil. Reduce heat; simmer, uncovered, about 1 hour or until lamb is tender. Stir in chickpeas and tomato.
4 Stir in blended flour and the extra water; stir over high heat until sauce boils and thickens. Stir in parsley; serve with lime wedges, if desired.
per serving 37.5g fat; 2877kJ (687 cal)
TIPS Ask your butcher to bone the leg of lamb for you. Recipe can be made a day ahead and refrigerated, covered.

lamb chops and lentil stew with vegetable mash

preparation time 20 minutes
cooking time 1 hour 45 minutes
serves 4

1 cup (200g) brown lentils
1 tablespoon vegetable oil
1.5kg lamb neck chops
2 medium brown onions (300g), chopped coarsely
2 cloves garlic, crushed
4 rindless bacon rashers (280g), chopped coarsely
1 teaspoon caraway seeds
2 teaspoons ground cumin
½ cup (125ml) dry red wine
⅓ cup (90g) tomato paste
2 cups (500ml) beef stock
425g can diced tomatoes
½cup coarsely chopped fresh coriander

SWEET POTATO AND CARROT MASH
2 medium sweet potatoes (800g), chopped coarsely
2 medium carrots (240g), chopped coarsely
1 teaspoon ground cumin
⅓ cup (80ml) buttermilk

1 Cook lentils in large saucepan of boiling water, uncovered, about 15 minutes or until tender; drain.
2 Preheat oven to moderate (180°C/160°C fan-assisted).
3 Meanwhile, heat oil in large flameproof casserole dish; cook chops, in batches, until browned. Cook onion, garlic and bacon in same heated pan, stirring, until onion is just browned and bacon is crisp. Add spices; cook, stirring, until fragrant. Add wine, paste, stock and undrained tomatoes; bring to a boil.
4 Return chops to dish; stir in lentils, Cook, covered, in moderate oven 1 hour 10 minutes.
5 Meanwhile, make sweet potato and carrot mash.
6 Stir coriander into stew just before serving with mash.

SWEET POTATO AND CARROT MASH
Boil, steam or microwave sweet potato and carrot, separately, until tender; drain. Dry-fry cumin in small frying pan until fragrant. Mash vegetables in large bowl with cumin and buttermilk until smooth.
per serving 47.9g fat; 3896kJ (932 cal)

lamb madras with roti

preparation time 50 minutes
cooking time 2 hours
serves 8

2 tablespoons groundnut oil
1.5kg diced lamb
2 medium brown onions (300g), chopped coarsely
2 cloves garlic, crushed
1 tablespoon ground cumin
2 tablespoons ground coriander
2 teaspoons garam masala
1 teaspoon chilli powder
1 cinnamon stick
5 medium tomatoes (1kg), chopped coarsely
3 cups (750ml) beef stock
400ml coconut cream

ROTI
1½ cups (225g) besan flour
1½ cups (240g) wholemeal plain flour
1½ cups (225g) plain flour
1½ teaspoons salt
80g ghee
2 tablespoons chopped fresh coriander
1 cup (250ml) warm water, approximately

1 Heat half of the oil in large heavy-base saucepan; cook lamb, in batches, until browned all over.
2 Heat remaining oil in same pan; cook onion and garlic, stirring, until onion is soft. Add spices, chilli and cinnamon; cook, stirring, about 2 minutes or until fragrant.
3 Return lamb to pan with tomato and stock; bring to a boil. Reduce heat; simmer, uncovered, 1½ hours.
4 Add coconut cream; simmer, uncovered, about 10 minutes or until sauce is just thickened. Discard cinnamon stick. Serve curry with roti.

ROTI
Sift flours and salt into large bowl; rub in ghee. Stir in coriander and just enough of the water to form a soft dough. Knead on floured surface about 5 minutes or until dough is smooth and elastic. Divide dough into 16 pieces; roll each piece into a 17cm-round roti. During preparation, stack rotis between pieces of plastic wrap; cover completely with cling film to avoid rotis drying out. Cook rotis, in batches, on heated oiled grill plate (or grill or barbecue) until browned both sides and puffed slightly.
per serving 37.4g fat; 3289kJ (787 cal)
TIP Pass each roti over a naked flame just before serving to make it puff and become more supple.

Perfectly suited to a relaxed style of eating and entertaining, barbecue is the definitive casual food, from the Asian-influenced lime chicken on lemongrass skewers to the hearty flavours of veal T-bone with buttered spinach and roast tomatoes.

barbeque

rosemary and garlic kebabs

japanese-style lamb kebabs

lamb thai red curry skewers

lamb, haloumi and allspice kebabs

rosemary and garlic lamb kebabs

preparation time 20 minutes
cooking time 20 minutes
makes 8 kebabs

8 x 15cm stalks fresh rosemary
1 clove garlic, crushed
1 tablespoon lemon juice
1 tablespoon olive oil
500g diced lamb

1 Pull enough leaves from bottom of rosemary stalks to make 2 tablespoons of finely chopped leaves; toss in small bowl with garlic, juice and oil.
2 Thread lamb onto rosemary stalk skewers; brush with rosemary oil mixture.
3 Cook kebabs on heated oiled grill plate (or grill or barbecue) until browned all over and cooked as desired.
per serving 15.6g fat; 1024kJ (245 cal)
TIPS Serve with warmed pitta bread or steamed rice, if desired. Soak bamboo skewers in cold water for at least 1 hour before using to prevent them scorching and splintering.

japanese-style lamb kebabs

preparation time 20 minutes
cooking time 20 minutes
makes 8 kebabs

½ cup (125ml) japanese soy sauce
½ cup (125ml) sake
¼ cup (60ml) mirin
2 tablespoons white sugar
500g diced lamb
1 medium carrot (120g), sliced thinly
6 spring onions, cut into 3cm lengths

1 Combine sauce, sake, mirin and sugar in small saucepan; bring to a boil. Reduce heat; simmer, uncovered, until sauce reduces by a third. Cool 10 minutes.
2 Meanwhile, thread lamb, carrot and onion, alternately, onto skewers.
3 Cook kebabs on heated oiled grill plate (or grill or barbecue), brushing with half of the sauce occasionally, until browned all over and cooked as desired. Serve yakitori with remaining sauce.
per serving 11.1g fat; 1229kJ (294 cal)
TIPS Serve with warmed pitta bread or steamed rice, if desired. Soak bamboo skewers in cold water for at least 1 hour before using to prevent them scorching and splintering.

lamb thai red curry skewers

preparation time 20 minutes
cooking time 20 minutes
makes 8 kebabs

2 tablespoons thai red curry paste
1 tablespoon fish sauce
1 tablespoon brown sugar
1 tablespoon lime juice
500g diced lamb
1 medium red pepper (200g), diced into 2cm pieces
1 lime, cut into 8 wedges

1 Combine paste, sauce, sugar and juice in small bowl.
2 Thread lamb and pepper, alternately, onto skewers; thread one lime wedge on each skewer. Brush skewers with half of the curry paste mixture.
3 Cook kebabs on heated oiled grill plate (or grill or barbecue), brushing with remaining curry paste mixture occasionally, until browned all over and cooked as desired.
per serving 14.7g fat; 1124kJ (269 cal)
TIPS Serve with warmed pitta bread or steamed rice, if desired. Soak bamboo skewers in cold water for at least 1 hour before using to prevent them scorching and splintering.

lamb, haloumi and allspice kebabs

preparation time 20 minutes
cooking time 20 minutes
makes 8 kebabs

½ teaspoon ground allspice
1 teaspoon cracked black pepper
1 clove garlic, crushed
2 tablespoons lemon juice
2 tablespoons olive oil
500g diced lamb
200g haloumi cheese, diced into 2cm pieces

1 Place allspice, pepper, garlic, juice and oil in medium bowl; add lamb, turn to coat in mixture. Thread lamb and cheese, alternately, onto skewers.
2 Cook kebabs on heated oiled grill plate (or grill or barbecue) until browned all over and cooked as desired.
per serving 28.7g fat); 1710kJ (409 cal)
TIPS Serve with warmed pitta bread or steamed rice, if desired. Soak bamboo skewers in cold water for at least 1 hour before using to prevent them scorching and splintering.

lamb cutlets with char-grilled vegetable salad

preparation time 10 minutes
cooking time 15 minutes
serves 4

⅓ cup (80ml) olive oil
350g sweet potatoes, sliced thinly
2 tablespoons balsamic vinegar
1 clove garlic, crushed
12 french-trimmed lamb cutlets (600g)
150g marinated char-grilled aubergine, sliced thickly
150g marinated char-grilled pepper, sliced thickly
125g char-grilled artichokes, quartered, optional
2 cups loosely packed fresh flat-leaf parsley leaves
2 tablespoons lemon juice

1 Combine one tablespoon of the oil with sweet potatoes in medium bowl. Cook sweet potatoes on heated, oiled barbecue (or grill plate or frying pan) until browned lightly and cooked through.
2 Combine another tablespoon of the oil with vinegar and garlic in small bowl; brush over lamb. Cook lamb on heated, oiled barbecue (or grill plate or frying pan) until browned lightly and cooked as desired.
3 In large bowl, toss sweet potatoes with aubergines, peppers, artichokes and parsley. Drizzle with combined juice and remaining oil. Serve lamb accompanied with vegetable mixture.
per serving 49.4g fat; 2533kJ (606 cal)
TIP This recipe is best made close to serving.

barbecued veal with tomato, capers and basil

preparation time 15 minutes
cooking time 20 minutes
serves 6

9 baby aubergines (540g), halved lengthways
6 small courgettes (540g), sliced thickly
⅓ cup (80ml) extra virgin olive oil
6 veal cutlets (1kg)
2 medium plum tomatoes (150g), deseeded,
  chopped finely
½ small red onion (50g), chopped finely
1 clove garlic, crushed
2 tablespoons drained small capers
1 tablespoon balsamic vinegar
1 tablespoon fresh baby basil leaves

1 Brush aubergines and courgettes with half of the oil; cook, in batches, on heated grill plate (or grill or barbecue) until browned and tender. Transfer to a plate; cover to keep warm.
2 Cook veal on heated, oiled grill plate (or grill or barbecue) until browned and cooked as desired. Transfer to a plate, cover veal; stand 10 minutes.
3 Meanwhile, combine tomato, onion, garlic, capers, vinegar and remaining oil in small bowl.
4 Divide aubergines and courgettes among plates; top with cutlets and tomato mixture, sprinkle with basil leaves.
per serving 16.7g fat; 1162kJ (278 cal)
TIP Antipasto aubergines and courgettes may be used instead of fresh for a quicker alternative.

basil and oregano steak with char-grilled vegetables

preparation time 20 minutes
cooking time 30 minutes
serves 4

2 teaspoons finely chopped fresh oregano
¼ cup finely chopped fresh basil
1 tablespoon finely grated lemon rind
2 tablespoons lemon juice
4 anchovy fillets, drained, chopped finely
4 beef sirloin steaks (1kg)
2 baby fennel bulbs (260g), quartered
3 small courgettes (270g), chopped coarsely
1 large red pepper (350g), sliced thickly
200g portobello mushrooms, sliced thickly
4 baby aubergines (240g), chopped coarsely
2 small red onions (200g), sliced thickly
2 teaspoons olive oil
¼ cup (60ml) lemon juice. extra
2 tablespoons fresh oregano leaves

1 Combine chopped oregano, basil, rind, the 2 tablespoons of lemon juice and anchovy in large bowl, add beef; toss beef to coat in marinade. Cover; refrigerate until required.
2 Meanwhile, combine fennel, courgette, pepper, mushroom, aubergine, onion and oil in large bowl; cook vegetables, in batches, on heated, lightly oiled grill plate (or grill or barbecue) until just tender. Add extra lemon juice and oregano leaves to bowl with vegetables; toss gently to combine. Cover to keep warm.
3 Cook beef mixture on same grill plate (or grill or barbecue) until cooked as desired; serve with char-grilled vegetables.
per serving 26.1g fat; 2153kJ (515 cal)

Dress the vegetables with lemon juice and oregano for added flavour.

new york steaks with lemon thyme butter

preparation time 15 minutes (plus refrigeration time)
cooking time 45 minutes
serves 4

4 large potatoes (1.2kg), cut into wedges
2 medium red onions (340g), cut into wedges
1 medium lemon (140g), cut into wedges
2 teaspoons fresh thyme leaves
¼ cup (60ml) olive oil
4 New York-cut beef steaks (880g)

LEMON THYME BUTTER
60g butter, softened
2 teaspoons finely grated lemon rind
1 teaspoon finely chopped fresh thyme
1 clove garlic, crushed

1 Preheat oven to hot (220°C/200°C fan-assisted).
2 Make lemon thyme butter.
3 Combine potato, onion, lemon, thyme and oil in large deep baking dish. Bake, uncovered, in hot oven, stirring occasionally, about 45 minutes or until potato is browned and crisp.
4 Meanwhile, cook beef, in batches, on heated, oiled grill plate (or grill or barbecue) until browned both sides and cooked as desired.
5 Serve beef with potato and onion mixture, topped with lemon thyme butter.

LEMON THYME BUTTER
Combine ingredients in small bowl. Cover; refrigerate until firm.
per serving 46.4g fat; 3306kJ (791 cal)
TIP New York-cut steaks are also known as boneless sirloin steaks.

veal t-bone with buttered spinach and roast tomatoes

preparation time 15 minutes
cooking time 1 hour
serves 4

12 small tomatoes on vine (1.5kg)
4 veal T-bone steaks (850g)
50g butter
2 cloves garlic, crushed
900g spinach, trimmed
¼ cup shredded fresh basil leaves
2 tablespoons olive oil
50g pecorino cheese, shaved

1 Preheat oven to moderately low.
2 Place tomatoes in large oiled baking dish. Roast, uncovered, in moderately low oven about 1 hour or until tomatoes soften.
3 Meanwhile, cook veal on heated oiled barbecue plate until browned both sides and cooked as desired.
4 Melt butter in large saucepan; cook garlic and spinach until spinach just wilts.
5 Serve veal with spinach and tomatoes. Spoon over combined basil and oil; sprinkle with cheese.
per serving 26g fat; 1804kJ (432 cal)

lime chicken on lemongrass skewers

preparation time 20 minutes (plus marinating time)
cooking time 15 minutes
serves 6

6 x 30cm-long fresh lemongrass stalks
⅓ cup (80ml) groundnut oil
1 tablespoon grated lime rind
¼ cup chopped fresh coriander
6 single chicken breast fillets (1kg)
¼ cup (60ml) lime juice
2 fresh red thai chillies, deseeded, chopped finely
⅓ cup (80ml) macadamia oil
1 tablespoon raw sugar
1 clove garlic, crushed

1 Cut 3cm off the end of each lemongrass stalk; reserve stalks. Chop the 3cm pieces finely; combine in large shallow dish with groundnut oil, rind and coriander.
2 Cut each chicken fillet into three strips crossways; thread three strips onto each lemongrass stalk 'skewer'. Place skewers in dish with lemongrass marinade; turn skewers to coat chicken in marinade. Cover; refrigerate 3 hours or overnight.
3 Cook skewers on heated oiled barbecue, uncovered, until chicken is browned all over and tender. Meanwhile, combine remaining ingredients in screw-top jar; shake well. Serve with chicken skewers.
per serving 33.6g fat; 1907kJ (456 cal)

yakitori chicken

preparation time 15 minutes
cooking time 10 minutes
serves 4

1kg chicken breast fillets
¼ cup (60ml) mirin
½ cup (125ml) light soy sauce
2 teaspoons grated fresh ginger
2 cloves garlic, crushed
¼ teaspoon freshly ground black pepper
1 tablespoon sugar

1 Cut chicken into 2cm pieces.
2 Combine chicken with remaining ingredients in large bowl. Drain chicken over small bowl; reserve marinade.
3 Thread chicken onto 12 bamboo skewers. Cook skewers on heated oiled barbecue plate, turning and brushing occasionally with reserved marinade during cooking, until chicken is browned all over and cooked through.
per serving 13.8g fat; 1614kJ (386 cal)
TIPS Mirin is a somewhat sweet rice wine used in many Asian, especially Japanese, dishes. You can substitute sherry or sweet white wine for mirin, if you prefer.
You will need to soak 12 bamboo skewers in water for at least an hour before use, to prevent them from splintering and scorching.

barbecued chicken with sweet chilli vinegar sauce

preparation time 20 minutes (plus refrigeration time)
cooking time 20 minutes (plus cooling time)
serves 4

1kg chicken thigh fillets
2 tablespoons groundnut oil
½ cup (125ml) coconut milk

PASTE
4 cloves garlic, crushed
1 teaspoon cracked black peppercorns
2 teaspoons white sugar
2 teaspoons ground turmeric
2 teaspoons hot paprika
1 tablespoon chopped fresh coriander root
1 teaspoon curry powder
2 fresh small red thai chillies, chopped
1 tablespoon groundnut oil

SWEET CHILLI VINEGAR SAUCE
6 fresh small red thai chillies, chopped coarsely
4 cloves garlic, quartered
1 cup (250ml) white vinegar
½ cup (110g) caster sugar
1 teaspoon coarse cooking salt
1 teaspoon tamarind paste

1 Using mortar and pestle, crush ingredients for paste.
2 Cut chicken in half, combine with paste and oil in large bowl; cover, refrigerate 3 hours or overnight.
3 Cook chicken on barbecue (or grill or grill plate), basting frequently with coconut milk, until browned and cooked through.
4 Meanwhile, make sweet chilli vinegar sauce.
5 Serve chicken with sauce, and salad greens, if desired.

SWEET CHILLI VINEGAR SAUCE
Place ingredients in small saucepan, stir over heat, without boiling, until sugar is dissolved. Bring to a boil, simmer, uncovered, about 15 minutes or until slightly thickened; cool 5 minutes. Blend or process mixture until chopped finely.
per serving 38.3g fat; 2759kJ (660 cal)
TIPS Paste can be made a week ahead; keep, covered, in refrigerator. Sauce can be made a day ahead; keep, covered, in refrigerator.
Chicken best cooked just before serving.

tandoori chicken

preparation time 10 minutes (plus marinating time)
cooking time 15 minutes
serves 6

½ cup (140g) low-fat plain yogurt
1 tablespoon lemon juice
½ teaspoon finely grated fresh ginger
1 clove garlic, crushed
½ teaspoon caster sugar
½ teaspoon paprika
¼ teaspoon ground cumin
¼ teaspoon ground coriander
¼ teaspoon ground turmeric
pinch chilli powder
2 x 200g single chicken breast fillets

TOMATO AND CORIANDER SALSA
1 small tomato (130g), chopped finely
½ small red onion (50g), chopped finely
1 teaspoon sugar
1 tablespoon chopped fresh coriander

1 Combine yogurt, juice, ginger, garlic, sugar, paprika and spices in large bowl. Add chicken; turn to coat in marinade. Refrigerate 3 hours or overnight.
2 Cook chicken on heated barbeque, or oiled grill plate, brushing with marinade, until browned both sides and tender. Serve chicken sliced thickly, with tomato and coriander salsa, and steamed rice, if desired.

TOMATO AND CORIANDER SALSA
Combine ingredients in small bowl.
per serving 12.5g fat; 1457kJ (349 cal)
TIP Chicken is best marinated a day ahead and refrigerated, covered.

chicken tikka with cucumber-mint raita

preparation time 15 minutes
cooking time 10 minutes
serves 4

1kg chicken breast fillets
½ cup (150g) tikka paste

CUCUMBER-MINT RAITA
¾ cup (200g) plain yogurt
½ cucumber (130g), peeled, chopped finely
2 tablespoons chopped fresh mint
1 teaspoon ground cumin

1 Combine chicken with paste in large bowl.
2 Cook chicken, in batches, on heated oiled barbecue plate until browned all over and cooked through.
3 Serve sliced chicken with cucumber-mint raita on a bed of cabbage with mango chutney, if desired.

CUCUMBER-MINT RAITA
Combine ingredients in small bowl.
per serving 31.6g fat; 2148kJ (514 cal)
TIPS The word tikka actually refers to a bite-size piece of meat, poultry, fish or vegetable.
Ready-made tikka paste can be found in jars in most supermarkets. You can also serve this recipe in the traditional manner, by threading the chopped or sliced chicken breast fillets onto bamboo skewers before grilling or barbecuing. You will need to soak 12 bamboo skewers in water for at least an hour before use, to prevent them from splintering and scorching.

cumin fish cutlets with coriander chilli sauce

preparation time 15 minutes
cooking time 10 minutes
serves 6

6 firm white fish cutlets (1.2kg)
2 teaspoons cumin seeds

CORIANDER CHILLI SAUCE
8 spring onions, chopped coarsely
3 cloves garlic, crushed
3 fresh red thai chillies, seeded, chopped finely
1 tablespoon finely chopped coriander root
2 tablespoons brown sugar
2 tablespoons fish sauce
¼ cup (60ml) lime juice

1 Sprinkle one side of each cutlet with seeds. Cook fish on heated oiled barbecue plate, until browned on both sides and just cooked through.
2 Serve fish with coriander chilli sauce and lime, if desired.

CORIANDER CHILLI SAUCE
Using the 'pulse' button, blend or process onion, garlic, chilli, coriander root and sugar until chopped finely. Add sauce and juice; blend until combined.
per serving 4.3g fat; 915kJ (218 cal)
TIP This recipe is best made just before serving.

salmon with grilled corn salsa

preparation time 20 minutes
cooking time 25 minutes
serves 6

6 salmon fillets or cutlets (1.2kg)

CORN SALSA
2 trimmed corn cobs (500g)
2 medium red peppers (400g)
1 small red onion (100g), chopped finely
1 fresh red thai chilli, deseeded, chopped finely
1 tablespoon olive oil
¼ cup chopped fresh coriander

1 Cook salmon on heated oiled barbecue plate until browned both sides and cooked as desired. Salmon is best served a little rare in the centre.
2 Serve salmon with corn salsa and grilled bread, if desired.

CORN SALSA
Cook corn on heated oiled barbecue plate, covered loosely with a piece of foil, about 20 minutes or until browned all over and tender. Using a sharp knife, cut kernels from cobs. Quarter peppers; remove and discard seeds and membranes. Cook on heated oiled barbecue plate until skin blisters and blackens. Cover pepper pieces with plastic or paper 5 minutes. Peel away and discard skin; chop pepper flesh finely. Combine corn, pepper, onion, chilli, oil and coriander in medium bowl.
per serving 18.5g fat; 1766kJ (422 cal)
TIPS Barbecuing corn gives it a distinctive smoky flavour.
Corn salsa can be made 3 hours ahead.

barbecued sweet and sour fish fillets

preparation time 20 minutes
cooking time 20 minutes
serves 4

1 small pineapple (900g), chopped coarsely
1 large red pepper (350g), chopped coarsely
1 medium green pepper (200g), chopped coarsely
1 medium red onion (170g), sliced thinly
4 firm white fish fillets (800g)
2 tablespoons caster sugar
½ cup (125ml) white vinegar
2 tablespoons soy sauce
1 fresh long red chilli, sliced thinly
4cm piece fresh ginger (20g), grated finely
3 spring onions, sliced thinly

1 Cook pineapple, peppers and red onion on heated, lightly oiled grill plate (or grill or barbecue) until browned all over and tender.
2 Meanwhile, cook fish on heated, lightly oiled flat plate (or large non-stick frying pan) until cooked as desired.
3 Combine sugar, vinegar, soy, chilli and ginger in large bowl. Place pineapple, peppers and red onion in bowl with dressing; toss gently to combine. Divide mixture among serving plates; top with fish and spring onion.
per serving 6g fat; 1434kJ (343 cal)

herbed swordfish kebabs

preparation time 30 minutes
cooking time 15 minutes
serves 8

2kg swordfish steaks
4 medium lemons (560g)
⅓ cup chopped fresh coriander
½ cup chopped fresh flat-leaf parsley
½ cup chopped fresh chives
½ teaspoon freshly ground black pepper
2 tablespoons groundnut oil

1 Remove and discard skin from fish; cut fish into 3cm pieces.
2 Using zester, remove as much of the rind as possible from lemons. Squeeze ⅔ cup (160ml) juice from the lemons.
3 Combine fish in large bowl with rind, juice, herbs, pepper and oil; toss to mix well.
4 Thread fish onto 16 skewers; place, in single layer, in large shallow dish. Pour any remaining marinade over skewers. Cover; refrigerate 3 hours or overnight. Cook skewers on heated oiled barbecue plate until browned all over and cooked through. Serve with baby spinach leaves, if desired.
per serving 11.8g fat; 1346kJ (322 cal)
TIP You will need to soak 16 bamboo skewers in water for at least an hour before use, to prevent them from splintering and scorching.

swordfish with thai dressing

preparation time 5 minutes
cooking time 10 minutes
serves 4

4 swordfish steaks (720g)
THAI DRESSING
⅓ cup (80ml) sweet chilli sauce
½ cup (125ml) lime juice
1 tablespoon fish sauce
2 teaspoons finely chopped lemongrass
2 tablespoons chopped fresh coriander
½ cup chopped fresh mint
1 teaspoon grated fresh ginger

1 Cook fish on heated oiled barbecue plate until browned both sides and cooked as desired.
2 Drizzle thai dressing over fish; serve with mixed salad leaves and lemon, if desired.

THAI DRESSING
Combine ingredients in screw-top jar; shake well.
per serving 4.7g fat; 918kJ (219 cal)
TIP This recipe is best made just before serving.

char-grilled prawns with mango chilli salsa

preparation time 15 minutes
cooking time 5 minutes
serves 4

1kg uncooked large prawns

MANGO CHILLI SALSA
¼ cup (60ml) lime juice
2 fresh small red thai chillies, chopped finely
¼ cup (60ml) olive oil
2 teaspoons fish sauce
2 teaspoons grated palm sugar
1 medium mango (430g), chopped
1 medium green mango (430g), sliced thinly
1 small red onion (100g), sliced thinly
½ cup firmly packed fresh coriander leaves

1 Make mango chilli salsa.
2 Cook prawns in their shells on heated, oiled grill plate (or grill or barbecue) until changed colour and cooked through.
3 Serve prawns with mango chilli salsa.

MANGO CHILLI SALSA
Combine juice, chilli, oil, sauce and sugar in medium bowl; stir until the sugar is dissolved. Add mangoes, onion and coriander; toss gently.
per serving 14.8g fat; 1405kJ (336 cal)
TIPS Salsa can be prepared three hours ahead.
Palm sugar can be substituted with brown sugar.

skewered lemon prawns

preparation time 15 minutes (plus marinating time)
cooking time 5 minutes
serves 8

24 large uncooked king prawns (1.5kg)
⅓ cup (80ml) olive oil
1 tablespoon grated lemon rind
lemon wedges, to serve

1 Remove head and back vein from prawns. Remove legs, leaving shell intact. Cut along the underside length of prawn, without cutting all the way through. Thread prawns onto skewers.
2 Place prawns in large dish; pour over oil and lemon rind. Cover; marinate in refrigerator 3 hours.
3 Cook prawns on heated oiled grill plate (or grill or barbecue), flesh-side down, until browned lightly; turn. Cook until just cooked through; serve with lemon. Return meat to soup, stir until heated through.
per serving 9.7g fat; 686kJ (164 cal)
TIPS Recipe can be prepared 6 hours ahead.
You will need to soak 24 bamboo skewers in water for at least an hour before use, to prevent them from splintering and scorching.

vegetable kebabs with balsamic dressing

preparation time 20 minutes
cooking time 20 minutes
serves 6

250g cherry tomatoes
1 large green pepper (350g), chopped coarsely
6 small flat mushrooms (600g), quartered
6 yellow patty-pan squash (240g), halved
3 baby aubergine (180g), sliced thickly
3 small courgettes (270g), sliced thickly
1 medium brown onion (150g), sliced thickly
500g haloumi cheese, cubed
60g baby rocket leaves

BALSAMIC DRESSING
⅓ cup (80ml) olive oil
¼ cup (60ml) balsamic vinegar
1 teaspoon sugar

1 Thread tomatoes, vegetables and cheese onto
12 skewers.
2 Cook kebabs, in batches, on heated oiled barbecue
plate until browned all over.
3 Serve kebabs on rocket leaf salad drizzled with
balsamic dressing.

BALSAMIC DRESSING
Combine ingredients in screw-top jar; shake well.
per serving 40.8g fat; 2402kJ (575 cal)
*TIP You will need to soak 12 bamboo skewers in water
for at least an hour before use, to prevent them from
splintering and scorching.*

barbecued mixed vegetables

preparation time 15 minutes
cooking time 20 minutes
serves 10

1 large sweet potato (500g), sliced thickly
2 large red onions (600g)
½ cup (125ml) olive oil
3 medium red peppers (600g), quartered, deseeded
3 medium yellow peppers (600g), quartered,
   deseeded
6 medium courgettes (720g), sliced thickly
400g chestnut mushrooms

1 Boil, steam or microwave sweet potato until almost
tender; drain. Cut each onion into 12 wedges, leaving
the root end intact.
2 Cook sweet potato and onion on heated oiled
barbecue plate, brushing with oil, until browned on one
side; turn vegetables and repeat.
3 Cook pepper, courgette and mushrooms on heated
oiled barbecue plate, brushing with oil, until browned
and tender.
per serving 11.9g fat; 789kJ (189 cal)
TIP This recipe is best made just before serving.

pasta, pizza
and risotto

Pasta and rice are two of the easiest dishes to cook and they'll complement almost anything. Here are some delicious creations like pappardelle with chicken and creamy mushroom sauce, chilli prawn linguine, and risotto primavera.

chilli prawn linguine

spaghetti with mussels and clams

spaghetti puttanesca

spaghetti with pesto

chilli prawn linguine

preparation time 15 minutes
cooking time 15 minutes
serves 4

500g linguine
⅓ cup (80ml) olive oil
400g prawns
3 fresh red thai chillies, deseeded, chopped finely
2 cloves garlic, crushed
½ cup chopped fresh flat-leaf parsley
2 teaspoons finely grated lemon rind

1 Cook pasta in large saucepan of boiling water, uncovered, until just tender; drain.
2 Meanwhile, heat oil in large frying pan; cook prawns, chilli and garlic, stirring, until prawns are just cooked through.
3 Remove from heat; stir in parsley and rind.
4 Combine pasta with prawn mixture in large bowl; toss gently.
per serving 20.5g fat; 2795kJ (669 cal)
TIPS This recipe is best made just before serving.
Spaghetti can be substituted for the linguine.

spaghetti with mussels and clams

preparation time 20 minutes
cooking time 15 minutes
serves 6

500g mussels
500g clams
¼ cup (60ml) dry white wine
¼ cup (60ml) water
500g spaghetti
⅓ cup (80ml) extra virgin olive oil
2 cloves garlic, crushed
1 fresh red thai chilli, chopped finely
2 medium tomatoes (380g), deseeded, chopped coarsely
½ cup chopped fresh flat-leaf parsley

1 Scrub mussels; remove beards. Rinse clams.
2 Combine wine and the water in large saucepan; bring to a boil. Add mussels and clams; reduce heat. Simmer, covered, until shells open; discard any that do not open. Cover seafood to keep warm. Strain cooking liquid through fine sieve into medium jug; reserve ⅓ cup (80ml) of the liquid.
3 Cook pasta in large saucepan of boiling water until tender; drain. Return to pan.
4 Meanwhile, heat oil in large frying pan; cook garlic and chilli, stirring, until fragrant. Add tomatoes and reserved cooking liquid; simmer, uncovered, until hot.
5 Add seafood to pasta with oil mixture and parsley; toss gently.
per serving 13.5g fat; 1814kJ (433 cal)
TIP This recipe is best made just before serving.

spaghetti puttanesca

preparation time 15 minutes
cooking time 20 minutes
serves 4

¼ cup (60ml) olive oil
2 cloves garlic, crushed
4 medium tomatoes (760g), chopped coarsely
½ cup finely chopped fresh parsley
12 stuffed olives, sliced thinly
45g canned anchovy fillets, chopped finely
1 tablespoon finely chopped fresh basil
pinch chilli powder
375g spaghetti

1 Heat oil in medium saucepan; cook garlic until just changed in colour.
2 Add tomato, parsley, olives, anchovy, basil and chilli powder; cook further 3 minutes.
3 Meanwhile, cook pasta in large saucepan of boiling water, uncovered, until just tender; drain.
4 Combine pasta in large warmed bowl, with sauce; toss gently.
per serving 16.9g fat; 2055kJ (491 cal)

spaghetti with pesto

preparation time 15 minutes
cooking time 15 minutes
serves 4

2 cups coarsely chopped fresh basil
2 tablespoons pine nuts, toasted
2 cloves garlic
⅓ cup (80ml) olive oil
¼ cup (20g) finely grated parmesan cheese
375g spaghetti

1 Blend or process basil, pine nuts and garlic until smooth. With processor operating, add oil in thin stream; process further 1 second.
2 Place basil mixture in medium bowl. Add cheese; mix until combined.
3 Cook pasta in large saucepan of boiling water, uncovered, until just tender; drain.
4 Combine pasta with pesto in large warmed bowl; toss gently.
per serving 26.5 fat; 2363kJ (564 cal)
TIP Pesto can be made 2 weeks ahead and refrigerated in sterilised jar with a thin layer of olive oil over top, or frozen, in freezer container, for up to 3 months.

spaghetti with herbed ricotta

preparation time 10 minutes
cooking time 15 minutes
serves 4

500g spaghetti
450g fresh ricotta
3 egg yolks
¾ cup (180ml) milk
⅓ cup firmly packed, coarsely chopped fresh
   flat-leaf parsley
¼ cup firmly packed, coarsely chopped fresh basil
3 spring onions, chopped finely
2 cloves garlic, crushed
¼ cup (20g) finely grated pepato cheese
freshly ground black pepper

1 Cook pasta in large saucepan of boiling water, uncovered, until just tender; drain.
2 Whisk ricotta, yolks and milk in large bowl until smooth; stir in herbs, onion, garlic and cheese.
3 Add pasta to ricotta mixture; toss gently to combine. Sprinkle with pepper to serve.
per serving 21.7g fat; 2863kJ (684 cal)
TIPS Pepato can be substituted with another hard cheese, such as romano or an aged provolone.
Feel free to use other herbs, such as chives or oregano, instead of the basil.

farfalle with baked salmon, caperberries and dill

preparation time 25 minutes
cooking time 30 minutes
serves 8

2 large red onions (600g)
1 cup (160g) caperberries, rinsed, drained
cooking-oil spray
1 fresh red thai chilli, deseeded, chopped finely
¼ cup loosely packed, finely chopped fresh dill
2 teaspoons olive oil
1kg piece skinless salmon fillet
500g farfalle pasta
⅔ cup (160ml) dry white wine
2 tablespoons lemon juice
½ cup (125ml) single cream
250g baby rocket leaves, trimmed

1 Preheat oven to moderately hot.
2 Cut each onion into eight wedges; place, in single layer, in large baking dish with caperberries. Spray lightly with cooking-oil spray; roast, uncovered, in moderately hot oven about 25 minutes or until onion is just softened.
3 Meanwhile, combine chilli and half of the dill in small bowl with olive oil. Place salmon on large baking-parchment-lined oven tray; brush salmon both sides with chilli mixture. Roast, uncovered, in moderately hot oven about 10 minutes or until salmon is just tender and cooked as desired.
4 Cook pasta, uncovered, in large pan of boiling water until just tender. While pasta is cooking, combine wine and juice in small saucepan; bring to a boil. Reduce heat; simmer, uncovered, about 5 minutes or until liquid reduces by half. Add cream and remaining dill.
5 Place pasta, flaked salmon, onion mixture and dill cream sauce in large bowl with baby rocket leaves; toss gently to combine.
per serving 15g fat; 2090kJ (500 cal)

fettuccine carbonara

preparation time 10 minutes
cooking time 10 minutes
serves 4

4 bacon rashers (280g), chopped coarsely
375g fettuccine
3 egg yolks, beaten
1 cup (250ml) cream
½ cup (40g) finely grated parmesan cheese
2 tablespoons coarsely chopped fresh chives

1 Cook bacon in small heated frying pan, stirring, until crisp; drain.
2 Just before serving, cook pasta in large saucepan of boiling water, uncovered, until just tender; drain.
3 Combine pasta in warmed large bowl with yolks, cream and cheese; sprinkle with chives and freshly ground black pepper, if desired.
per serving 42g fat; 3222kJ (770 cal)
TIP Pancetta or prosciutto can be substituted for the bacon, and grated romano or pepato can be substituted for the parmesan.

fettuccine with rocket pesto and fresh tomato salsa

preparation time 10 minutes
cooking time 15 minutes
serves 4

500g fettuccine
8 cloves garlic, quartered
½ cup loosely packed, chopped fresh basil
120g rocket, chopped coarsely
⅔ cup (160ml) olive oil
½ cup (40g) finely grated parmesan cheese
3 medium tomatoes (570g), chopped coarsely
2 tablespoons lemon juice
2 fresh red thai chillies, sliced thinly
⅓ cup (50g) pine nuts, toasted

1 Cook pasta in large saucepan of boiling water, uncovered, until just tender; drain.
2 Meanwhile, blend or process garlic, basil, rocket and oil until smooth.
3 Combine pasta, rocket pesto, cheese, tomato, juice and chilli in large saucepan; cook, stirring, until hot. Add nuts; toss gently to combine.
per serving 50.3g fat; 3780kJ (904 cal)
TIP You could substitute baby spinach leaves for the rocket to give a milder-flavoured pesto.

pappardelle with chilli and semi-dried tomato sauce

preparation time 15 minutes
cooking time 25 minutes
serves 6

2 medium brown onions (300g), chopped coarsely
2 cloves garlic, quartered
1 cup (150g) semi-dried tomatoes in oil, drained
¼ cup (70g) tomato paste
2 fresh red thai chillies, deseeded, chopped finely
2 cups (500ml) beef stock
375g pappardelle
¼ cup coarsely chopped fresh flat-leaf parsley
freshly ground black pepper

1 Blend or process onion, garlic, tomatoes, tomato paste and chilli until mixture forms a paste.
2 Heat large non-stick frying pan; cook tomato mixture, stirring, 10 minutes. Stir in stock; bring to a boil. Reduce heat; simmer sauce, uncovered, about 10 minutes or until thickened slightly. [Can be made 2 days ahead to this stage and refrigerated, covered, or frozen for up to 6 months.]
3 Meanwhile, cook pasta in large saucepan of boiling water, uncovered, until just tender; drain.
4 Just before serving, gently toss pasta through sauce; sprinkle with parsley and pepper.
per serving 2.9g fat; 1147kJ (274 cal)
TIP Pappardelle is the widest ribbon pasta available; any long pasta such as fettuccine or tagliatelle can be substituted.

creamy squash and sage ravioli

preparation time 15 minutes
cooking time 25 minutes
serves 6

¼ cup (60ml) olive oil
16 fresh sage leaves
½ large butternut squash (900g), peeled, sliced
1 medium leek (350g), chopped finely
1 tablespoon shredded fresh sage leaves, extra
1 tablespoon white balsamic vinegar
300ml cream
900g fresh or frozen ricotta ravioli

1 Heat 2 tablespoons of the oil in large frying pan, fry sage leaves until bright green; remove with slotted spoon or tongs, drain on absorbent paper.
2 Heat remaining oil in same pan; add squash, cook in batches until browned on both sides and just tender. Turn squash carefully to prevent it breaking; cover to keep warm.
3 Add leek to frying pan; cook, stirring, about 5 minutes or until softened.
4 Add shredded extra sage, balsamic and cream; bring to a boil then simmer, uncovered, until sauce has thickened slightly.
5 Meanwhile, cook pasta in large saucepan of boiling water, uncovered, until just tender; drain.
6 Combine drained pasta with squash and cream mixture; serve topped with fried sage leaves.
per serving 38.9g fat; 2241kJ (536 cal)
TIPS This recipe is best made close to serving.
White balsamic vinegar is slightly sweet, and is available in the vinegar section in supermarkets.

pappardelle with chicken and creamy mushroom sauce

preparation time 15 minutes
cooking time 12 minutes
serves 6

2 tablespoons olive oil
1 clove garlic, crushed
1 small onion (80g), chopped finely
250g chestnut mushrooms, sliced thinly
1 cup (250ml) cream
2 teaspoons finely chopped fresh rosemary
50g butter, chopped
500g pappardelle
200g cooked chicken, shredded thinly
½ cup (50g) walnut pieces, toasted
¾ cup (60g) finely grated parmesan cheese
¼ cup chopped fresh flat-leaf parsley

1 Heat oil in large frying pan; cook garlic and onion, stirring, until onion softens. Add mushroom; cook, stirring, until tender.
2 Add cream and rosemary to pan. Bring to a boil; reduce heat. Simmer, uncovered, about 3 minutes or until sauce thickens; stir in butter.
3 Meanwhile, cook pasta in large saucepan of boiling water, uncovered, until just tender. Drain pasta; return to pan.
4 Add hot cream sauce to hot pasta with chicken, nuts, half of the cheese, and parsley; toss gently until combined.
5 Serve immediately, topped with remaining cheese.
per serving 44g fat; 3078kJ (735 cal)
TIP This recipe is best made just before serving.

ricotta and pepper ravioli with rocket dressing

preparation time 40 minutes
cooking time 30 minutes
serves 6

3 large red peppers (1kg)
2 spring onions, chopped finely
1 clove garlic, crushed
2½ cups (500g) ricotta cheese
72 wonton wrappers
300g baby rocket leaves
½ cup (125ml) olive oil
2 tablespoons lemon juice
2 tablespoons balsamic vinegar
2 teaspoons sugar
1 clove garlic, quartered, extra
¼ cup (20g) shaved parmesan cheese

1 Quarter peppers; remove and discard seeds and membrane. Roast under grill or in very hot oven, skin-side up, until skin blisters and blackens. Cover pepper quarters in plastic or paper 5 minutes. Peel away and discard skin; chop pepper flesh finely.

2 Combine pepper, onion, garlic and ricotta in a medium bowl.

3 Place a level tablespoon of the pepper filling in the centre of 36 wonton wrappers; brush edges lightly with a little water. Top each with remaining wonton wrappers; press edges together to seal the ravioli.

4 Reserve approximately a fifth of the rocket. Blend or process remaining rocket, oil, juice, vinegar, sugar and extra garlic until pureed. Strain into medium jug; discard pulp.

5 Cook ravioli, in batches, in large saucepan of boiling water, uncovered, until tender; drain. Serve ravioli drizzled with rocket dressing; top with reserved rocket and parmesan.

per serving 30.9g fat; 1913kJ (458 cal)
TIP Make the ravioli a day ahead and refrigerate, on a covered tray, until just before you want to cook them.

gnocchi with roasted squash and burnt butter

preparation time 5 minutes
cooking time 15 minutes
serves 4

500g trimmed butternut squash
1kg gnocchi
100g butter
1 tablespoon olive oil
1 clove garlic, crushed
1 tablespoon shredded fresh sage

1 Preheat oven to moderate.
2 Cut squash into 1cm cubes. Place on oiled oven tray; roast, uncovered, in moderate oven about 15 minutes or until just tender.
3 Meanwhile, cook gnocchi in large saucepan of boiling water, uncovered, until just tender; drain. Keep warm.
4 Melt butter with oil in medium frying pan; cook garlic, stirring, 2 minutes. Add sage; cook, stirring, until butter foams.
5 Combine squash, gnocchi and butter mixture in large bowl; stir gently.
per serving 27.8g fat; 2634kJ (630 cal)
TIP Squash can be cooked in the microwave oven to reduce cooking time.

cheese and spinach tortellini with gorgonzola sauce

preparation time 5 minutes
cooking time 15 minutes
serves 4

30g butter
2 tablespoons plain flour
1 cup (250ml) milk
¾ cup (180ml) cream
100g gorgonzola cheese, chopped coarsely
750g cheese and spinach tortellini
¼ cup loosely packed fresh flat-leaf parsley
freshly ground black pepper

1 Melt butter in medium saucepan; cook flour, stirring, about 2 minutes or until mixture bubbles and thickens.
2 Gradually stir in milk and cream; bring to a boil. Reduce heat; simmer, uncovered, until sauce boils and thickens. Remove from heat; stir in cheese.
3 Meanwhile, cook pasta in large saucepan of boiling water, uncovered, until just tender; drain.
4 Combine pasta with sauce; sprinkle with parsley and pepper.
per serving 43.8g fat; 3017kJ (721 cal)
TIPS Ravioli or gnocchi can be substituted for the tortellini.
It's best to choose a ricotta and spinach filled tortellini (or the even simpler ricotta filled version) when making this sauce, as it doesn't marry overly well with meat-filled pastas.

pasta with fresh tomato sauce

preparation time 15 minutes
cooking time 5 minutes
serves 8

375g fresh lasagne sheets, sliced thickly
2 tablespoons extra virgin olive oil
6 medium tomatoes (1.2kg), peeled, deseeded, chopped coarsely
¼ cup loosely packed, chopped fresh basil
2 cloves garlic, crushed
2 teaspoons red wine vinegar
1 fresh red thai chilli, deseeded, chopped finely
80g low-fat feta cheese, crumbled

1 Cook pasta in large saucepan of boiling water, uncovered, until just tender; drain. Sprinkle half of the oil over pasta; toss gently to combine.
2 Combine tomato, basil, garlic, remaining oil, vinegar and chilli in medium bowl.
3 Divide pasta among serving plates. Spoon tomato mixture over pasta; sprinkle with cheese.
per serving 6.3g fat; 535kJ (128 cal)
TIP To peel tomatoes, slice a cross in the bottom of each tomato. Place tomatoes in large bowl of boiling water 1 minute; drain. Rinse under cold running water; peel.

rigatoni with aubergine sauce

preparation time 10 minutes
cooking time 20 minutes
serves 4

¼ cup (60ml) olive oil
1 medium brown onion (150g), chopped finely
2 trimmed sticks celery (150g), chopped finely
1 clove garlic, crushed
2 tablespoons brandy
1 medium aubergine (300g), sliced thinly
2⅓ cups (580ml) bottled tomato pasta sauce
½ cup (140g) tomato paste
½ cup (125ml) water
375g rigatoni pasta
¼ cup (20g) finely grated parmesan cheese

1 Heat oil in large saucepan; cook onion, celery and garlic, stirring, until onion softens. Add brandy; cook, stirring, until brandy evaporates. Add aubergine; cook, stirring, until aubergine is tender.
2 Stir in sauce, paste and the water; bring to a boil. Reduce heat; simmer, uncovered, about 10 minutes or until sauce thickens slightly. [Can be made 2 days ahead to this stage and refrigerated, covered.]
3 Meanwhile, cook pasta in large saucepan of boiling water, uncovered, until just tender; drain. Place pasta in large warmed bowl with half of the aubergine sauce; toss gently to combine. Divide pasta among serving plates; top each with remaining sauce. Serve with cheese.
per serving 16.9g fat; 2420kJ (578 cal)
TIP Before serving, warm large bowls and platters, by placing in a sink of very hot water 10 minutes; dry before using.

pasta shells with lamb and peas

preparation time 25 minutes
cooking time 35 minutes
serves 4

2 tablespoons olive oil
1 medium brown onion (150g), chopped finely
1 clove garlic, crushed
600g minced lamb
2 fresh small red thai chillies, sliced thinly
500g orecchietti pasta
2 cups (300g) shelled fresh peas
3 medium tomatoes (450g), deseeded, chopped finely
⅓ cup (80ml) extra virgin olive oil

GREMOLATA
½ cup finely chopped fresh flat-leaf parsley
1 clove garlic, crushed
2 teaspoons finely grated lemon rind

1 Make gremolata.
2 Heat oil in large frying pan; add onion and garlic, cook, stirring, until onion is soft. Add lamb and chilli; cook, stirring, about 10 minutes or until lamb is well browned. Cover to keep warm.
3 Meanwhile, cook pasta in large saucepan of boiling water, uncovered, until just tender. Reserve ¼ cup (60ml) of the cooking liquid; drain pasta.
4 Boil, steam or microwave peas until tender; drain.
5 Toss pasta in large bowl with lamb mixture, peas, reserved liquid, tomato and oil. Serve sprinkled with gremolata.

GREMOLATA
Combine all ingredients in small bowl.
per serving 39.5g fat; 3929kJ (940 cal)
TIPS You will need about 800g fresh peas in the pod for this recipe.
The mince mixture and gremolata can be prepared several hours ahead. Reheat mince just before serving.

risotto primavera

mushroom risotto

baked squash and spinach risotto

mushroom and rocket risotto

risotto primavera

preparation time 10 minutes
cooking time 25 minutes
serves 4

20g butter
2 teaspoons olive oil
1 medium leek (350g), sliced thinly
1 clove garlic, crushed
2 cups (400g) arborio rice
¾ cup (180ml) dry white wine
1½ cups (375ml) vegetable stock
2½ cups (625ml) water
150g sugar snap peas
300g asparagus, sliced thickly
100g yellow patty-pan squash, quartered
⅔ cup (50g) finely grated parmesan cheese
⅓ cup (80ml) cream

1 Heat butter and oil in large saucepan; cook leek and garlic, stirring, until leek softens.
2 Add rice, wine, stock and the water; bring to a boil. Reduce heat; simmer, covered, 15 minutes, stirring occasionally.
3 Stir in peas, asparagus and squash; cook, covered, about 5 minutes or until rice is just tender.
4 Just before serving, stir in cheese and cream.
per serving 20.4g fat; 2632kJ (630 cal)
TIP Medium-grain rice can be used instead of arborio.

mushroom risotto

preparation time 15 minutes
cooking time 45 minutes
serves 6

1 cup (250ml) olive oil
2 tablespoons fresh sage leaves
500g mixed mushrooms, sliced thinly
3 cloves garlic, crushed
60g butter, chopped
2 medium brown onions (300g), chopped finely
2 cups (400g) arborio rice
1.5 litres (6 cups) vegetable stock
½ cup (40g) finely grated parmesan cheese

1 Heat oil in small saucepan; carefully cook a few of the sage leaves until bright green. Remove from pan with slotted spoon; drain on absorbent paper. Repeat with remaining sage leaves; reserve.
2 Transfer 2 tablespoons of the oil to large saucepan; cook mushroom, stirring, until browned and just tender. Add garlic; stir until fragrant. Remove mushroom mixture from pan; reserve.
3 Heat half of the butter in same pan; cook onion, stirring, over low heat until soft but not coloured. Add rice; stir until rice is coated in butter mixture.
4 Meanwhile, bring stock to a boil in large saucepan. Reduce heat; simmer. Add 1 cup (250ml) of the stock to rice mixture; cook, stirring, over low heat until liquid is absorbed. Continue adding stock, in 1-cup batches, stirring, until liquid is absorbed after each addition. Total cooking time should be about 30 minutes or until rice is just tender.
5 Stir in cheese, remaining butter and reserved mushroom mixture. Risotto should be creamy; add a little boiling water, if necessary, and serve topped with reserved sage leaves.
per serving 21.2g fat; 2017kJ (412 cal)
TIPS Mushroom can be cooked 3 hours ahead.
The risotto is best made just before serving.

baked squash and spinach risotto

preparation time 15 minutes
cooking time 35 minutes
serves 4

500g butternut squash, chopped coarsely
2 tablespoons olive oil
1½ cups (375ml) chicken stock
1.25 litres (5 cups) water
1 large brown onion (200g), chopped coarsely
2 cloves garlic, crushed
2 cups (400g) arborio rice
½ cup (125ml) dry white wine
500g spinach, trimmed, chopped coarsely
½ cup (80g) pine nuts, toasted
½ cup (40g) grated parmesan cheese
½ cup (125ml) cream

1 Preheat oven to hot. Combine squash with half of the oil in baking dish. Bake, uncovered, in hot oven about 20 minutes or until tender; reserve.
2 Meanwhile, combine stock and the water in large saucepan; bring to a boil. Reduce heat; simmer.
3 Heat remaining oil in large saucepan; cook onion and garlic, stirring, until onion is soft. Add rice; stir to coat in oil mixture. Add wine; stir until almost evaporated.
4 Stir in 1 cup (250ml) of the hot stock mixture; cook, stirring, over low heat until liquid is absorbed. Continue adding stock mixture, in 1-cup batches, stirring, until liquid is absorbed after each addition. Total cooking time should be about 30 minutes or until rice is just tender.
5 Add spinach, pine nuts, cheese and cream; cook, stirring, until spinach wilts. Gently stir in reserved baked squash.
6 Serve topped with parmesan cheese flakes, if desired.
per serving 41.6g fat; 3504kJ (837 cal)
TIPS Squash can be baked 3 hours ahead.
The risotto is best made just before serving.

mushroom and rocket risotto

preparation time 10 minutes
cooking time 35 minutes
serves 4

2 cups (500ml) chicken stock
3½ cups (875ml) water
50g butter
2 tablespoons olive oil
250g button mushrooms, sliced thickly
2 cloves garlic, crushed
2 medium brown onions (300g), sliced thinly
2 cups (400g) arborio rice
¼ cup chopped fresh flat-leaf parsley
¾ cup (60g) grated parmesan cheese
30g butter, chopped, extra
250g rocket, trimmed

1 Combine stock and the water in large saucepan; bring to a boil then reduce heat to simmer gently.
2 Meanwhile, heat half of the butter and half of the oil in another large saucepan; add mushroom, cook, stirring, until browned lightly. Add garlic; cook, stirring, until fragrant. Remove from pan; cover to keep warm.
3 Heat remaining butter and remaining oil in same pan; cook onion, stirring, until soft. Add rice, stir over medium heat until rice is coated in butter mixture. Stir in ½ cup (125ml) of the stock mixture; cook, stirring, over low heat until liquid is absorbed.
4 Continue adding stock mixture, in ½-cup batches, stirring after each addition until liquid is absorbed. The total cooking time should be about 20 minutes or until rice is tender.
5 Stir in mushroom mixture, parsley, cheese, extra butter and rocket. Top with extra parmesan cheese flakes, if desired.
per serving 93.6g fat; 5229kJ (1251 cal)
TIP This recipe is best made close to serving.

leek and asparagus risotto

preparation time 15 minutes
cooking time 45 minutes
serves 8

1½ cups (375ml) dry white wine
1.5 litres (6 cups) chicken stock
1 tablespoon olive oil
2 medium leeks (700g), sliced thinly
2 cloves garlic, crushed
3 cups (600g) arborio rice
500g asparagus, trimmed, chopped coarsely
⅓ cup (25g) finely grated parmesan cheese
1 tablespoon shredded fresh basil

1 Combine wine and stock in large saucepan; bring to a boil. Reduce heat; simmer, covered, to keep hot.
2 Meanwhile, heat oil in large saucepan; cook leek and garlic, stirring, until leek softens.
3 Add rice; stir to coat in leek mixture. Stir in 1 cup (250ml) of the hot stock mixture; cook, stirring, over low heat until liquid is absorbed. Continue adding stock mixture, in 1-cup batches, stirring, until liquid is absorbed after each addition. Total cooking time should be about 30 minutes or until rice is just tender.
4 Add asparagus; cook, stirring, until asparagus is just tender. Just before serving, stir in cheese. Serve sprinkled with basil.
per serving 4.7g fat; 1550kJ (371 cal)
TIP Fresh sugar snap peas can be substituted for the asparagus.

asparagus, bacon and parmesan tortiglioni

preparation time 15 minutes
cooking time 25 minutes
serves 4

500g tortiglioni pasta
500g asparagus, chopped coarsely
2 teaspoons olive oil
5 bacon rashers (350g), sliced thinly
1 clove garlic, crushed
100g butter, chopped
¼ cup coarsely chopped fresh flat-leaf parsley
½ cup (40g) grated parmesan cheese
½ cup (50g) grated mozzarella cheese

1 Cook pasta in large saucepan of boiling water, uncovered, until just tender. Drain; return to pan.
2 Meanwhile, boil, steam or microwave asparagus until just tender; drain.
3 Heat oil in large frying pan; add bacon, cook, stirring, until crisp. Add garlic, cook until fragrant.
4 Add bacon mixture to drained pasta with butter, asparagus, parsley and a quarter of the combined cheeses; toss gently.
5 Preheat grill to hot. Transfer pasta mixture to shallow 2.5 litre (10-cup) ovenproof dish. Sprinkle top of pasta with remaining cheese, grill until browned lightly.
per serving 32g fat; 3219kJ (770 cal)

lasagne

preparation time 40 minutes
cooking time 2 hours 10 minutes
serves 6

1 tablespoon olive oil
1 medium onion (150g), chopped finely
1 medium carrot (120g), chopped finely
1 trimmed stick celery (75g), chopped finely
2 cloves garlic, crushed
500g minced beef
⅓ cup (80ml) dry red wine
850g canned tomatoes
2 tablespoons tomato paste
½ cup (125ml) water
4 slices prosciutto (60g), chopped finely
1 tablespoon coarsely chopped fresh oregano
2 tablespoons coarsely chopped fresh parsley
18 fresh lasagne sheets
½ cup (40g) grated parmesan cheese

CHEESE SAUCE
60g butter
⅓ cup (50g) plain flour
1 litre (4 cups) milk
¾ cup (60g) grated parmesan cheese
pinch ground nutmeg

1 Heat oil in large frying pan; cook onion, carrot, celery and garlic, stirring, until onion is soft. Add beef; cook, stirring, until browned. Add wine; bring to a boil. Stir in undrained crushed tomatoes, paste and the water; reduce heat. Simmer, uncovered, about 1 hour or until mixture is thick. Stir in prosciutto and herbs; cool slightly.
2 Place six lasagne sheets into greased shallow 3-litre (12 cup) ovenproof dish. Spread with half of the meat sauce; drizzle with 1 cup (250ml) of the cheese sauce. Repeat layers again.
3 Top with remaining pasta sheets. Spread with remaining cheese sauce; sprinkle with cheese. Bake in moderate oven about 45 minutes or until pasta is tender and lasagne is browned.

CHEESE SAUCE
Heat butter in large saucepan; cook flour, stirring over heat until flour bubbles and thickens. Remove from heat; gradually stir in milk. Cook, until mixture boils and thickens. Remove from heat; stir in cheese and nutmeg. Cool 10 minutes.
per serving 32.4g fat; 2934kJ (701 cal)
TIP Recipe best made a day ahead; can be made 3 days ahead and refrigerated, covered, or frozen for up to 2 months.

chicken and prosciutto cannelloni

preparation time 30 minutes
cooking time 1 hour 10 minutes
serves 8

50g butter
¼ cup (35g) plain flour
⅔ cup (160ml) milk
1½ cups (375ml) chicken stock
½ cup (40g) finely grated parmesan cheese
400g fontina cheese, grated coarsely
1 tablespoon olive oil
2 medium brown onions (300g), chopped finely
3 cloves garlic, crushed
1 kg minced chicken
2 tablespoons finely chopped fresh sage
850g canned tomatoes
½ cup (125ml) dry white wine
¼ cup (70g) tomato paste
3 teaspoons sugar
12 fresh lasagne sheets
24 slices prosciutto (360g)

1 Heat butter in medium saucepan; cook flour, stirring, until flour thickens and bubbles. Gradually stir in milk and stock; cook, stirring, until sauce boils and thickens. Remove from heat; stir in parmesan and a quarter of the fontina cheese.

2 Heat oil in large saucepan; cook onion and garlic, stirring, until onion is soft. Add chicken; cook, stirring, until browned. Stir in sage. Combine chicken and cheese sauce in large bowl; cool.

3 Combine undrained crushed tomatoes, wine, paste and sugar in same large pan; cook, stirring, 10 minutes. Cool 10 minutes; blend or process, in batches, until smooth.

4 Cut pasta sheets and prosciutto slices in half crossways. Place two pieces of prosciutto on each piece of pasta. Top each with ¼ cup chicken mixture; roll to enclose filling. Repeat with remaining pasta, prosciutto and chicken mixture.

5 Oil two 3-litre (12 cup) ovenproof dishes. Pour a quarter of the tomato sauce into base of each prepared dish; place half of the pasta rolls, seam-side down, in each dish. Pour remaining tomato sauce over rolls; sprinkle each dish with remaining fontina. [Can be made 2 days ahead to this stage and refrigerated, covered, or frozen for up to 2 months.]

6 Bake cannelloni, covered, in moderate oven 30 minutes. Uncover, bake further 15 minutes or until cheese melts and browns. Serve with a green salad, if desired.

per serving 40.3g fat; 2998kJ (716 cal)
TIP Pancetta or double-smoked ham can be substituted for the prosciutto.

turkish-style pizza with minted yogurt

preparation time 15 minutes
cooking time 35 minutes
serves 6

1 tablespoon olive oil
1 medium brown onion (150g), chopped finely
1 clove garlic, crushed
500g minced beef or lamb
¼ teaspoon cayenne pepper
2 teaspoons ground cumin
½ teaspoon ground cinnamon
1½ teaspoons mixed spice
1 teaspoon grated lemon rind
2 tablespoons lemon juice
1 cup (250ml) beef stock
2 medium tomatoes (300g), chopped finely
⅓ cup (50g) pine nuts, toasted
¼ cup finely chopped fresh parsley
¼ cup finely chopped fresh mint
2 x 430g turkish breads
200g plain yogurt
1 tablespoon finely chopped fresh mint, extra

1 Preheat oven to hot (220°C/200°C fan-assisted).
2 Heat oil in large frying pan, add onion and garlic; cook, stirring, until onion is soft. Add mince; cook until browned. Add pepper and spices; stir until fragrant.
3 Add rind, juice, stock and tomatoes to pan; cook, stirring over medium heat until most of the liquid is evaporated. Remove from heat, stir in pine nuts and chopped herbs.
4 Place bread on oven trays; press mince mixture evenly over top of bread leaving 3cm border.
5 Cover pizzas with foil; bake in hot oven 10 minutes. Remove foil; bake further 10 minutes until browned lightly.
6 Cut into thick slices; serve topped with combined yogurt and extra chopped mint.
per serving 21.9g fat; 2767kJ (662 cal)
TIPS Pizza is best baked just before serving.
Mince mixture can be made a day ahead.

mushroom pizza

preparation time 10 minutes
cooking time 15 minutes
serves 4

4 x 15cm pizza bases
1½ cups (185g) grated pizza cheese
150g flat mushrooms, sliced thinly
100g feta cheese, crumbled
2 tablespoons finely chopped fresh chives

1 Preheat oven to hot. Place pizza bases on oven tray. Sprinkle half the pizza cheese over bases. Divide mushroom, feta cheese, chives and remaining pizza cheese among bases.
2 Bake, uncovered, in hot oven about 15 minutes or until pizza tops are browned lightly and bases are crisp.
per serving 22.1g fat; 2325kJ (556 cal)
TIPS We used a Greek feta, which crumbles well and has a sharp taste, for this recipe.
Any fresh or frozen pizza bases would be suitable.

napoletana pizza

preparation time 20 minutes (plus standing time)
cooking time 30 minutes
serves 6

300g mozzarella, sliced thinly
¼ cup coarsely torn basil
BASIC PIZZA DOUGH
2 teaspoons (7g) instant yeast
½ teaspoon salt
2½ cups (375g) plain flour
1 cup (250ml) warm water
1 tablespoon olive oil
BASIC TOMATO PIZZA SAUCE
1 tablespoon olive oil
1 small white onion (80g), chopped finely
2 cloves garlic, crushed
425g canned tomatoes
¼ cup (70g) tomato paste
1 teaspoon sugar
1 tablespoon fresh oregano

1 Halve basic pizza dough; roll out each half on lightly floured surface to form 30cm round. Place on two oiled pizza trays. Spread each with half of the basic tomato pizza sauce; top with cheese.
2 Bake, uncovered, in moderately hot oven about 15 minutes or until crust is golden and cheese is bubbling. Sprinkle each with basil before serving.

BASIC PIZZA DOUGH
Combine yeast, salt and sifted flour in large bowl; mix well. Gradually stir in the water and oil. Knead on well floured surface about 10 minutes or until smooth and elastic. Place dough in large oiled bowl; stand in warm place about 30 minutes or until dough doubles in size. Knead dough on lightly floured surface until smooth. Roll out dough as required or to fit pizza tray.

BASIC TOMATO PIZZA SAUCE
Heat oil in medium frying pan; cook onion, stirring occasionally, over low heat until soft and transparent. Stir in garlic, undrained, crushed tomatoes, paste, sugar and oregano. Simmer, uncovered, about 15 minutes or until mixture thickens. [Can be made 2 days ahead and refrigerated, covered, or frozen for up to 6 months.]
per serving 18.1g fat; 1890kJ (451 cal)
TIPS Basic pizza dough can be made 3 hours ahead and refrigerated, covered. Remove from refrigerator 10 minutes before using.
Purchased pizza bases can be used in place of the basic pizza dough.

salami and rocket pizza

preparation time 10 minutes
cooking time 15 minutes
serves 4

2 x 26cm pizza bases
⅔ cup (160ml) tomato pasta sauce
250g mozzarella cheese, sliced thinly
125g salami, sliced thinly
50g baby rocket leaves

1 Preheat oven to hot.
2 Place pizza bases on oven trays. Spread sauce evenly over bases; top with cheese and salami. Bake, uncovered, in hot oven about 15 minutes or until cheese melts and bases are crisp.
3 Just before serving, top pizzas with rocket and freshly ground pepper, if desired.
per serving 30.3g fat; 2818kJ (673 cal)
TIPS Pizza is best made just before serving.
Any fresh or frozen pizza bases would be suitable.

roasted tomato, goat's cheese and chicken pizza

preparation time 25 minutes
cooking time 35 minutes
serves 2

500g cherry tomatoes, halved
2 tablespoons balsamic vinegar
2 tablespoons brown sugar
2 chicken breast fillets (340g)
30cm round homemade or purchased pizza base
2 tablespoons coarsely chopped fresh coriander
80g goat's cheese
40g rocket

1 Place tomatoes on baking tray lined with baking parchment; drizzle with combined vinegar and sugar. Bake, uncovered, in very hot oven about 25 minutes or until tomatoes are soft.
2 Meanwhile, cook chicken on heated oiled grill plate (or grill or barbecue) until browned both sides and cooked through. Cool 5 minutes; cut into thin slices. Place pizza base on baking tray; bake, uncovered, in hot oven about 10 minutes or until browned lightly.
3 Top pizza with tomato, chicken, coriander and crumbled cheese. Bake, uncovered, in very hot oven, 10 minutes or until pizza is browned and crisp.
4 Just before serving, top with rocket.
per serving 17.6g fat; 3278kJ (783 cal)
TIPS Lebanese bread can be substituted for prepared pizza base.
Use baking parchment to prevent the skin of the tomatoes sticking to oven tray.

vegetarian

There are so many choices when it comes to mouth-watering vegetarian food – from rich, flavoursome dishes to light, healthy meals. Try the red onion, cheese and vegetable frittata, chickpea corn enchiladas, or the spinach and ricotta pie.

char-grilled polenta cakes

spinach and ricotta pie

frittata with onions and courgettes

asparagus and gruyere tart

char-grilled polenta cakes

preparation time 15 minutes (plus refrigeration time)
cooking time 20 minutes
serves 8

cooking-oil spray
1 litre (4 cups) water
1 teaspoon salt
1 cup (170g) polenta
2 tablespoons wholegrain mustard
2 trimmed corn cobs (500g)
1 medium red pepper (200g), chopped finely
1 medium red onion (170g), chopped finely
½ cucumber (130g), chopped finely
¼ cup loosely packed, chopped fresh flat-leaf
  parsley
1 teaspoon finely grated lime rind
⅓ cup (80ml) lime juice
2 tablespoons olive oil
3 cloves garlic, crushed
1 tablespoon sweet chilli sauce

1 Lightly spray 23cm-square shallow cake tin with cooking-oil spray. Bring the water and salt to a boil in large saucepan. Add polenta; cook, stirring, about 10 minutes or until polenta thickens. Add mustard; stir until combined. Spread polenta into cake tin. Cover; refrigerate about 30 minutes or until firm.
2 Meanwhile, boil, steam or microwave corn until just tender; drain. Cool; using sharp knife, remove kernels from cob. Combine corn in medium bowl with remaining ingredients.
3 Turn polenta onto board; cut into eight rectangles. Heat large lightly oiled non-stick frying pan; cook polenta, in batches, until browned both sides. Serve polenta cakes with corn salsa.
per serving 6.3g fat; 753kJ (180 cal)
TIP You can reduce preparation and cooking times by substituting the fresh corn for a 420g can of corn kernels, drained.

spinach and ricotta pie

preparation time 10 minutes
cooking time 30 minutes
serves 4

200g baby spinach leaves
2 tablespoons olive oil
1 medium brown onion (150g), chopped coarsely
1 clove garlic, crushed
2 teaspoons finely grated lemon rind
¼ cup chopped fresh flat-leaf parsley
¼ cup chopped fresh dill
2 tablespoons chopped fresh mint
1½ cups (300g) ricotta cheese
2 sheets ready-rolled puff pastry

1 Preheat oven to very hot.
2 Boil, steam or microwave spinach until just wilted; drain on absorbent paper. Squeeze out excess liquid.
3 Heat oil in small frying pan; cook onion and garlic until onion softens.
4 Combine spinach, onion mixture, rind, herbs and cheese in large bowl; mix well.
5 Oil two oven trays and place in oven about 5 minutes to heat. Place a sheet of pastry on each tray; divide spinach mixture between sheets, leaving a 3cm border. Using a metal spatula, fold pastry border roughly over edge of filling.
6 Bake pies in very hot oven about 20 minutes or until pastry browns.
per serving 36.8g fat; 2184kJ (522 cal)
TIP Taking the Greek pie, spanakopita, as our inspiration, we've simplified the recipe by replacing the traditional filo pastry with ready-rolled puff pastry.
For best results, use a pizza tray with holes in the base – this will make it possible to cook the pastry evenly.

frittata with onions and courgettes

preparation time 10 minutes
cooking time 30 minutes (plus cooling time)
serves 4

20g butter, melted
2 tablespoons olive oil
2 medium brown onions (300g), sliced thinly
6 eggs, beaten lightly
¼ cup (60ml) cream
¾ cup (60g) grated parmesan cheese
2 small courgettes (180g), sliced thinly
1 tablespoon finely shredded fresh basil

1 Brush base and sides of deep 19cm-square cake tin with butter. Heat oil in medium frying pan. Cook onion, stirring, until soft; cool.
2 Combine onion, egg, cream, cheese, courgettes and basil in medium bowl. Pour mixture into prepared tin; bake, uncovered, in moderate oven about 25 minutes or until browned lightly and firm.
per serving 13g fat; 672kJ (161 cal)
TIP Recipe can be made a day ahead and refrigerated, covered.

asparagus and gruyere tart

preparation time 25 minutes (plus refrigeration and freezing time)
cooking time 55 minutes (plus cooling time)
serves 4

25g butter
1 small white onion (80g), sliced thinly
12 asparagus spears, halved crossways
2 eggs
1 teaspoon plain flour
¾ cup (180ml) cream
50g gruyere cheese, grated coarsely

PASTRY SHELL
¾ cup (110g) plain flour
75g butter
1 tablespoon finely grated parmesan cheese
pinch of paprika
1 egg yolk
2 teaspoons iced water

1 Make pastry. Increase oven temperature to moderately hot (200°C/180°C fan-assisted).
2 Heat butter in large frying pan; cook onion over low heat without browning, about 10 minutes until very soft.
3 Add asparagus to small pan of boiling water, cook 1 minute; drain. Place into bowl of iced water; drain.
4 Whisk eggs, flour and cream in medium jug.
5 Place onion in pastry base, top with asparagus and cheese. Place tart on an oven tray, gently pour egg mixture over asparagus; carefully place tart in oven.
6 Bake in moderately hot oven about 20 minutes or until browned lightly and set.

PASTRY SHELL
Process flour, butter, parmesan and paprika until crumbly. Add yolk and iced water; pulse until mixture just comes together. Knead pastry on lightly floured surface until smooth. Wrap pastry in cling film; refrigerate 30 minutes. Roll pastry until large enough to line 10cm x 34cm rectangular loose-base flan tin. Lift pastry into tin, ease into sides, trim edges. Freeze 30 minutes. Preheat oven to moderate (180°C/160°C fan-assisted). Cover pastry with baking parchment, fill with dried beans or rice, place on oven tray. Bake in moderate oven 15 minutes, remove paper and beans or rice, bake further 10 minutes; cool.
per serving 48.9g fat; 2445kJ (585 cal)

grilled herb polenta with semi-dried tomato and olive salad

preparation time 15 minutes
cooking time 30 minutes (plus refrigeration time)
serves 4

2 cups (500ml) water
2 cups (500ml) vegetable stock
1 cup (170g) polenta
⅓ cup (25g) finely grated parmesan cheese
1 tablespoon finely chopped fresh flat-leaf parsley
1 tablespoon finely chopped fresh basil

SEMI-DRIED TOMATO AND OLIVE SALAD
100g baby cos lettuce, trimmed, leaves torn roughly
1⅓ cups (200g) drained semi-dried tomatoes
4 spring onions, sliced thinly
¼ cup (50g) thinly sliced pitted black olives

SPICED MAYONNAISE
¾ cup (225g) mayonnaise
pinch of cayenne pepper
¼ teaspoon ground cumin
¼ teaspoon ground coriander
¼ teaspoon ground turmeric
1 tablespoon lemon juice

1 Combine the water and stock in medium saucepan; bring to a boil. Gradually add polenta to liquid, stirring constantly. Reduce heat; cook, stirring, about 10 minutes or until polenta thickens. Stir in cheese, parsley and basil.
2 Spread polenta evenly into deep 19cm-square cake tin; cool 10 minutes. Cover; refrigerate about 3 hours or until firm.
3 Turn polenta onto board; trim edges. Cut into four squares, cut each square diagonally into two triangles. Cook polenta, in batches, on heated, oiled grill plate (or grill or barbecue) until browned both sides.
4 Meanwhile, make semi-dried tomato and olive salad. Make spiced mayonnaise.
5 Divide polenta among serving plates; top with salad, drizzle with spiced mayonnaise mixture.

SEMI-DRIED TOMATO AND OLIVE SALAD
Combine ingredients in medium bowl.

SPICED MAYONNAISE
Whisk ingredients in small bowl.
per serving 25.7g fat; 2257kJ (540 cal)

Gently fold the cheese and herbs into the polenta until well combined

Serve the salad separately, with a small bowl of mayonnaise on the side

courgette fritters with tzatziki

*preparation time 20 minutes (plus refrigeration
  and standing time)*
cooking time 20 minutes
makes 24

4 medium courgettes (480g), grated coarsely
1 teaspoon salt
1 medium brown onion (150g), chopped finely
¾ cup (45g) stale breadcrumbs
2 eggs, beaten lightly
1 tablespoon finely chopped fresh oregano
1 tablespoon finely chopped fresh mint
2 tablespoons extra virgin olive oil

TZATZIKI
2 cups (560g) thick Greek-style yogurt
½ cucumber (130g)
1 clove garlic, crushed
2 tablespoons finely chopped fresh mint
2 tablespoons lemon juice

1 Make tzatziki.
2 Combine courgettes and salt. Stand 15 minutes, then squeeze out excess liquid. Combine courgettes with onion, breadcrumbs, egg, oregano and mint.
3 Preheat oven to very low (120°C/100°C fan-assisted).
4 Heat oil in non-stick frying pan over medium heat; drop in tablespoonfuls of courgette mixture, flatten slightly; cook until browned lightly both sides and cooked through. Transfer to oven tray; place in very low oven to keep warm. Repeat with remaining mixture.
5 Serve fritters with tzatziki.

TZATZIKI
Line a sieve with absorbent paper. Add yogurt, place over a bowl. Cover, refrigerate at least 4 hours. Halve cucumber lengthways; remove seeds. Coarsely grate flesh and skin. Squeeze out excess liquid. Combine yogurt, cucumber, garlic, mint and juice in medium bowl.
per fritter 3.3g fat; 242kJ (58 cal)
TIP Fritters can be made several hours ahead.

red onion, cheese and vegetable frittata

preparation time 15 minutes
cooking time 25 minutes
serves 4

2 tablespoons olive oil
2 medium red onions (340g), sliced thinly
1 clove garlic, crushed
2 medium courgettes (240g), grated
250g button mushrooms, sliced thinly
1 tablespoon chopped fresh chives
2 tablespoons chopped fresh basil
1 teaspoon freshly ground black pepper
8 eggs, beaten lightly
1 cup (100g) grated mozzarella cheese

1 Heat oil in 23cm non-stick frying pan; cook onion and garlic, stirring, until onion is soft.
2 Stir in courgette and mushroom. Cook, stirring, until vegetables are tender; stir in herbs and pepper. Reduce heat; pour in egg.
3 Cook egg mixture over low heat, without stirring, until base is browned lightly and top is almost set; sprinkle with cheese. Place pan under grill on high heat until top is set and browned lightly. Cut into wedges.
4 Serve with salad, if desired.
per serving 25.6g fat; 1488kJ (356 cal)
TIP This recipe is best made just before serving.

supreme cottage loaf

preparation time 1 hour (plus standing time)
cooking time 50 minutes (plus refrigeration time)
serves 8

23cm-round cottage loaf
2 large red peppers (700g)
1 large aubergine (500g)
2 tablespoons coarse cooking salt
1 small sweet potato (250g)
1 large courgette (150g)
cooking-oil spray
⅓ cup firmly packed fresh basil leaves
¾ cup (180g) ricotta
¼ cup (20g) coarsely grated parmesan

SUN-DRIED TOMATO PUREE
1 cup (150g) sun-dried tomatoes in oil, drained
2 cloves garlic, crushed
¼ cup lightly packed fresh oregano leaves
1 tablespoon wholegrain mustard
¼ cup (60ml) olive oil

1 Make sun-dried tomato puree.
2 Cut a lid from top of loaf, remove soft bread from inside of loaf, leaving 2cm shell. Brush sun-dried tomato puree inside lid and bread shell.
3 Quarter peppers, remove seeds and membranes. Roast under grill or in very hot oven (240°C/220°C fan-assisted), skin-side up, until skin blisters and blackens. Cover pepper pieces in plastic or paper 5 minutes, peel away skin.
4 Cut aubergine into 1.5cm slices, sprinkle all over with salt; stand 30 minutes. Rinse aubergine under cold water; drain on absorbent paper.
5 Preheat grill. Cut sweet potato and courgette into 5mm slices. Spray aubergine, sweet potato and courgette slices with oil; grill, in batches, until browned lightly.
6 Place sweet potato inside bread shell; top with basil leaves, pepper, courgette, combined cheeses and aubergine. Replace lid, wrap loaf completely in cling film, place on oven tray, top with another oven tray, weight with heavy cans; refrigerate overnight.
7 Preheat oven to very hot (240°C/220°C fan-assisted).
8 Discard cling film; place loaf on oven tray. Bake about 5 minutes or until crisp.

SUN-DRIED TOMATO PUREE
Blend or process tomatoes, garlic, oregano and mustard until almost smooth. With motor operating, gradually add oil, in a thin stream, until combined.
per serving 13.3g fat; 1413kJ (338 cal)
TIP Loaf must be made a day ahead and heated on day of serving.

stuffed peppers

preparation time 20 minutes
cooking time 45 minutes
serves 4

2 tablespoons olive oil
1 medium brown onion (150g), chopped finely
1 clove garlic, crushed
½ small aubergine (115g), chopped finely
1 tablespoon coarsely chopped fresh
flat-leaf parsley
1 tablespoon coarsely chopped fresh oregano
2 teaspoons drained capers, chopped coarsely
4 medium plum tomatoes (300g), chopped finely
¼ cup (15g) stale breadcrumbs
¼ cup (20g) grated parmesan cheese
2 medium red peppers (400g)

1 Heat half of the oil in large saucepan; cook onion and garlic, stirring, until onion is soft. Stir in aubergine, herbs, capers and tomato; cook, stirring, 3 minutes. Transfer mixture to large bowl; cool.
2 Stir in breadcrumbs and cheese.
3 Cut peppers in half lengthways; remove seeds and membranes. Brush skin with remaining oil; place peppers on baking tray. Fill pepper with tomato mixture; bake, uncovered, in moderate oven about 40 minutes or until peppers are tender.
per serving 11.6g fat; 724kJ (173 cal)
TIP Recipe can be prepared a day ahead and refrigerated, covered.

spinach and cheese quesadillas

preparation time 20 minutes
cooking time 10 minutes
serves 8

⅔ cup (130g) low-fat cottage cheese
100g spinach leaves, trimmed
1 medium avocado (250g), chopped finely
1 cup (200g) canned mexican-style beans, drained
125g can corn kernels, drained
2 medium tomatoes (380g), deseeded, chopped
   finely
1 small red onion (100g), chopped finely
2 medium courgettes (240g), grated coarsely
16 small flour tortillas
1½ cups (150g) coarsely grated low-fat mozzarella

1 Blend or process cottage cheese and spinach until smooth. Combine avocado, beans, corn, tomato, onion and courgettes in medium bowl.
2 Place eight tortillas on lightly oiled oven tray; divide spinach mixture among tortillas, leaving 2cm border around edge. Divide avocado mixture among tortillas, sprinkling it over spinach mixture. Top each with one of the remaining tortillas.
3 Sprinkle mozzarella over quesadilla stacks; place under preheated grill until cheese just melts and browns lightly.
per serving 11.8g fat; 1177kJ (282 cal)
TIPS Quesadillas are filled tortillas which are grilled or fried and served with fresh salsa. We used small flour tortillas measuring approximately 16cm in diameter; they are sometimes labelled 'fajita tortillas' on the package.

vegetable pasties with roasted tomato sauce

preparation time 45 minutes
cooking time 2 hours 5 minutes
serves 4

10 large plum tomatoes (900g), quartered
2 teaspoons brown sugar
⅓ cup (80ml) olive oil
2 tablespoons red wine vinegar
2 large red peppers (700g), halved
30g butter
2 large courgettes (300g), sliced thinly
7 flat mushrooms (560g), sliced thinly
1 clove garlic, crushed
1 tablespoon port
5 sheets ready-rolled puff pastry
1 egg yolk
1 tablespoon milk
50g baby spinach leaves

1 Preheat oven to moderate (180°C/160°C fan-assisted).

2 Combine tomato, sugar, half of the oil and half of the vinegar in large bowl; place tomato pieces on oven tray. Roast, uncovered, in moderate oven 1 hour 40 minutes. Remove from oven; return to same bowl; crush with potato masher. Cover to keep warm.

3 While tomato is roasting, place pepper, skin-side up, on oven tray. Roast, uncovered, in moderate oven about 40 minutes or until softened. Place pepper in plastic bag; close tightly, cool. Discard skin, membrane and seeds; slice thinly.

4 Meanwhile, melt butter in large frying pan; cook courgettes, stirring, about 5 minutes or until softened. Place courgettes in small bowl; cover to keep warm. Place mushroom and garlic in same pan; cook, stirring, about 5 minutes or until mushroom softened. Add port; cook, stirring, until liquid evaporates.

5 Cut four of the pastry sheets into 16cm squares; cut remaining sheet into quarters. Place one of the small squares on oiled oven tray; centre a 9cm round cutter on pastry. Layer a quarter of the mushroom mixture, a quarter of the courgette and a quarter of the pepper on pastry; remove cutter. Brush border with combined egg yolk and milk; top with one of the large squares, press edges together to seal.

6 Using sharp knife, cut around pasties, leaving 5mm border; mark pastry with swirl design from centre to side, taking care not to cut through pastry. Brush lightly with egg mixture. Repeat process with remaining pastry, vegetables and egg mixture. Bake, uncovered, in moderate oven about 25 minutes or until pastry is browned lightly.

7 Meanwhile, combine spinach, remaining oil and remaining vinegar in medium bowl; toss gently. Divide salad among serving plates; serve with pasties and roasted tomato sauce.

per serving 74.3g fat; 4728kJ (1131 cal)

The roast tomato pieces should be soft and caramelised

vegetable and feta free-form tarts

preparation time 30 minutes (plus standing time)
cooking time 50 minutes
serves 4

1 small aubergine (230g), chopped coarsely
coarse cooking salt
1 tablespoon olive oil
1 medium brown onion (150g), sliced thinly
2 medium courgette (240g), sliced thinly
4 sheets ready-rolled shortcrust pastry
¼ cup (65g) bottled pesto
120g feta cheese, crumbled
8 cherry tomatoes, halved
1 tablespoon finely chopped fresh basil
1 egg, beaten lightly

1 Place aubergine in sieve or colander; sprinkle all over with salt, then stand sieve over sink or large bowl for 15 minutes. Rinse aubergine well under cold running water, drain; pat dry with absorbent paper.
2 Preheat oven to moderate (180°C/160°C fan-assisted).
3 Heat oil in large non-stick frying pan; cook onion, stirring, until softened. Add aubergine and courgette to pan; cook, stirring, until vegetables are softened.
4 Using a plate as a guide, cut a 20cm round from each pastry sheet; place rounds on oven trays. Spread equal amounts of pesto in centre of each round, leaving a 4cm border around the outside edge.
5 Divide vegetables among rounds over pesto; top each with equal amounts of cheese, tomato and basil. Using hands, turn the 4cm edge on each round over filling; brush around pastry edge with egg.
6 Bake, uncovered, in moderate oven about 40 minutes or until pastry is browned lightly.
per serving 57.6g fat; 3578kJ (856 cal)
TIP Allowing the aubergine to stand a while covered with salt will help withdraw most of the vegetable's slightly bitter juice; it also helps prevent the aubergine from absorbing too much oil when it's cooked. Be sure to rinse the aubergine well under cold running water to remove as much of the salt as possible, and to dry it thoroughly with absorbent paper before cooking.

soft polenta with braised vegetables

preparation time 15 minutes
cooking time 15 minutes
serves 4

2½ cups (625ml) water
1 cup (170g) polenta
½ cup (40g) finely grated parmesan cheese
1 tablespoon olive oil
1 medium brown onion (150g), sliced thinly
1 clove garlic, crushed
200g button mushrooms, halved
2 medium green courgettes (240g), sliced thickly
8 medium yellow patty-pan squash (100g),
    quartered
600ml bottled tomato pasta sauce
¾ cup (180ml) vegetable stock

1 Bring the water to a boil in medium saucepan. Sprinkle polenta gradually into the water, stirring constantly. Cover, reduce heat to low; cook, stirring occasionally, about 10 minutes or until polenta thickens. Add cheese, stir until melted.
2 Meanwhile, heat oil in medium saucepan; cook onion and garlic, stirring, until onion softens. Add mushrooms; cook, stirring, 3 minutes. Add courgettes and squash; cook, stirring, 2 minutes. Add sauce and stock; bring to a boil. Reduce heat; simmer, covered, about 8 minutes or until vegetables are just tender.
3 Serve polenta with braised vegetables.
per serving 10.5g fat; 1462kJ (349 cal)
TIPS Braised vegetables can be prepared in advance and refrigerated, covered; reheat just before serving. Serve with a tossed green salad and crusty Italian bread, such as ciabatta.

spicy dhal

preparation time 15 minutes (plus standing time)
cooking time 45 minutes
serves 4

½ cup (100g) yellow split peas
½ cup (100g) green split peas
½ cup (100g) red lentils
2 tablespoons ghee
2 teaspoons black mustard seeds
½ teaspoon black onion seeds
2 medium brown onions (300g), chopped coarsely
4 cloves garlic, crushed
4cm piece fresh ginger (20g), grated
1 tablespoon ground cumin
1 tablespoon ground coriander
1 teaspoon ground turmeric
1 teaspoon chilli powder
2 x 400g cans chopped tomatoes
2½ cups (625ml) vegetable stock
⅓ cup (80ml) cream
2 tablespoons coarsely chopped fresh coriander

1 Rinse peas under cold water; drain. Put peas in small bowl, cover with water; stand 30 minutes; drain.
2 Rinse lentils under cold water; drain.
3 Heat ghee in large heavy-based frying pan; cook seeds, stirring, until they start to pop. Add onion, garlic and ginger; cook, stirring, until onion is browned lightly.
4 Add ground spices; cook, stirring, until fragrant. Add peas, lentils, undrained tomatoes and stock; bring to a boil. Reduce heat; simmer, covered, about 30 minutes or until lentils are tender.
5 Add cream; stir over low heat until just heated through. Serve dahl sprinkled with chopped coriander.
per serving 20.1g fat; 1881kJ (450 cal)
TIP Dhal can be prepared a day ahead; keep, covered, in refrigerator.

Accompany any meal with a selection of delicious side dishes – a plate of crunchy garlic potatoes, a cool asparagus, avocado and macadamia salad, or a bowl of steaming cauliflower with chilli and pine nuts – and you'll transform a snack into a feast.

side dishes
and salads

roast potatoes with aïoli

mediterranean grilled vegetables with tomato vinaigrette

roast tomatoes with garlic crumbs

roast vegetables with feta

roast potatoes with aïoli

preparation time 10 minutes
cooking time 40 minutes
serves 10

1kg tiny new potatoes, quartered
2 tablespoons olive oil
1 teaspoon sea salt
¼ teaspoon hot paprika

AÏOLI
2 egg yolks
6 gloves garlic, peeled, quartered
1 teaspoon sea salt
¾ cup (180ml) olive oil

1 Preheat oven to very hot.
2 Combine potato, oil and salt in large baking dish. Roast, uncovered, in very hot oven about 40 minutes or until potato is browned and crisp. Sprinkle with paprika.
3 Serve potato with aïoli.

AÏOLI
Blend or process egg yolks, garlic and salt until smooth. With the motor operating, gradually add oil; process until thick. A little lemon juice can be added to taste, if desired.
per serving 21.3g fat; 1074kJ (256 cal)
TIP The aïoli can be made a day ahead. The potatoes are best roasted just before serving.

mediterranean grilled vegetables with tomato vinaigrette

preparation time 20 minutes (plus standing time)
cooking time 1 hour
serves 6

5 medium trimmed beetroot (825g)
2 medium aubergines (600g)
1 tablespoon salt
6 medium flat mushrooms (600g)
300g feta cheese, crumbled
½ cup loosely packed fresh basil leaves

TOMATO VINAIGRETTE
4 large plum tomatoes (360g), halved
cooking-oil spray
¼ cup (60ml) olive oil
2 tablespoons white wine vinegar
1 teaspoon salt

1 Preheat oven to hot.
2 Wrap beetroot individually in foil; place in baking dish. Bake in hot oven about 50 minutes or until tender; cool 5 minutes. Wearing gloves, peel while still warm and cut into 1cm slices.
3 Cut aubergine into 1cm slices; place in colander. Sprinkle with salt; stand 30 minutes. Rinse aubergine under cold running water; drain on absorbent paper.
4 Cook aubergine and mushrooms, in batches, on heated oiled grill plate (or grill or barbecue) until browned on both sides.
5 Divide tomato vinaigrette among serving plates; top with mushroom, aubergine, beetroot, cheese and basil.

TOMATO VINAIGRETTE
Place tomato on oiled oven tray; coat with cooking-oil spray. Bake in hot oven about 40 minutes or until browned lightly. Blend or process tomato with oil, vinegar and salt until pureed. Push vinaigrette through food mill or fine sieve into large bowl; discard pulp.
per serving 22.5g fat; 1549kJ (371 cal)
TIPS Tomato vinaigrette can be made a day ahead and refrigerated, covered.
You need approximately 1.5kg of untrimmed fresh beetroot for this recipe.

roast tomatoes with garlic crumbs

preparation time 5 minutes
cooking time 25 minutes
serves 4

6 large plum tomatoes (540g), halved lengthways
2 teaspoons balsamic vinegar
1 teaspoon caster sugar
1 teaspoon salt
1 tablespoon olive oil
1 clove garlic, crushed
½ cup (35g) stale breadcrumbs
1 tablespoon olive oil, extra

1 Preheat oven to hot.
2 Place tomatoes, cut-side up, in single layer on lightly greased oven tray. Brush tomatoes with vinegar; sprinkle with sugar and salt. Bake in hot oven about 20 minutes or until tender.
3 Heat oil in medium frying pan; cook garlic and breadcrumbs, stirring, about 5 minutes or until crumbs are golden brown. Remove from heat; drain on absorbent paper. Serve tomatoes, sprinkled with garlic crumbs and drizzled with extra oil.
per serving 9.6g fat; 568kJ (136 cal)

roast vegetables with feta

preparation time 15 minutes
cooking time 20 minutes
serves 4

4 baby aubergines (240g), sliced thinly lengthways
1 large yellow pepper (350g), sliced thickly
250g butternut squash, peeled, sliced thinly
2 tablespoons olive oil
2 tablespoons pine nuts, toasted
70g semi-dried tomatoes, drained
40g feta cheese, crumbled
2 teaspoons balsamic vinegar

1 Preheat oven to very hot.
2 Combine aubergines, pepper, squash and oil in large baking dish. Cook vegetables in very hot oven about 20 minutes or until tender. Add nuts and tomatoes. Serve vegetables sprinkled with feta and vinegar.
per serving 18.3g fat; 1032kJ (247 cal)

garlic roast peppers with olive croutes

preparation time 15 minutes
cooking time 1 hour 40 minutes
serves 4

1 medium red onion (170g)
2 medium red peppers (400g)
2 medium green peppers (400g)
2 medium yellow peppers (400g)
½ cup (125ml) olive oil
10 unpeeled cloves garlic
⅓ cup (50g) pine nuts, toasted
150g feta cheese

TOMATO SALSA
1 medium red onion (170g)
400g can tomatoes
½ teaspoon sugar
⅓ cup (80ml) water

OLIVE CROUTES
1 large loaf crusty bread
½ cup (125ml) olive oil
¼ cup (65g) olive paste

1 Preheat oven to moderate.
2 Cut onion into eight wedges. Quarter peppers; remove and discard seeds and membranes.
3 Combine onion, peppers, oil and garlic in large baking dish; bake, uncovered, in moderate oven 1 hour.
4 Add tomato salsa and pine nuts; bake 30 minutes, turning vegetables occasionally.
5 Serve vegetables with crumbled cheese and olive croutes.

TOMATO SALSA
Cut onion into eight wedges. Combine onion, undrained crushed tomatoes and remaining ingredients in large saucepan; simmer, uncovered, until thickened.

OLIVE CROUTES
Cut bread into 1.5cm slices; place bread on oven tray. Brush with combined oil and paste; toast in moderately hot oven about 10 minutes.

per serving 75.2g fat; 4082kJ (976 cal)
TIP Recipe can be prepared a day ahead. Vegetables should be refrigerated, covered, and croutes stored in an airtight container.

caponata

preparation time 15 minutes
cooking time 20 minutes (plus cooling and standing time)
serves 6

2 medium red peppers (400g)
3 trimmed celery stalks (300g)
2 small red onions (200g)
2 medium tomatoes (300g)
2 medium aubergines (600g)
1 tablespoon olive oil
1 clove garlic, chopped finely
cooking-oil spray
½ cup (110g) white sugar
1 cup (250ml) red wine vinegar
½ cup (80g) sultanas
100g pitted black olives
⅓ cup (50g) pine nuts, toasted
1½ tablespoons capers, rinsed, drained

1 Cut peppers, celery, onions, tomatoes and aubergines into 2cm pieces.
2 Heat oil in large frying pan, cook peppers, celery, onion, tomato and garlic, in batches, until soft; transfer to large bowl.
3 Spray aubergine all over with oil, cook aubergine in batches, until browned. Add to pepper mixture.
4 Place sugar in medium frying pan over low heat. Cook, without stirring or boiling, until dissolved, swirling pan occasionally. Cook about 5 minutes or until browned lightly. Add vinegar, bring to a boil; reduce heat, simmer, uncovered, until liquid is reduced by a third; cool to room temperature.
5 Add vinegar mixture to vegetables with sultanas, olives, nuts and capers; stir until combined. Stand for 1 hour at room temperature before serving.

per serving 10g fat; 1137kJ (272 cal)
TIP This recipe can be made a day ahead.

spicy potato wedges

preparation time 5 minutes
cooking time 25 minutes
serves 4

1kg potatoes, washed
2 tablespoons sumac
2 tablespoons olive oil

1 Preheat oven to very hot (240°C/220°C fan-assisted). Lightly grease oven tray.
2 Cut potatoes into wedges; combine in large microwave-safe bowl with sumac and oil.
3 Cook, covered, in microwave oven, on HIGH (100%), 5 minutes.
4 Place wedges, in single layer, on tray. Roast about 20 minutes or until wedges are crisp. Sprinkle with sea salt flakes, if desired.
per serving 9.3g fat; 915kJ (219 cal)
TIP Sumac, a granular spice ranging in colour from terracotta to almost-black purple, is used extensively from the eastern Mediterranean through to Pakistan. Its tart astringency adds a delightful piquancy to food without the heat of chilli. Available from Middle Eastern food stores.

garlic potatoes

preparation time 10 minutes
cooking time 55 minutes
serves 4

1kg salad potatoes
8 cloves garlic
1 teaspoon salt

1 Preheat oven to hot.
2 Boil, steam or microwave potatoes until just tender; drain. Cut potatoes in half lengthways; place in oiled baking dish with garlic. Sprinkle with salt.
3 Bake, uncovered, in hot oven about 45 minutes or until potato is brown and crisp. Squeeze two of the roasted garlic cloves over potato; shake gently to combine.
per serving 0.4g fat; 706kJ (169 cal)

potato crush

preparation time 10 minutes
cooking time 15 minutes
serves 6

1kg tiny new potatoes, unpeeled
½ cup (120g) soured cream
40g butter, softened

1 Boil, steam or microwave potatoes until tender; drain.
2 Mash half of the potatoes with all the soured cream and butter in large bowl.
3 Stir in one of the flavour variations (below).
4 Using back of a fork or potato masher, gently crush remaining potatoes until skins burst and flesh is just flattened; fold into mash mixture.

ORIGINAL POTATO CRUSH
Combine 6 coarsely chopped drained cornichons, 3 coarsely chopped spring onions, ¼ cup coarsely chopped fresh flat-leaf parsley and 1 tablespoon coarsely chopped drained capers in small bowl. Add to Step 3, above.
per serving 13.7g fat; 1116kJ (267 cal)

CAESAR CRUSH
Cook 3 finely chopped bacon rashers in non-stick frying pan until crisp; drain on absorbent paper. Combine with 4 finely chopped anchovies, 1 crushed garlic clove, 3 thinly sliced spring onions and ½ cup shaved parmesan in small bowl. Add to Step 3, above.
per serving 17.6g fat; 1246kJ (298 cal)

HERB AND MUSTARD CRUSH
Combine 1 tablespoon wholegrain mustard, ¼ cup coarsely chopped fresh chives, ¼ cup coarsely chopped fresh flat-leaf parsley, 2 tablespoons coarsely chopped fresh basil and 2 tablespoons coarsely chopped fresh dill in small bowl. Add to Step 3, above.
per serving 13.7g fat; 978kJ (234 cal)

roasted sweet potato mash

preparation time 10 minutes
cooking time 1 hour 5 minutes
serves 8

4 large sweet potatoes (2kg), chopped coarsely
2 tablespoons olive oil
1 cup (250ml) buttermilk
20g butter

1 Preheat oven to moderately hot.
2 Combine sweet potatoes in large baking dish with oil; cook, uncovered, in moderately hot oven about 1 hour or until sweet potatoes are tender.
3 Blend or process sweet potatoes with remaining ingredients until pureed. Transfer to medium saucepan; reheat, stirring, until hot.
per serving 7.7g fat; 910kJ (218 cal)
TIPS Make the mash just before serving.
Add a little lemon juice or a few tablespoons of freshly chopped herbs such as thyme, dill or even flat-leaf parsley, if desired.

buttery mashed celeriac

preparation time 15 minutes
cooking time 20 minutes
serves 8

4 large sweet potatoes (2kg), chopped coarsely
2 tablespoons olive oil
1 cup (250ml) buttermilk
20g butter

1 Preheat oven to moderately hot.
2 Combine sweet potatoes in large baking dish with oil; cook, uncovered, in moderately hot oven about 1 hour or until sweet potatoes are tender.
3 Blend or process sweet potatoes with remaining ingredients until pureed. Transfer to medium saucepan; reheat, stirring, until hot.
per serving 7.7g fat; 910kJ (218 cal)
TIPS Make the mash just before serving.
Add a little lemon juice or a few tablespoons of a freshly chopped herb such as thyme, dill or even flat-leaf parsley, if desired.

cauliflower with chilli and pine nuts

preparation time 10 minutes
cooking time 10 minutes
serves 8

1 small cauliflower (1kg)
2 tablespoons extra virgin olive oil
2 cloves garlic, crushed
2 tablespoons pine nuts
2 teaspoons chopped dried chilli
2 tablespoons chopped fresh flat-leaf parsley

1 Separate cauliflower into pieces. Boil, steam or microwave cauliflower until almost tender. Drain; pat dry.
2 Heat oil in medium frying pan; cook garlic, pine nuts and chilli, stirring, over low heat until fragrant and nuts are browned lightly.
3 Add cauliflower; cook, stirring, until well coated with oil mixture.
4 Add parsley; stir until combined.
per serving 7.5g fat; 385kJ (92 cal)
TIP This recipe is best made just before serving.

asparagus with garlic breadcrumbs and chopped eggs

preparation time 10 minutes
cooking time 10 minutes
serves 8

80g butter
2 tablespoons honey
2 cloves garlic, crushed
1 cup (70g) stale breadcrumbs
1kg fresh asparagus, trimmed
2 hard-boiled eggs, chopped finely
⅓ cup chopped fresh flat-leaf parsley

1 Melt half of the butter and half of the honey in large frying pan. Add garlic and breadcrumbs; cook, stirring, until breadcrumbs are browned and crisp.
2 Boil, steam or microwave asparagus until just tender; drain.
3 Serve asparagus scattered with breadcrumb mixture, egg and parsley; drizzle with combined remaining melted butter and honey.
per serving 9.9g fat; 621kJ (149 cal)
TIPS This recipe is best made just before serving, so breadcrumbs stay crisp.
One of the easiest ways to dice an egg is to use an egg slice. After slicing in one direction, hold egg and turn at a 90-degree angle; slice a second time, cutting egg into cubes. If you don't have an egg slice, you can use a grater.

beans and sugar snap peas with lemon and capers

preparation time 10 minutes
cooking time 10 minutes
serves 4

300g butter beans
200g sugar snap peas
2 tablespoons drained tiny capers
¼ cup (60ml) lemon juice
2 tablespoons chopped fresh dill

1 Boil, steam or microwave beans and peas, separately, until just tender; drain.
2 Heat large oiled frying pan; cook capers, stirring, until browned lightly. Add juice, beans and peas; stir until vegetables are hot. Stir in dill.
per serving 0.6g fat; 167kJ (40 cal)

ginger chicken salad

preparation time 30 minutes
cooking time 55 minutes (plus cooling time)
serves 6

1.8kg chicken
1 cup (250ml) soy sauce
1 cup (250ml) water
¼ cup (55g) white sugar
1 teaspoon sesame oil
1 teaspoon five-spice powder
2cm piece fresh ginger (10g), sliced
1 clove garlic, crushed
500g broccoli, chopped coarsely
1 medium red pepper (200g), sliced
410g can baby corn, drained
3 spring onions, sliced

GINGER DRESSING
⅓ cup (80ml) groundnut oil
2 teaspoons honey
2 teaspoons white vinegar
1 teaspoon soy sauce
4cm piece fresh ginger (20g), grated

1 Rinse chicken, pat dry with absorbent paper inside and out. Combine sauce, the water, sugar, oil, five-spice, ginger and garlic in large saucepan. Add chicken, bring to a boil, uncovered. Reduce heat, cover; simmer, about 40 minutes or until cooked, turning once. Remove from heat; stand chicken in covered saucepan until cold. Drain chicken; remove meat from bones; slice meat.

2 Boil, steam or microwave broccoli until tender; drain, rinse under cold water, drain.

3 Meanwhile, combine ingredients for ginger dressing in screw-top jar; shake well.

4 Combine chicken, broccoli, pepper, corn and onion in large bowl. Pour dressing over salad just before serving.

per serving 37.7g fat; 2383kJ (570 cal)

TIP Cook chicken, allow time to cool and serve on the same day, if possible. Use a saucepan just large enough to hold the chicken.

smoked chicken and pear salad

preparation time 15 minutes
serves 4

150g radicchio lettuce, torn
100g mignonette lettuce, torn
200g smoked cooked chicken, sliced thinly
1 large pear (330g), sliced thinly
1 medium red onion (170g), sliced thinly
¼ cup (60ml) red wine vinegar
1 tablespoon balsamic vinegar
⅓ cup (80ml) olive oil
¼ teaspoon white sugar

1 Combine both lettuces, chicken, pear and onion in large bowl.
2 Combine the remaining ingredients in a screw-top jar; shake well.
3 Drizzle dressing over lettuce mixture; toss gently to combine.
per serving 21.9g fat; 1262kJ (302 cal)
TIPS The dressing can be made a day ahead.
The recipe is best assembled just before serving.
You can use a store-bought barbecue chicken in this recipe, if preferred.

warm potato and smoked chicken salad

preparation time 20 minutes
cooking time 15 minutes
serves 4

700g salad potatoes
500g frozen broad beans
500g smoked chicken breasts, sliced thinly
1 large red onion (300g), sliced thinly
100g rocket
2 tablespoons drained baby capers, rinsed
PARSLEY DRESSING
½ cup firmly packed fresh flat-leaf parsley leaves
⅓ cup (80ml) olive oil
2 tablespoons lemon juice
1 clove garlic, crushed
1 teaspoon dijon mustard

1 Boil or steam potatoes and beans, separately, until tender.
2 Meanwhile, make parsley dressing.
3 Combine remaining ingredients in large bowl.
4 Cut hot potatoes into thin wedges; peel beans. Add potato, beans and parsley dressing to salad; toss gently to combine.

PARSLEY DRESSING
Blend or process parsley and oil until chopped finely. Transfer to small bowl; whisk in juice, garlic and mustard.
per serving 246g fat; 1956kJ (468 cal)
TIPS Use a sturdy brush to scrub the potatoes well before cooking. Some kitchenware stores stock brushes especially designed for cleaning potatoes.
You can use thin slices of cooked chicken as a substitute for the smoked chicken, if preferred.
This recipe can be prepared several hours ahead.

thai chicken and lychee salad

preparation time 20 minutes
serves 4

3 cups (480g) shredded cooked chicken
565g can lychees in syrup, drained, halved
1 small red onion (100g), sliced thinly
8 spring onions, sliced thinly
2 cups (160g) beansprouts
½ cup firmly packed fresh mint leaves
½ cup firmly packed fresh coriander leaves
1 teaspoon finely grated lime rind
1 teaspoon sambal oelek
¼ cup (60ml) lime juice
1 teaspoon sesame oil
1 tablespoon brown sugar
2 teaspoons fish sauce

1 Combine chicken, lychees, onions, sprouts, mint and coriander in large bowl.
2 Combine remaining ingredients in screw-top jar; shake well. Drizzle dressing over salad; toss gently to combine.
per serving 7.6g fat; 1112kJ (266 cal)
TIP You need to buy a barbecued chicken weighing about 900g for this recipe.

salad of greens, chicken livers, bacon and apple

preparation time 15 minutes
cooking time 15 minutes
serves 4

4 bacon rashers (280g), rind removed, sliced thinly
1 tablespoon olive oil
500g chicken livers, halved, trimmed
200g lamb's lettuce
250g baby spinach leaves
1 medium apple (150g), halved, sliced into thin
   wedges

CRANBERRY DRESSING
4 shallots (100g), chopped finely
2 tablespoons red wine vinegar
⅓ cup (80ml) olive oil
¼ cup (80g) whole berry cranberry sauce, warmed

1 Combine ingredients for cranberry dressing in small bowl.
2 Cook bacon, stirring, in large frying pan until crisp; drain on absorbent paper.
3 Heat oil in same clean pan; cook liver, over high heat, about 5 minutes or until browned and cooked as desired (do not overcook or liver will be dry and tasteless). Drain on absorbent paper.
4 Place bacon, liver, lettuce, leaves, apple and dressing in large bowl; toss gently to combine. Return meat to soup, stir until heated through.
per serving 33g fat; 2027kJ (485 cal)

chicken caesar salad

preparation time 20 minutes
cooking time 35 minutes
serves 4

1 long french bread stick
⅓ cup (80ml) olive oil
2 cloves garlic, crushed
600g chicken breast fillets
4 bacon rashers (280g), rind removed
1 large cos lettuce, trimmed, torn
6 spring onions, sliced thinly
¼ cup coarsely chopped fresh flat-leaf parsley
100g parmesan cheese, shaved

CAESAR DRESSING
1 egg
1 clove garlic, quartered
2 tablespoons lemon juice
1 teaspoon dijon mustard
6 anchovy fillets, drained
⅔ cup (160ml) olive oil
1 tablespoon hot water, approximately

1 Preheat oven to moderate (180°C/160°C fan-assisted).
2 Make caesar dressing.
3 Halve bread lengthways; slice halves on the diagonal into 1cm-thick slices. Combine oil and garlic in large bowl, add bread; toss bread to coat in mixture. Place bread, in single layer, on oven trays; toast in moderate oven about 10 minutes or until croûtes are browned lightly.
4 Meanwhile, cook chicken, in batches, on heated, oiled grill plate (or grill or barbecue) until browned lightly and cooked through. Cook bacon on same grill plate until browned and crisp; drain on absorbent paper. Slice chicken thinly; slice bacon thinly.
5 Combine half the chicken, half the bacon, half the croûtes and half the dressing in large bowl with lettuce and half the onion, half the parsley and half the cheese; toss gently.
6 Divide salad among serving bowls; top with remaining chicken, bacon, croûtes, onion, parsley and cheese, drizzle with remaining dressing.

CAESAR DRESSING
Blend or process egg, garlic, juice, mustard and anchovies until smooth. With motor operating, add oil in a thin, steady stream until dressing thickens. If thinner dressing is preferred, stir in as much of the water as desired.
per serving 76.5g fat; 4661kJ (1115 cal)
TIP Caesar dressing and croûtes can be prepared a day ahead. Cover and refrigerate dressing; store croûtes in airtight container.

The croutes add a wonderful crisp contrast in this classic salad

beef salad with blue-cheese dressing

preparation time 10 minutes (plus standing time)
cooking time 20 minutes
serves 4

500g tiny new potatoes, quartered
1 tablespoon olive oil
4 fillet steaks (500g)
300g green beans, trimmed, halved crossways
200g baby plum tomatoes, halved
100g baby rocket leaves

BLUE-CHEESE DRESSING
¼ cup (60ml) olive oil
2 cloves garlic, crushed
¼ cup (60ml) orange juice
60g blue cheese, crumbled

1 Preheat oven to very hot.
2 Place potato, in single layer, in large shallow baking dish; drizzle with oil. Roast, uncovered, in very hot oven about 20 minutes or until lightly browned and tender.
3 Make blue-cheese dressing.
4 Cook steaks on heated oiled grill plate (or grill or barbecue) until browned both sides and cooked as desired. Cover; stand 5 minutes.
5 Meanwhile, boil, steam or microwave beans until just tender; drain.
6 Slice steak thinly. Combine steak, beans and potato in large bowl with tomato and rocket, drizzle with blue-cheese dressing; toss gently to combine.

BLUE-CHEESE DRESSING
Combine ingredients in screw-top jar; shake well.
per serving 31.9g fat; 2143kJ (512 cal)

italian fennel and beef salad with balsamic vinaigrette

preparation time 15 minutes (plus standing time)
cooking time 15 minutes
serves 4

100g bean thread noodles
4 rib-eye steaks (800g)
2 medium fennel bulbs (600g), sliced thinly
1 medium red onion (170g), sliced thinly
150g baby rocket leaves
1¼ cups (100g) shaved parmesan cheese

BALSAMIC VINAIGRETTE
¼ cup (60ml) lemon juice
2 cloves garlic, crushed
¼ cup (60ml) olive oil
2 tablespoons balsamic vinegar
1 tablespoon coarsely chopped fresh thyme

1 Place noodles in medium heatproof bowl; cover with boiling water, stand until just tender, drain.
2 Make balsamic vinaigrette.
3 Cook steaks on heated oiled grill plate (or grill or barbecue) until browned both sides and cooked as desired. Cover; stand 5 minutes.
4 Cut noodles into 5cm lengths; place in large bowl with fennel, onion and rocket. Slice steak thinly, add to noodles with balsamic vinaigrette; toss gently to combine. Serve salad topped with cheese.

BALSAMIC VINAIGRETTE
Combine ingredients in screw-top jar; shake well.
per serving 34.8g fat; 2610kJ (624 cal)
TIP Recipe can be made three days ahead; keep, covered, in refrigerator.

thai char-grilled beef salad

preparation time 20 minutes (plus refrigeration time)
cooking time 15 minutes
serves 4

600g piece beef rump steak
2 teaspoons sesame oil
⅓ cup (80ml) kecap manis
1 cup loosely packed fresh mint leaves
1 cup loosely packed fresh coriander leaves
½ cup loosely packed fresh thai basil leaves
6 spring onions, sliced thinly
5 shallots (125g), sliced thinly
250g cherry tomatoes, halved
1 cucumber (400g), deseeded, sliced thinly
10 kaffir lime leaves, shredded finely
100g mixed salad leaves

SWEET AND SOUR DRESSING
½ cup (125ml) lime juice
¼ cup (60ml) fish sauce
2 teaspoons white sugar
2 fresh small red thai chillies, sliced thinly

1 Place beef in shallow dish; brush all over with combined oil and kecap manis. Cover; refrigerate 30 minutes.
2 Meanwhile, combine herbs, onion, shallot, tomato and cucumber in large bowl; toss gently.
3 Combine ingredients for sweet and sour dressing in screw-top jar; shake well.
4 Cook beef on heated oiled grill plate (or grill or barbecue) until browned lightly and cooked as desired. Cover beef; stand 10 minutes then slice thinly.
5 Place beef, lime leaves and salad leaves in large bowl with herb mixture. Add sweet and sour dressing; toss gently to combine.
per serving 11.7g fat; 1225kJ (293 cal)
TIPS Thai basil, also known as horapa, has small leaves, purplish stems and a sweet licorice flavour; it is one of the basic flavours that typify Thai cuisine.
Rib-eye, boneless sirloin or fillet steaks are all good substitutes for rump in this recipe.

warm salmon, risoni and pea salad

preparation time 15 minutes
cooking time 15 minutes
serves 4

250g risoni pasta
2 cups (250g) frozen peas
1 tablespoon olive oil
500g salmon fillets
8 spring onions, chopped
100g baby spinach leaves

DILL DRESSING
¼ cup (60ml) olive oil
2 teaspoons grated lemon rind
¼ cup (60ml) lemon juice
½ teaspoon white sugar
1 teaspoon dijon mustard
1 tablespoon coarsely chopped fresh dill

1 Make dill dressing.
2 Cook pasta in large saucepan of boiling water until almost tender. Add peas to pan with pasta and cook until peas and pasta are just tender; drain. Transfer to a large bowl.
3 Meanwhile, heat oil in large non-stick frying pan. Add salmon; cook until browned lightly and cooked as desired. Remove from pan; stand 5 minutes. Remove skin and any bones; break salmon into large chunks.
4 Add onion, spinach and dill dressing to pasta; toss well. Add salmon, toss gently to combine.

DILL DRESSING
Combine ingredients in screw-top jar; shake well.
per serving 28.2g fat; 2508kJ (600 cal)
TIP This recipe can be made three hours ahead and served cold.

spicy potato salad

preparation time 10 minutes
cooking time 30 minutes (plus cooling time)
serves 6

6 medium potatoes (1.2kg), chopped coarsely
¼ cup (60ml) groundnut oil
1 teaspoon black mustard seeds
1 teaspoon cumin seeds
1 teaspoon ground cumin
½ teaspoon sweet paprika
1½ teaspoons ground turmeric
¼ teaspoon chilli flakes
1 clove garlic, crushed
2 tablespoons lemon juice
¼ cup chopped fresh coriander

1 Preheat oven to hot. Boil, steam or microwave potato until just tender; rinse under cold running water. Drain potato; cool.
2 Combine potato, oil, seeds, spices, garlic and juice in baking dish. Cook in hot oven about 20 minutes or until potato is brown. Top with coriander to serve.
per serving 10.2g fat; 960kJ (230 cal)
TIP Recipe can be made 3 hours ahead and refrigerated, covered.

crispy noodle and cabbage salad

preparation time 15 minutes
serves 4

3 cups (240g) finely shredded white cabbage
3 cups (240g) finely shredded red cabbage
300g packet crunchy noodles
8 spring onions, chopped finely
½ cup chopped fresh flat-leaf parsley
2 tablespoons sesame seeds, toasted

SOY AND SWEET CHILLI DRESSING
1 tablespoon sesame oil
1 tablespoon groundnut oil
2 tablespoons white vinegar
2 tablespoons light soy sauce
½ cup (125ml) sweet chilli sauce

1 Place cabbage, noodles, onion, parsley and seeds in large bowl.
2 Pour over dressing; toss to combine.

SOY AND SWEET CHILLI DRESSING
Combine ingredients in screw-top jar; shake well.
per serving 22.8g fat; 1464kJ (350 cal)
TIPS Make salad just before serving or the noodles will lose their crispness; either flat or round crunchy noodles can be used in this recipe.
The dressing can be made a day ahead and refrigerated, covered.

roasted vegetable and haloumi salad

preparation time 15 minutes
cooking time 45 minutes
serves 4

1 medium sweet potato (400g), chopped coarsely
2 large carrots (360g), quartered lengthways
2 medium parsnips (500g), halved lengthways
2 cloves garlic, crushed
¼ cup (60ml) extra virgin olive oil
2 large red onions (600g), cut into wedges
4 baby aubergines (240g), halved lengthways
4 fresh long red chillies, halved
250g haloumi cheese, sliced
75g baby spinach leaves

LEMON AND BASIL DRESSING
½ cup (125ml) extra virgin olive oil
2 tablespoons lemon juice
¼ cup coarsely chopped fresh basil
1 teaspoon white sugar

1 Preheat oven to hot (220°C/200°C fan-assisted).
2 Combine sweet potato, carrot, parsnip and half the combined garlic and olive oil on large shallow oven tray. Combine onion, aubergine, chilli and remaining oil mixture on separate shallow oven tray. Roast sweet potato mixture in hot oven about 45 minutes and onion mixture about 30 minutes, or until vegetables are cooked and browned lightly.
3 Meanwhile, make lemon and basil dressing.
4 Just before serving, heat lightly oiled grill plate; cook cheese until browned lightly on both sides.
5 Combine roasted vegetables with spinach; divide among serving plates. Top with cheese and drizzle with lemon and basil dressing.

LEMON AND BASIL DRESSING
Blend or process ingredients until smooth.
per serving 53.6g fat; 2880kJ (689 cal)
TIP Lemon and basil dressing can be made several hours ahead.

tomatoes and goat's cheese in walnut dressing

two-tomato salad

beetroot and mozzarella salad

grilled haloumi, tomato and aubergine salad

tomatoes and goat's cheese in walnut dressing

preparation time 15 minutes
serves 6

8 medium vine tomatoes (1.5kg), sliced thickly
150g goat's cheese, sliced thickly
¼ cup (25g) walnuts, toasted, chopped coarsely
¼ cup (60ml) olive oil
1 clove garlic, crushed
1½ tablespoons raspberry vinegar
2 teaspoons dijon mustard
2 teaspoons coarsely chopped fresh thyme
2 teaspoons sugar

1 Place a slice of tomato on each serving plate; top with a slice of cheese.
2 Repeat, sprinkling nuts and combined remaining ingredients between layers.
per serving 18.5g fat; 938kJ (224 cal)
TIPS Hazelnuts can be substituted for walnuts in this recipe and, if you have hazelnut or walnut oil at hand, use one of these, rather than the olive oil.
Sample a few different goat's cheeses before you decide on one; they vary greatly in texture and taste.

two-tomato salad

preparation time 10 minutes
cooking time 1 hour 45 minutes
serves 4

400g cherry tomatoes
250g yellow teardrop tomatoes, halved
½ cup baby basil leaves
2 tablespoons balsamic vinegar

1 Combine tomatoes and basil in medium serving bowl. Add vinegar just before serving. Sprinkle with freshly ground black pepper, if desired.
per serving 0.2g fat; 93kJ (22 cal)

beetroot and mozzarella salad

preparation time 25 minutes
cooking time 30 minutes (plus cooling time)
serves 4

2 medium red peppers (400g)
8 baby red beetroot (200g)
8 baby golden beetroot (200g)
150g mozzarella cheese, chopped coarsely
2 medium oranges (480g), peeled, segmented
2 tablespoons red wine vinegar
1 tablespoon extra virgin olive oil
120g mixed salad leaves
8 slices crusty bread, toasted

1 Preheat oven to moderately hot. Quarter peppers; remove and discard seeds and membranes. Roast in moderately hot oven, skin-side up, until skin blisters and blackens; cover pepper pieces with plastic or paper 5 minutes. Peel away and discard skin; slice pepper flesh into wide strips.
2 Remove stems from beetroot; cook beetroot in boiling water about 10 minutes or until tender; cool. Peel beetroot.
3 Combine pepper, mozzarella, orange, vinegar and oil. Arrange salad leaves on serving plates; top with pepper mixture and beetroot. Serve with toast.

per serving 13.6g fat; 2159kJ (517 cal)
TIPS All red beetroot can be substituted for golden beetroot, and bocconcini can be substituted for mozzarella.
Ciabatta, a crusty Italian bread, is ideal for this recipe.

grilled haloumi, tomato and aubergine salad

preparation time 20 minutes
cooking time 25 minutes
serves 4

½ cup (125ml) olive oil
4 baby aubergines (240g), sliced thinly
4 medium plum tomatoes (300g), halved lengthways
400g haloumi cheese, sliced thinly
250g rocket, chopped coarsely
¼ cup firmly packed fresh basil leaves
2 tablespoons red wine vinegar
2 teaspoons chopped drained capers

1 Heat 1 tablespoon of the oil in large frying pan or grill pan. Cook aubergine until browned both sides; remove from pan.
2 Add tomato to same pan; cook, cut-side down, until browned and softened slightly. Remove from pan.
3 Heat another tablespoon of the oil in same pan; cook haloumi until browned lightly both sides.
4 Combine aubergine, tomato, haloumi, rocket and basil in large bowl with remaining oil, vinegar and capers.

per serving 59.1g fat; 2681kJ (641 cal)
TIP This recipe is best made just before serving.

pasta, pepper and goat's cheese salad

preparation time 10 minutes
cooking time 20 minutes
serves 4

375g large spiral pasta
2 medium red peppers (400g)
2 medium yellow peppers (400g)
150g goat's cheese, crumbled
⅓ cup (35g) walnuts, toasted, chopped coarsely
½ cup loosely packed fresh basil leaves
¼ cup (60ml) red wine vinegar
⅓ cup (80ml) olive oil
1 clove garlic, crushed
2 teaspoons wholegrain mustard

1 Cook pasta in large saucepan of boiling water, uncovered, until just tender; drain. Rinse under cold water; drain.
2 Meanwhile, quarter peppers; remove and discard seeds and membranes. Roast under grill or in very hot oven, skin-side up, until skin blisters and blackens. Cover pepper pieces with plastic or paper 5 minutes. Peel away and discard skin; slice pepper flesh thickly.
3 Place pasta and pepper in large bowl with cheese, nuts, basil and combined remaining ingredients; toss gently to combine.
per serving 31.5g fat; 2703kJ (647 cal)
TIP Feta or any soft, crumbly cheese can be substituted for the goat's cheese, and toasted pecan halves can be used instead of walnuts.

avocado and artichoke salad

preparation time 15 minutes (plus refrigeration time)
serves 4

1 medium avocado (250g), sliced
8 bottled artichoke hearts in oil, drained, quartered
1 cucumber (260g), sliced thinly
1 small mignonette lettuce, torn

LIME AND BASIL VINAIGRETTE
¼ cup (60ml) olive oil
¼ cup (60ml) lime juice
1 fresh small red thai chilli, chopped finely
1 tablespoon finely shredded fresh basil
½ teaspoon white sugar

1 Combine ingredients for lime and basil vinaigrette in screw-top jar; shake well.
2 Combine avocado, artichoke and cucumber in medium bowl, add vinaigrette; cover, refrigerate 2 hours.
3 Place lettuce in bowl. Serve avocado mixture sprinkled over lettuce.
per serving 24.1g fat; 1028kJ (246 cal)

asparagus, avocado and macadamia salad

preparation time 10 minutes
cooking time 5 minutes (plus cooling time)
serves 8

750g asparagus, halved
150g rocket leaves
1 large avocado (320g), sliced thinly
½ cup (75g) macadamias, toasted, chopped
  coarsely
2 tablespoons sherry vinegar
¼ cup (60ml) macadamia (or olive) oil

1 Cook asparagus, in batches, on heated oiled grill plate (or grill or barbecue), until just tender; cool.
2 Combine asparagus on serving platter with rocket, avocado and nuts.
3 Just before serving, drizzle with the combined vinegar and oil.
per serving 20.6g fat; 852kJ (204 cal)
TIP This recipe can be prepared 3 hours ahead; add the avocado and dressing just before serving.

baked ricotta with roasted pepper salad

preparation time 15 minutes
cooking time 30 minutes (plus standing time)
serves 8

200g low-fat ricotta cheese
2 tablespoons finely grated parmesan cheese
1 egg, beaten lightly
1 teaspoon coarsely chopped fresh sage
3 fresh bay leaves, chopped coarsely
2 medium red peppers (400g)
2 medium yellow peppers (400g)
250g mixed salad leaves
¼ cup (60ml) balsamic vinegar
1 tablespoon olive oil
1 tablespoon honey

1 Preheat oven to moderately low.
2 Oil eight holes of a 12-hole ⅓-cup (80ml) non-stick muffin tray. Combine cheeses and egg in small bowl. Divide ricotta mixture among prepared holes; sprinkle with combined herbs.
3 Place muffin tray in large baking dish; add enough boiling water to come halfway up side of tray. Bake ricotta, uncovered, in moderately low oven about 30 minutes or until set. Stand 10 minutes before turning ricotta out.
4 Meanwhile, quarter peppers; remove and discard seeds and membranes. Roast under grill or in very hot oven, skin-side up, until skin blisters and blackens. Cover pepper pieces with plastic or paper 5 minutes. Peel away and discard skin; slice pepper flesh thickly.
5 Place pepper and salad leaves in large bowl with combined remaining ingredients. Divide salad among serving plates; top each with a baked ricotta.
per serving 5.8g fat; 430kJ (103 cal)
TIP Dried bay leaves and ¼ teaspoon crumbled dried sage can be substituted for the fresh varieties.

roast squash, sesame and rocket salad

preparation time 15 minutes
cooking time 25 minutes
serves 6

600g trimmed butternut squash
cooking-oil spray
1 tablespoon honey
1 tablespoon sesame seeds
500g asparagus, halved
150g rocket leaves
1 small red onion (100g), sliced thinly
1 tablespoon sesame oil
1 tablespoon cider vinegar
1 teaspoon honey, extra

1 Preheat oven to very hot.
2 Cut squash into 1.5cm wide strips.
3 Place squash, in single layer, in baking dish lined with baking parchment; spray lightly with cooking-oil spray. Roast, uncovered, in very hot oven about 20 minutes or until squash is just tender. Drizzle with honey; sprinkle with seeds. Roast 5 minutes, uncovered, or until seeds are browned lightly.
4 Meanwhile, boil, steam or microwave asparagus until just tender; drain. Rinse under cold water; drain.
5 Combine squash, asparagus, rocket and onion in large bowl. Drizzle with combined remaining ingredients; toss salad gently.
per serving 5.3g fat; 505kJ (121 cal)
TIPS Reserve any seeds or honey from squash pan and add to dressing.
You will need a piece of squash weighing approximately 750g for this recipe.

Tropical fruit mini pavlovas, crème brulée,
berry tiramisu – these are just a few of the
classic recipes you'll find here. What better
way to complete the perfect casual feast
than with a divinely decadent dessert?

desserts

chocolate jaffa tart

chocolate self-saucing pudding

decadent chocolate roulade

rich chocolate meringue torte

chocolate jaffa tart

preparation time 30 minutes (plus refrigeration time)
cooking time 55 minutes
serves 8

1½ cups (225g) plain flour
¼ cup (40g) icing sugar
125g chilled unsalted butter, chopped
2 egg yolks
2 teaspoons iced water, approximately
3 eggs
1 tablespoon finely grated orange rind
⅔ cup (160ml) whipping cream
¾ cup (165g) caster sugar
60g dark chocolate, melted
2 tablespoons cocoa powder
2 tablespoons Grand Marnier
140g dark chocolate, chopped coarsely, extra
¼ cup (60ml) whipping cream, extra
20 Ferrero Rocher chocolates, halved

1 Grease 24cm-round loose-based flan tin.
2 Blend or process flour, icing sugar and butter until crumbly. Add egg yolks and enough of the water to make ingredients just come together. Knead pastry on floured surface until smooth. Cover with cling film; refrigerate 30 minutes.
3 Roll pastry, between sheets of baking parchment, until large enough to line prepared tin; lift pastry into tin. Press into side; trim edge. Cover; refrigerate 30 minutes.
4 Preheat oven to moderately hot.
5 Cover pastry with baking parchment; fill with dried beans or rice. Place on baking tray; bake in moderately hot oven 10 minutes. Remove paper and beans. Bake further 10 minutes or until pastry is browned lightly; cool.
6 Meanwhile, whisk eggs, rind, cream, caster sugar, chocolate, sifted cocoa powder and liqueur in medium bowl until combined.
7 Reduce oven temperature to moderate. Pour chocolate mixture into pastry case. Bake in moderate oven about 30 minutes or until filling is set; cool.
8 Place extra chocolate and cream in small saucepan; stir over low heat until smooth. Spread warm chocolate mixture over top of cold tart; refrigerate until set. Just before serving, decorate with Ferrero Rocher halves.
TIP Use a rolling pin to trim the edges of the pastry after it has been eased into the tin; this makes a tidier cut than a knife.

chocolate self-saucing pudding

preparation time 10 minutes
cooking time 40 minutes
serves 6

1 cup (150g) self-raising flour
½ teaspoon bicarbonate of soda
½ cup (50g) cocoa powder
1¼ cups (275g) firmly packed brown sugar
80g butter, melted
½ cup (120g) soured cream
1 egg, beaten lightly
2 cups (500ml) boiling water

1 Preheat oven to moderate (180°C/160°C fan-assisted). Grease deep 1.5-litre (6-cup) ovenproof dish.
2 Sift flour, soda, half of the cocoa and ½ cup of the sugar into medium bowl; stir in combined butter, soured cream and egg.
3 Spread mixture into prepared dish. Sift remaining cocoa and remaining sugar evenly over mixture; gently pour over the boiling water. Bake, uncovered, in moderate oven about 40 minutes. Stand 5 minutes before serving.
TIP Serve with vanilla ice-cream, if desired.

decadent chocolate roulade

preparation time 15 minutes (plus refrigeration time)
cooking time 20 minutes (plus cooling time)
serves 8

1 tablespoon caster sugar
200g dark eating chocolate, chopped
¼ cup (60ml) hot water
1 teaspoon dry instant coffee
4 eggs, separated
½ cup (110g) caster sugar, extra
300ml whipping cream
120g raspberries

1 Preheat oven to moderate (180°C/160°C fan-assisted). Grease 25cm x 30cm swiss roll tin; line base with baking parchment, extending paper 5cm over two long sides of tin. Place a piece of parchment, cut the same size as swiss roll tin, on work surface; sprinkle evenly with caster sugar.
2 Combine chocolate, the hot water and coffee in medium heatproof bowl. Stir over medium saucepan of simmering water until smooth; remove from heat.
3 Beat egg yolks and extra sugar in small bowl with an electric mixer until thick and creamy. Fold egg mixture into warm chocolate mixture.
4 Beat egg whites in small clean bowl with electric mixer until soft peaks form. Gently fold egg whites, in two batches, into chocolate mixture. Spread into prepared tin; bake in moderate oven about 15 minutes.
5 Turn cake onto sugared paper, peeling baking parchment away; use serrated knife to cut away crisp edges from all sides. Cover cake with tea towel; cool.
6 Beat cream in small bowl with electric mixer until firm peaks form. Spread cake evenly with cream; sprinkle evenly with raspberries. Roll cake, from long side, by lifting paper and using it to guide the roll into log shape. Cover roll; refrigerate 30 minutes before serving.

rich chocolate meringue torte

preparation time 15 minutes
cooking time 1 hour 30 minutes (plus cooling time)
serves 8

8 egg whites
1 cup (220g) caster sugar
¼ cup (25g) cocoa powder
60g dark chocolate, chopped finely
¼ cup (60g) soft dried figs, chopped finely
¼ cup (60g) soft prunes, chopped finely
¾ cup (50g) stale breadcrumbs
1 tablespoon icing sugar
1 tablespoon cocoa powder, extra

1 Preheat oven to very low. Grease 22cm springform cake tin; line base with baking parchment. Flour side of tin; shake away excess.
2 Beat egg whites in large bowl with electric mixer until soft peaks form. Gradually add caster sugar; beat until sugar dissolves between additions.
3 Fold in sifted cocoa, chocolate, dried fruit and breadcrumbs. Spoon mixture into prepared tin. Bake in very low oven about 1½ hours or until firm; cool in oven with door ajar.
4 Dust cake with sifted icing sugar and extra cocoa.
TIP This recipe can be made 2 days ahead.

choc-cherry cheesecake

preparation time 30 minutes (plus refrigeration time)
cooking time 50 minutes
serves 10

125g plain chocolate biscuits
75g butter, melted
2 x 250g packets cream cheese, softened
1/3 cup (75g) caster sugar
2 eggs
200g dark chocolate, melted
2 x 85g plain chocolate Bounty bars, chopped coarsely
425g can pitted black cherries in syrup, drained

1 Grease 24cm springform tin.
2 Blend or process biscuits until mixture resembles fine breadcrumbs. Add butter; process until just combined. Using one hand, press biscuit mixture evenly over base of prepared tin. Cover; refrigerate about 30 minutes or until firm.
3 Preheat oven to moderate.
4 Meanwhile, beat cheese and sugar in medium bowl with electric mixer until smooth; add eggs, one at a time, beating well between additions. Gradually beat in chocolate; fold Bounty bars and cherries into cheesecake mixture.
5 Place tin on oven tray. Spread cheesecake mixture into tin; bake in moderate oven about 50 minutes or until set. Remove from oven; cool to room temperature. Cover; refrigerate 3 hours or overnight.
6 Serve cheesecake decorated with chocolate roses, if desired.
TIPS Use absorbent paper to soak up liquid from the cherries.
Chocolate should be cool, but not set, before it is added to the cheesecake mixture.
To make chocolate roses, melt your choice of chocolate then spread evenly over marble or a foil-covered surface. When chocolate is almost set, drag ice-cream scoop over surface of chocolate to make roses.

pear tart tatin

preparation time 20 minutes (plus refrigeration time)
cooking time 1 hour 15 minutes
serves 6

3 large firm pears (990g)
90g butter, chopped
½ cup (110g) firmly packed brown sugar
⅔ cup (160ml) cream
¼ cup (35g) toasted pecans, chopped coarsely

PASTRY
1¼ cups (185g) plain flour
⅓ cup (55g) icing sugar
90g butter, chopped
1 egg yolk
1 tablespoon water

1 Peel and core pears; cut lengthways into quarters.
2 Melt butter with brown sugar in large frying pan. Add cream, stirring, until sugar dissolves; bring to a boil. Add pear; reduce heat, simmer, turning occasionally, about 45 minutes or until tender.
3 Meanwhile, make pastry.
4 Preheat oven to hot (220°C/200°C fan-assisted). Place pears, round-side down, in deep 22cm-round cake tin; pour over caramelised pan liquid, sprinkle with nuts.
5 Roll pastry between sheets of baking parchment until slightly larger than circumference of prepared tin. Remove top paper, turn pastry onto pears. Remove remaining paper; tuck pastry between pear quarters and side of tin.
6 Bake, uncovered, in hot oven about 25 minutes or until pastry is browned lightly. Cool 5 minutes; turn tart onto plate, serve with whipped cream, if desired.

PASTRY
Blend or process flour, icing sugar and butter until mixture is crumbly. Add egg yolk and the water; process until ingredients just come together. Enclose in cling film; refrigerate 30 minutes.

plum clafoutis

preparation time 15 minutes
cooking time 40 minutes
serves 4

1½ cups (375ml) low-fat custard
¼ cup (35g) self-raising flour
1 egg yolk
2 egg whites
825g can whole plums, drained, halved, pitted
2 teaspoons icing sugar

1 Preheat oven to moderate.
2 Combine custard, flour and egg yolk in medium bowl.
3 Beat egg whites in small bowl of electric mixer on highest speed until soft peaks form; fold gently into custard mixture. Pour mixture into 24cm-round ovenproof pie dish.
4 Pat plums dry with absorbent paper; arrange, cut-side down, over custard. Place pie dish on oven tray.
5 Bake in moderate oven, uncovered, about 40 minutes or until firm.
6 Just before serving, dust with sifted icing sugar. Serve with vanilla ice-cream, if desired.
TIP Canned apricots or peaches can be substituted for the plums.

summer berry and almond tart

preparation time 30 minutes (plus refrigeration time)
cooking time 50 minutes (plus cooling time)
serves 8

1⅔ cups (250g) plain flour
⅓ cup (55g) icing sugar
2 teaspoons grated orange rind
150g chilled butter, chopped
1 egg
350g fresh mixed berries

FILLING
90g butter
1 teaspoon vanilla essence
½ cup (110g) caster sugar
1 egg
1 tablespoon plain flour
1 cup (100g) ground almonds

1 Process flour, icing sugar, rind and butter until combined. Add egg; process until pastry just comes together.
2 Shape pastry into round. Cover; refrigerate 1 hour.
3 Roll pastry between two sheets of baking parchment until large enough to line base and side of 26cm-round loose-base flan tin. Ease pastry into tin, pressing lightly into side. Trim edge with sharp knife or rolling pin. Place tin on oven tray; refrigerate 15 minutes.
4 Preheat oven to moderate. Cover pastry with baking parchment; fill with dried beans or rice. Bake in moderate oven 10 minutes. Remove paper and beans. Bake further 5 minutes or until pastry is golden brown; cool.
5 Spoon filling into pastry base; scatter berries over filling. Bake in moderate oven 35 minutes or until filling is golden and firm; cool.
6 Serve with whipped cream and dusted with icing sugar, if desired.

FILLING
Beat butter, vanilla and sugar in small bowl with electric mixer until pale. Beat in egg until combined; stir in flour and ground almonds.
TIPS Pastry suitable to freeze.
This recipe can be made a day ahead.

lemon curd crepe cake

preparation time 30 minutes (plus refrigeration time)
cooking time 40 minutes
serves 10

¾ cup (110g) plain flour
3 eggs
1 tablespoon vegetable oil
1⅓ cups (330ml) milk
2 teaspoons finely grated lemon rind
¾ cup (180ml) lemon juice
1½ cups (330g) caster sugar
6 eggs, beaten lightly, extra
125g butter, chopped
2 teaspoons gelatine
2 tablespoons water

1 Line base and side of deep 20cm-round cake tin with cling film.

2 Place flour in medium bowl; make well in centre. Gradually whisk in combined eggs, oil and milk; strain batter into large jug. Cover; stand crepe batter 30 minutes.

3 Heat greased crepe pan or small heavy-based non-stick frying pan over high heat; pour about 2 tablespoons of batter into pan, tilting pan so batter coats base evenly. Cook, over low heat, loosening edge with spatula until crepe is browned lightly. Turn crepe; brown other side. Remove from pan; repeat with remaining batter to make 12 crepes.

4 Combine rind, juice, sugar, strained extra egg and butter in large heatproof bowl. Place bowl over large saucepan of simmering water; cook, stirring, about 15 minutes or until lemon curd coats the back of a spoon.

5 Sprinkle gelatine over the water in small heatproof jug. Stand jug in small saucepan of simmering water; stir until gelatine dissolves. Stir gelatine mixture into warm lemon curd.

6 Place one crepe in prepared pan; spread with ¼ cup lemon curd. Continue layering with remaining crepes and curd, finishing with crepe layer. Cover; refrigerate overnight or until firm. Cut into wedges; top with crystallised lemon rind, if desired.

TIPS Simmering water should not touch the base of the heatproof bowl while making the lemon curd.
This cake is best assembled a day before serving.
You need approximately three large lemons for this recipe.

mini apple charlottes with caramel sauce

preparation time 25 minutes
cooking time 30 minutes
serves 4

4 large apples (800g)
¼ cup (50g) firmly packed brown sugar
¼ cup (60ml) orange juice
1 loaf sliced raisin bread (560g)
80g butter, melted

CARAMEL SAUCE
50g butter
½ cup (100g) firmly packed brown sugar
⅓ cup (80ml) orange juice

1 Grease four 1-cup (250ml) metal moulds.
2 Peel and core apples; cut into thin wedges. Cook apple with sugar and juice in large frying pan, stirring until apple browns and mixture bubbles and thickens.
3 Preheat oven to hot. Remove crusts from bread. Cut one 5.5cm round from each of four bread slices; cut each of remaining slices into three strips. Brush one side of each bread piece with butter. Place a round, buttered-side down, in each mould; line side of each mould with bread strips, buttered-side against side of mould, slightly overlapping edges. Firmly pack warm apple mixture into moulds. Fold end of each bread strip into centre of charlotte to enclose filling; press firmly to seal.
4 Place moulds on oven tray; bake, uncovered, in hot oven about 15 minutes until golden brown. Turn, top-side up, onto serving plates; drizzle with caramel sauce.

CARAMEL SAUCE
Melt butter in small frying pan. Add sugar; stir until dissolved. Add juice; cook, stirring, until sauce thickens slightly.
TIPS It's best if the raisin bread is a few days old. You can also use plain white bread instead of the raisin bread.

apricot almond crumbles

preparation time 15 minutes
cooking time 30 minutes
serves 6

825g can apricot halves in natural juice
1 tablespoon brandy
½ cup (75g) self-raising flour
¾ teaspoon ground ginger
¼ cup (30g) ground almonds
¼ cup (55g) brown sugar
¼ cup (55g) caster sugar
90g butter, chopped

1 Preheat oven to moderate (180°C/160°C fan-assisted).
2 Drain apricots over a small jug or bowl; reserve ½ cup (125ml) juice.
3 Slice apricots and divide among six ¾-cup (180ml) ovenproof dishes; place dishes on oven tray. Combine brandy with reserved juice; pour over apricots.
4 Sift flour and ginger into medium bowl; stir in almonds and sugars, then rub in butter with fingertips.
5 Sprinkle crumble mixture over fruit and bake in moderate oven about 30 minutes or until browned lightly. Serve hot with ice-cream or cream, if desired.
TIP This recipe is best made close to serving.

apple pie

preparation time 45 minutes (plus refrigeration time)
cooking time 35 minutes (plus cooling time)
serves 8

1½ cups (225g) plain flour
¾ cup (110g) self-raising flour
⅓ cup (50g) cornflour
½ cup (60g) custard powder
185g chilled butter, chopped
1 tablespoon white sugar
1 egg, separated
⅓ cup (80ml) iced water, approximately
2 tablespoons apricot jam
2 teaspoons white sugar, extra

FILLING
7 large green-skinned apples (1.5kg)
½ cup (125ml) water
¼ cup (55g) white sugar
½ teaspoon ground cinnamon
1 teaspoon finely grated lemon rind

1 Make filling.
2 Sift flours and custard powder into large bowl; rub in butter, add sugar. Make well in centre, add egg yolk and enough of the water to mix to a firm dough; knead lightly. Cover; refrigerate 1 hour.
3 Preheat oven to moderately hot (200°C/180°C fan-assisted).
4 Roll out just over half of the pastry, on floured surface, until just large enough to line a 23cm pie plate. Lift pastry into pie plate; press into side, trim edge. Spread base of pastry with apricot jam, top with filling.
5 Roll out remaining pastry until large enough to cover pie. Brush edges of pie with a little lightly beaten egg white; cover with pastry. Press edges together firmly, trim and decorate. Brush pastry with egg white; sprinkle with extra sugar. Cut a few slits in pastry to allow steam to escape. Bake about 25 minutes or until golden brown.

FILLING
Peel, quarter and core apples; cut each quarter in half lengthways. Combine apples in large saucepan with the water, sugar, cinnamon and rind. Bring to a boil, simmer, covered, about 5 minutes or until apples are almost tender. Remove from heat; drain, cool to room temperature.

pecan, macadamia and walnut tarts

preparation time 20 minutes (plus refrigeration time)
cooking time 25 minutes
serves 4

1¼ cups (185g) plain flour
⅓ cup (55g) icing sugar
¼ cup (30g) ground almonds
125g chilled butter, chopped
1 egg yolk

FILLING
⅓ cup (50g) macadamias, toasted
⅓ cup (35g) pecans, toasted
⅓ cup (35g) walnuts, toasted
2 tablespoons brown sugar
1 tablespoon plain flour
40g butter, melted
2 eggs, beaten lightly
¾ cup (180ml) maple syrup

1 Grease four 10cm-round loose-based flan tins.
2 Blend or process flour, sugar and ground almonds with butter until combined. Add egg yolk; process until mixture just comes together. Knead on floured surface until smooth. Cover with cling film; refrigerate 30 minutes.
3 Divide pastry into quarters. Roll each piece, between sheets of baking parchment, into rounds large enough to line prepared tins; lift pastry into each tin. Press into sides; trim edges. Cover; refrigerate 1 hour.
4 Preheat oven to moderately hot. Place tins on oven tray; line each tin with baking parchment then fill with uncooked rice or dried beans. Bake, uncovered, in moderately hot oven 10 minutes; remove paper and rice. Bake further 7 minutes or until pastry cases are browned lightly; cool.
5 Reduce oven temperature to moderate. Divide filling among cases. Bake in moderate oven about 25 minutes or until set; cool.

FILLING
Combine ingredients in medium bowl; mix well.
TIP Do not use maple-flavoured syrups as a substitute for the 'real thing' in the nut filling.

panettone and butter pudding

preparation time 20 minutes (plus standing time)
cooking time 1 hour 30 minutes (plus cooling time)
serves 8

1kg panettone
90g butter, softened
3 cups (750ml) milk
300ml cream
½ cup (110g) caster sugar
5cm piece vanilla pod
2 egg yolks
3 eggs
¼ cup (80g) apricot jam
1 tablespoon Grand Marnier

1 Preheat oven to moderately low. Grease deep 22cm-round cake tin; line base and side with baking parchment.
2 Cut panettone in half lengthways, reserve half for another use. Cut in half lengthways again, then crossways into 1.5cm slices. Toast panettone lightly both sides; spread one side with butter while still warm.
3 Slightly overlap slices around sides of prepared tin; layer remaining slices in centre.
4 Combine milk, cream, sugar and split vanilla pod in medium saucepan; stir over heat until mixture comes to a boil. Strain into large jug. Cover; cool 10 minutes.
5 Beat egg yolks and eggs in large bowl; gradually beat in milk mixture. Pour custard over bread in tin.
6 Place cake tin in baking dish; add enough boiling water to dish to come halfway up side of tin.
7 Bake, uncovered, about 1¼ hours or until set. Stand pudding in tin 30 minutes before carefully turning out.
8 Combine jam and liqueur in small bowl; brush evenly over warm pudding. Serve with cream and raspberries.
TIPS Panettone is a sweet Italian celebration yeast bread; you can also use fruit bread.
This recipe is best made on day of serving, but will keep up to 2 days.

sticky date roll with butterscotch sauce

preparation time 15 minutes
cooking time 30 minutes
serves 12

2 tablespoons white sugar
1 cup (160g) pitted dates
¾ cup (180ml) boiling water
1 teaspoon bicarbonate of soda
50g butter, chopped
⅔ cup (150g) firmly packed brown sugar
2 eggs
¾ cup (110g) self-raising flour
300ml whipping cream

BUTTERSCOTCH SAUCE
½ cup (100g) firmly packed brown sugar
⅔ cup (160ml) whipping cream
100g butter, chopped

1 Preheat oven to moderate. Grease 25cm x 30cm swiss roll tin; line base and short sides of tin with baking parchment, bringing paper 5cm above edges of tin. Place a piece of baking parchment cut the same size as swiss roll tin on board or work top; sprinkle evenly with white sugar.
2 Combine dates, the water and soda in bowl of food processor. Place lid in position; stand 5 minutes. Add butter and brown sugar; process until almost smooth. Add eggs and flour; process until just combined. Pour mixture into prepared tin; bake in moderate oven about 15 minutes.
3 Turn cake onto sugared parchment, peel baking parchment away; working quickly, use serrated knife to cut away crisp edges from all sides.
4 Using hands and sugared parchment as a guide, gently roll cake loosely from a long side; hold for 30 seconds then unroll. Cover cake with tea towel; cool.
5 Beat cream in small bowl with electric mixer until firm peaks form. Fold ¼ cup of the butterscotch sauce into cream. Spread cake evenly with cream mixture. Roll cake, from same long side, by lifting parchment and using it to guide the roll into shape. Serve sticky date roll drizzled with remaining warmed butterscotch sauce.

BUTTERSCOTCH SAUCE
Combine ingredients in small saucepan; stir over heat until sugar dissolves and butter melts.
TIP Rolling and unrolling the cake, then cooling it flat, is not the traditional method for a swiss roll; however, our method helps minimise the likelihood of the cake splitting.

Roll filled cake using paper to guide into roll

Gently roll cake from long side

mars bar cheesecake

preparation time 30 minutes (plus refrigeration time)
cooking time 5 minutes
serves 8

250g plain chocolate biscuits
125g butter, melted
2 tablespoons brown sugar
20g butter, extra
300ml whipping cream
50g milk eating chocolate, chopped finely
3 teaspoons gelatine
¼ cup (60ml) water
2 x 250g packets cream cheese, softened
½ cup (110g) caster sugar
3 x 60g Mars bars, chopped finely

1 Blend or process biscuits until mixture resembles fine breadcrumbs. Add butter; process until just combined. Press biscuit mixture evenly over base and side of 20cm springform cake tin, place on tray; refrigerate about 30 minutes or until firm.

2 Meanwhile, make butterscotch sauce; combine brown sugar, extra butter and 2 tablespoons of the cream in small saucepan. Stir over low heat, without boiling, until sugar dissolves.

3 Make chocolate sauce; combine chocolate and another 2 tablespoons of the cream in another small saucepan; stir over low heat until chocolate melts.

4 Sprinkle gelatine over the water in small heatproof jug; stand jug in small saucepan of simmering water, stir until gelatine dissolves. Cool 5 minutes.

5 Beat cream cheese and caster sugar in medium bowl with electric mixer until smooth. Beat remaining cream in small bowl with electric mixer until soft peaks form. Stir gelatine mixture into cream cheese mixture with Mars bars; fold in cream.

6 Pour half of the cream cheese mixture into crumb crust; drizzle half of the butterscotch and chocolate sauces over top. Pull skewer backwards and forwards through mixture to create marbled effect. Repeat with remaining cream cheese mixture and sauces. Cover cheesecake; refrigerate about 3 hours or until set.

TIP This recipe can be made a day ahead; keep, covered, in refrigerator.

lemon cheesecake

preparation time 30 minutes (plus refrigeration time)
serves 8

250g packet plain sweet biscuits
125g butter, melted
250g packet cream cheese, softened
395g can sweetened condensed milk
2 teaspoons finely grated lemon rind
⅓ cup (80ml) lemon juice
1 teaspoon gelatine
1 tablespoon water

1 Blend or process biscuits until mixture resembles fine breadcrumbs. Add butter; process until combined. Press biscuit mixture evenly over base and side of 20cm springform cake tin, place on tray; refrigerate about 30 minutes or until firm.

2 Meanwhile, beat cream cheese in small bowl with electric mixer until smooth. Beat in condensed milk, rind and juice; beat until smooth.

3 Sprinkle gelatine over the water in small heatproof jug; stand jug in small saucepan of simmering water. Stir until gelatine dissolves; cool 5 minutes.

4 Stir gelatine mixture into lemon mixture. Pour mixture into crumb crust; cover cheesecake; refrigerate about 3 hours or until set.

TIP This recipe can be made a day ahead; keep, covered, in refrigerator.

crème brulée

preparation time 15 minutes (plus refrigeration time)
cooking time 40 minutes
serves 6

1 vanilla pod
3 cups (750ml) whipping cream
6 egg yolks
¼ cup (55g) caster sugar
⅓ cup (55g) icing sugar, approximately, sifted

1 Preheat oven to moderately low. Split vanilla pod in half lengthways. Using the point of a sharp knife, scrape seeds from pod; reserve seeds. Place pod and cream in medium saucepan; heat until just below boiling point.
2 Meanwhile, whisk egg yolks, caster sugar and vanilla seeds in medium heatproof bowl; gradually whisk in hot cream mixture. Place bowl over medium pan of simmering water – do not let water touch base of bowl. Stir over heat about 10 minutes or until mixture thickens slightly and coats the back of a spoon.
3 Remove pod. Place six ½-cup (125ml) ovenproof ramekins in baking dish; pour cream mixture into ramekins level with the top as they will shrink slightly. Add boiling water to baking dish to come ¾ of the way up side of ramekins. Bake in prepared oven about 20 minutes until custard is just set. Remove dishes from water; cool to room temperature. Cover; refrigerate 3 hours or overnight.
4 Place dishes in shallow baking dish filled with ice-cubes. Sprinkle each custard evenly with a heaped teaspoon of icing sugar; wipe edge of dishes. Place under hot grill until sugar is just melted, not coloured. Sprinkle custards with a second layer of icing sugar; place under hot grill until sugar is golden brown.
TIPS This recipe can be prepared a day ahead; grill the tops up to an hour before serving.

berry tiramisu

preparation time 15 minutes (plus refrigeration time)
serves 8

1¾ cups (430ml) whipping cream
¼ cup (40g) icing sugar
1 teaspoon finely grated orange rind
250g mascarpone
¼ cup (60ml) Cointreau
150g blueberries
240g raspberries
250g strawberries, quartered
1 cup (250ml) fresh orange juice
20 sponge finger biscuits (300g)

1 Beat cream, sugar and rind in small bowl, with electric mixer, until soft peaks form; fold in mascarpone and 2 teaspoons of the liqueur.
2 Combine berries and another 2 teaspoons of the liqueur in medium bowl.
3 Combine remaining liqueur and juice in medium bowl. Soak sponge fingers, one at a time, in juice mixture 30 seconds. Arrange half of the sponge fingers around base of 8-cup (2-litre) serving dish. Top with half of the cream mixture; sprinkle with half of the berry mixture.
4 Layer remaining sponge fingers over berries. Repeat cream and berry layers. Cover; refrigerate 6 hours or overnight.
TIP This recipe can be made a day ahead.

hazelnut crème caramel

preparation time 25 minutes (plus standing and refrigeration times)
cooking time 55 minutes
serves 6

125g hazelnuts
1 cup (250ml) milk
1½ cups (375ml) cream
¾ cup (165g) caster sugar
¾ cup (180ml) water
3 eggs
3 egg yolks
½ cup (110g) caster sugar, extra

1 Preheat oven to moderate. Place nuts in baking tin; bake in moderate oven about 8 minutes or until skins begin to split and nuts are toasted lightly. Place nuts in tea towel; rub vigorously to remove skins. Chop nuts coarsely. Reduce oven temperature to slow.
2 Bring milk, cream and nuts to a boil in medium saucepan; cover. Remove from heat; stand 20 minutes.
3 Meanwhile, combine sugar and the water in medium saucepan; stir over low heat, without boiling, until sugar dissolves. Brush down side of pan with pastry brush dipped in water to remove any sugar grains. Bring to a boil; boil, uncovered, without stirring, until mixture is caramel in colour. Remove from heat; divide between six ¾-cup (180ml) ovenproof moulds. The toffee will set immediately.
4 Combine eggs, egg yolks and extra sugar in medium bowl; whisk until just combined. Bring milk and cream back to a boil; gradually whisk into egg mixture until combined. Strain mixture into large jug; discard nuts.
5 Pour custard over toffee in moulds; place moulds into baking dish. Pour enough boiling water into baking dish to come ¾ of the way up side of moulds.
6 Bake, uncovered, in low oven 35 minutes. Custards are ready when only the centre has a slight wobble to it. Remove from baking dish; refrigerate at least 8 hours or overnight before serving. The refrigeration time allows the toffee to dissolve, which forms the sauce.
7 Gently pull custard away from side of moulds. Invert onto serving plates.
TIPS Cream mixture suitable to microwave.
This recipe is best made a day ahead.

white chocolate fondue

preparation time 10 minutes
cooking time 5 minutes
serves 4

180g white eating chocolate, chopped coarsely
½ cup (125ml) cream
1 tablespoon coconut-flavoured liqueur
1 cup (130g) strawberries
1 large banana (230g), chopped coarsely
150g fresh pineapple, chopped coarsely
8 slices (35g) almond bread
16 (100g) marshmallows

1 Combine chocolate and cream in small saucepan, stir over low heat until smooth; stir in liqueur. Transfer fondue to serving bowl.
2 Place fondue in centre of dining table; serve with remaining ingredients on a platter.
TIP Fondue can be served with any of your favourite fruits. Provide your guests with skewers so they are able to spear the fruit and marshmallows and dip them into the chocolate pot.

raspberry and chocolate mousse trifle

preparation time 30 minutes (plus refrigeration time)
serves 6

150g dark chocolate, chopped coarsely
½ cup (125ml) whipping cream
1 egg, separated
2 teaspoons caster sugar
85g packet raspberry jelly crystals
200g packaged chocolate sponge fingers
   (approximately 6)
¼ cup (60ml) coffee-flavoured liqueur
1 cup (135g) raspberries
300ml whipping cream, extra

1 Combine chocolate and cream in small saucepan; stir over heat, without boiling, until smooth. Remove from heat; whisk in egg yolk. Transfer to medium bowl.
2 Place egg white and sugar in small bowl; beat with electric mixer until sugar dissolves. Gently fold egg white mixture into chocolate mixture. Cover; refrigerate mousse 3 hours or overnight.
3 Meanwhile, make jelly according to manufacturer's instructions; refrigerate until jelly just begins to set.
4 Cut sponge fingers into 1.5cm slices. Place slices over base and around side of deep 2-litre (8-cup) large serving bowl; drizzle evenly with liqueur. Pour jelly over sponge fingers; refrigerate until jelly sets.
5 Sprinkle half of the raspberries over jelly; spread evenly with mousse. Top with whipped extra cream and remaining raspberries. Sprinkle with chocolate shavings, if desired.
TIPS Mousse can be prepared up to 2 days ahead; trifle can be assembled 1 day ahead.
If fresh raspberries are not available, frozen raspberries, thawed, can be substituted.
In step 3, jelly should set to the same consistency as an unbeaten egg white.

tiramisu torte

preparation time 30 minutes
cooking time 25 minutes
serves 12

6 eggs
1 cup (220g) caster sugar
½ cup (75g) plain flour
½ cup (75g) self-raising flour
½ cup (75g) cornflour
¼ cup (10g) instant coffee powder
1½ cups (375ml) boiling water
¾ cup (180ml) marsala
¼ cup (60ml) coffee-flavoured liqueur
300ml whipping cream
½ cup (80g) icing sugar
750g mascarpone cheese
500g caramelised almonds, chopped coarsely

1 Preheat oven to moderate.
2 Grease two deep 22cm-round cake tins; line bases with baking parchment.
3 Beat eggs in medium bowl with electric mixer about 10 minutes or until thick and creamy. Add caster sugar, about 1 tablespoon at a time, beating until sugar is dissolved between additions. Gently fold triple-sifted flours into egg mixture. Divide cake mixture evenly between prepared tins; bake in moderate oven about 25 minutes. Turn cakes, top-side up, onto wire racks to cool.
4 Meanwhile, dissolve coffee powder in the water in small heatproof bowl. Stir in marsala and liqueur; cool.
5 Beat cream and icing sugar in small bowl with electric mixer until soft peaks form; transfer to large bowl. Stir in mascarpone and ½ cup of the coffee mixture.
6 Split cooled cakes in half. Centre half of one cake on serving plate; brush with a quarter of the remaining coffee mixture then spread with about 1 cup of mascarpone cream. Repeat layering until last cake half is covered with mascarpone cream. Spread remaining mascarpone cream around side of cake; press almonds into side and top of cake. Refrigerate until ready to serve.
TIPS This cake is best made a day ahead and kept, refrigerated, in an airtight container.
Caramelised almonds are whole almonds that have been coated in a toffee mixture.

Spread mascarpone cream around cake

Press almonds into mascarpone cream

tropical fruit mini pavlovas

preparation time 20 minutes
cooking time 45 minutes (plus cooling time)
serves 8

6 egg whites
1½ cups (330g) caster sugar
300ml whipping cream
1 medium kiwi fruit (85g), peeled, halved,
 sliced thinly
1 small mango (300g), peeled, sliced thinly
2 passionfruit
shaved fresh coconut

1 Preheat oven to very low. Draw eight 8.5cm circles on a large sheet of baking parchment. Grease oven tray; place paper, pencil side down, on tray.
2 Beat egg whites in large bowl with electric mixer until soft peaks form. Gradually add sugar; continue beating about 10 minutes or until sugar dissolves.
3 Divide mixture evenly among circles; shape using a palette knife. Bake in very low oven about 45 minutes or until crisp and dry. Cool pavlovas in oven with door ajar.
4 Beat cream in small bowl with electric mixer until soft peaks form.
5 Just before serving, top pavlovas with cream, fruit and coconut.
TIPS To open a fresh coconut, pierce the 'eyes' with a strong metal skewer; drain liquid. Place coconut on ground and hit sharply with a hammer. Remove outer husk. Use vegetable peeler to shave flakes; flaked dry coconut can be substituted.
Pavlova shells can be made 3 days ahead and stored in an airtight container in a cool, dry place. Add cream and fruit just before serving.

warm lemon meringue pots

preparation time 20 minutes
cooking time 15 minutes
serves 4

2 tablespoons cornflour
½ cup (110g) caster sugar
¼ cup (60ml) lemon juice
½ cup (125ml) water
1 teaspoon finely grated lemon rind
2 eggs, separated
30g butter, chopped
2 tablespoons whipping cream
⅓ cup (75g) caster sugar, extra

1 Preheat oven to moderately hot.
2 Combine cornflour and sugar in small saucepan. Gradually add juice and the water; stir until smooth. Cook, stirring constantly, until mixture boils and thickens. Reduce heat; simmer, stirring, 1 minute. Remove from heat; stir in rind, egg yolks, butter and cream.
3 Divide mixture between four ½-cup (125ml) ovenproof dishes. Place dishes onto oven tray.
4 Beat egg whites in small bowl with electric mixer until soft peaks form. Gradually beat in extra caster sugar until dissolved.
5 Spoon meringue over filling. Bake in moderately hot oven about 5 minutes or until browned lightly. Serve with sponge finger biscuits, if desired.
TIP This recipe is best made just before serving.

coconut and vanilla parfait

margarita mousse

sticky pears

chocolate nut bavarois with raspberry sauce

coconut and vanilla parfait

preparation time 10 minutes
serves 4

⅓ cup (80ml) coconut cream
1.5 litres vanilla ice-cream, softened
2 tablespoons passionfruit pulp
⅓ cup (15g) flaked coconut, toasted

1 Combine coconut cream and ice-cream in large bowl. Divide mixture evenly between four parfait glasses. Top each parfait with passionfruit pulp and coconut.

margarita mousse

preparation time 20 minutes (plus refrigeration time)
cooking time 5 minutes
serves 6

¼ cup (55g) white sugar
1 tablespoon gelatine
2 tablespoons water
1 cup (220g) caster sugar
1¼ cups (300g) soured cream
300ml whipping cream
½ cup (120g) spreadable cream cheese
green food colouring
¼ cup (60ml) tequila
1 tablespoon Cointreau
1 teaspoon finely grated lime rind
¾ cup (180ml) lime juice
⅓ cup (80ml) orange juice

1 Place white sugar on saucer. Dip rims of six ¾-cup (180ml) glasses in bowl of cold water then into white sugar; refrigerate glasses.
2 Sprinkle gelatine over the water in small heatproof jug; stand jug in small saucepan of simmering water. Stir until gelatine dissolves; cool 5 minutes.
3 Beat caster sugar, soured cream, cream and cream cheese in medium bowl with electric mixer until sugar dissolves and mixture is fluffy. Beat in enough colouring to tint mixture a pale green.
4 Whisk tequila, liqueur, rind, juices and gelatine mixture into cream mixture. Divide mixture among prepared glasses; refrigerate about 2 hours or until mousse sets.
TIPS Mousse can be prepared a day ahead and refrigerated, covered, until ready to serve.
Gelatine mixture should be cool but not set, and should be approximately the same temperature as the cream mixture when they're combined; if not, the mousse can split into layers or become somewhat rubbery.

sticky pears

preparation time 10 minutes
cooking time 7 minutes
serves 4

40g butter
4 medium pears (920g), peeled, halved lengthways
⅓ cup (75g) firmly packed brown sugar
1 teaspoon ground cardamom
2 tablespoons green ginger wine
⅔ cup (160ml) double cream

1 Heat butter in large heavy-base frying pan; cook pear, sugar, cardamom and wine over high heat, stirring occasionally, about 5 minutes or until pears are browned. Serve hot pears with cream.

chocolate nut bavarois with raspberry sauce

preparation time 30 minutes (plus refrigeration time)
cooking time 5 minutes
serves 6

1 cup (250ml) milk
½ cup (165g) Nutella
4 egg yolks
¼ cup (55g) caster sugar
2 teaspoons gelatine
1 tablespoon water
300ml whipping cream

RASPBERRY SAUCE
200g raspberries
2 tablespoons icing sugar

1 Combine milk and Nutella in small saucepan. Stir over heat until Nutella melts; bring to a boil. Transfer to medium bowl.
2 Beat egg yolks and caster sugar in small bowl with electric mixer until thick and creamy; gradually stir into Nutella mixture.
3 Sprinkle gelatine over the water in small heatproof jug; stand in small saucepan of simmering water, stirring, until gelatine dissolves. Stir gelatine mixture into warm milk mixture; cool to room temperature.
4 Beat cream in small bowl with electric mixer until soft peaks form; fold into Nutella mixture. Divide bavarois mixture among six ¾-cup (180ml) serving glasses; refrigerate about 4 hours. Top with raspberry sauce.

RASPBERRY SAUCE
Push raspberries through sieve into small bowl; discard seeds. Stir in sugar.
TIPS If fresh raspberries are not available, you can use frozen raspberries, thawed, instead.

berry-mousse cake

preparation time 40 minutes (plus refrigeration time)
cooking time 20 minutes
serves 12

4 egg whites
¾ cup (165g) caster sugar
1½ cups (240g) ground almonds
¼ cup (35g) plain flour
300ml whipping cream
450g fresh raspberries
½ cup (160g) raspberry jam, warmed
¼ cup (60ml) Malibu

RASPBERRY MOUSSE
200g fresh raspberries
3 teaspoons gelatine
2 tablespoons water
125g white chocolate, melted
2 egg yolks
¼ cup (55g) caster sugar
1 tablespoon Malibu
300ml whipping cream

1 Preheat oven to moderate. Grease two 22cm springform tins; line bases with baking parchment.
2 Beat egg whites in medium bowl with electric mixer until soft peaks form. Gradually add sugar, beating between additions, until sugar dissolves; fold in dry ingredients.
3 Spread mixture equally between prepared tins; bake in moderate oven about 20 minutes. Stand cakes 5 minutes. Remove from tins; cool at room temperature.
4 Line base and side of clean 22cm springform tin with baking parchment; return one cake to tin. Pour mousse over cake; top with remaining cake. Cover; refrigerate 3 hours or overnight, until mousse sets.
5 Remove cake from tin. Beat cream in small bowl with electric mixer until soft peaks form; spread all over cake. Place raspberries on top of cake; brush raspberries with combined strained jam and liqueur.

RASPBERRY MOUSSE
Push raspberries through sieve into large bowl; discard seeds. Sprinkle gelatine over the water in small heatproof jug. Stand jug in small saucepan of simmering water; stir until gelatine dissolves. Combine gelatine mixture, chocolate, egg yolks, sugar and liqueur in small bowl; stir until smooth. Beat cream in small bowl with electric mixer until soft peaks form; fold cream and chocolate mixture into raspberry puree.
TIPS Prepare the raspberry mousse while cake is baking.
The cake, without the topping, can be made a day ahead.
Malibu is a liqueur made from rum and coconut. If you don't like the taste of coconut, substitute plain white rum for Malibu in this recipe.

Push raspberries through sieve into bowl

Combine mousse ingredients carefully

Place top cake layer over mousse in tin

mango baked alaska

preparation time 20 minutes (plus freezing time)
cooking time 3 minutes
serves 6

2 litres mango ice-cream, softened
¼ cup (60ml) orange juice
2 tablespoons orange-flavoured liqueur
16cm-round unfilled packaged sponge cake
1 large mango (600g), sliced thinly
4 egg whites
1 cup (220g) caster sugar

1 Line 15cm 1.375-litre pudding basin or bowl with cling film, extending film 5cm over edge of basin.
2 Pack ice-cream into prepared basin, cover with foil; freeze about 2 hours or until firm.
3 Preheat oven to very hot (240°C/220°C fan-assisted).
4 Combine juice and liqueur in small jug. Trim top of cake to flatten; split cake in half horizontally through centre. Place bottom layer of cake on oven tray; brush with half the juice mixture. Top with mango then remaining cake half; brush with remaining juice mixture.
5 Invert ice-cream from basin onto cake; working quickly, trim cake to exact size of ice-cream. Return to freezer.
6 Beat egg whites in small bowl with electric mixer until soft peaks form; gradually add sugar, beating until sugar dissolves between additions.
7 Remove bombe from freezer; spread meringue over to enclose bombe completely. Bake, uncovered, in very hot oven about 3 minutes or until browned lightly. Lift onto serving plate; serve immediately.
TIPS You can use Cointreau, Grand Marnier, Curaçao or any other orange-flavoured liqueur in this recipe.

almond and raspberry frozen puddings

preparation time 25 minutes (plus freezing time)
serves 8

3 eggs
⅓ cup (75g) caster sugar
600ml whipping cream
1 teaspoon vanilla extract
1 tablespoon cherry-flavoured liqueur
⅓ cup (45g) caramelised almonds, chopped
   coarsely
⅔ cup (70g) frozen raspberries
200g white eating chocolate, melted
fresh raspberries, for serving, optional

1 Beat eggs and sugar in small bowl with electric mixer about 5 minutes or until the mixture is very pale and fluffy. Transfer to large bowl.
2 Beat cream, extract and liqueur in clean small bowl with electric mixer until soft peaks form. Gently fold cream mixture into egg mixture along with nuts and frozen raspberries.
3 Divide mixture among eight ¾-cup (180ml) moulds. Cover; freeze overnight or until firm.
4 Wipe moulds with hot damp cloth; turn out onto plates. Spoon melted chocolate over top; serve with fresh raspberries, if desired.
TIPS This recipe can be made a week ahead.
We used kirsch in this recipe, but any cherry-flavoured liqueur may be used.

chocolate nougat frozen parfait

preparation time 20 minutes (plus freezing time)
serves 6

2 cups (400g) ricotta cheese
½ cup (110g) caster sugar
300ml whipping cream
200g dark chocolate, melted
150g almond nougat, chopped finely

1 Line base and two long sides of 14cm x 21cm loaf tin with foil or baking parchment, extending over edge of sides.
2 Blend or process ricotta and sugar until smooth; transfer to medium bowl. Beat cream in small bowl with electric mixer until soft peaks form. Fold cream into ricotta mixture; fold in chocolate and nougat.
3 Spoon mixture into prepared tin. Cover with foil; freeze overnight or until firm.
4 Turn out of tin; cut into slices. Stand 10 minutes before serving, to allow it to soften slightly.
5 Serve sliced with raspberries, if desired.
TIPS Chocolate suitable to microwave.
This recipe is best made a day ahead.

peanut butter and fudge ice-cream pie

preparation time 20 minutes (plus refrigeration time)
cooking time 10 minutes
serves 10

300g packet chocolate chip cookies
40g butter, melted
1 tablespoon milk
1 litre vanilla ice-cream
1⅓ cups (375g) crunchy peanut butter

HOT FUDGE SAUCE
200g dark chocolate, chopped coarsely
50g white marshmallows, chopped coarsely
300ml whipping cream

1 Grease 24cm-round loose-based flan tin.
2 Blend or process cookies until mixture resembles coarse breadcrumbs. Add butter and milk; process until combined.
3 Using one hand, press cookie mixture evenly over base and around side of prepared tin; refrigerate 10 minutes.
4 Beat softened ice-cream and peanut butter in large bowl with electric mixer until combined. Spoon pie filling into crumb crust. Cover; freeze pie 3 hours or overnight.
5 Drizzle slices of pie with hot fudge sauce to serve.

HOT FUDGE SAUCE
Combine ingredients in small saucepan; stir over heat, without boiling, until smooth.
TIPS Use a good quality ice-cream; various ice-creams differ from manufacturer to manufacturer, depending on the quantities of air and fat incorporated into the mixture.
Warm a large knife under hot water, quickly dry it and cut the pie while the knife is still hot.
Marshmallows come in a variety of sizes and colours; the largest white type is best for this recipe

vanilla ice-cream with choc-almond crunch

preparation time 20 minutes (plus refrigeration time)
cooking time 20 minutes
serves 6

2 egg yolks
⅓ cup (75g) caster sugar
1 cup (250ml) milk
300ml whipping cream
1 vanilla pod

CHOC-ALMOND CRUNCH
2 cups (440g) caster sugar
1 cup (250ml) water
200g dark chocolate, chopped coarsely
½ cup (40g) flaked almonds, toasted

1 Whisk egg yolks and sugar in medium bowl until light and fluffy.
2 Combine milk and cream in medium saucepan. Split vanilla pod in half lengthways; scrape seeds from pod. Add pod and seeds to pan; bring milk mixture almost to a boil.
3 Remove milk mixture from heat; discard vanilla pod. Whisking constantly, gradually pour milk mixture into egg mixture. Return custard mixture to same saucepan; cook over low heat, stirring constantly, until mixture begins to thicken and coats the back of a spoon (do not boil or mixture will curdle).
4 Return custard to same medium bowl. Cover surface completely with cling film; freeze about 4 hours or until ice-cream is firm.
5 Line 8cm x 25cm shallow cake tin with cling film. Blend or process ice-cream until smooth; spread into prepared tin. Cover with foil; freeze until firm. Turn ice-cream out of pan; cut into 12 slices. Serve with shards of choc-almond crunch.

CHOC-ALMOND CRUNCH
Combine sugar and the water in medium heavy-base saucepan; stir over low heat until sugar dissolves. Increase heat; bring to a boil. Boil, uncovered, without stirring, about 10 minutes or until syrup is a deep golden colour. Pour toffee mixture into 20cm x 30cm baking tin; stand 5 minutes. Sprinkle chocolate over hot toffee, spreading with a palette knife to completely cover toffee. Sprinkle with almonds; refrigerate until set. Break choc-almond crunch into shards.
TIP Milk chocolate can be used instead of dark chocolate, if preferred.

lemon baked alaska bombes

preparation time 40 minutes (plus refrigeration time)cooking time 20 minutes
serves 4

2¾ cups (680ml) vanilla ice-cream, slightly softened
30g unsalted butter
½ teaspoon finely grated lemon rind
1 tablespoon lemon juice
1 egg yolk
¼ cup (55g) caster sugar
⅓ cup (80ml) limoncello
½ cup (125ml) whipping cream
290g packet sponge cake
2 egg whites
⅓ cup (75g) caster sugar, extra

1 Line four ½-cup (125ml) moulds with cling film. Press ⅓ cup ice-cream firmly up and around inside of each mould to form cavity. Cover with foil; freeze 2 hours. Return remaining ice-cream to freezer.
2 Combine butter, rind, juice, egg yolk and sugar in small heatproof bowl; stir over small saucepan of simmering water until mixture thickens slightly. Stir in liqueur. Cover surface of lemon curd with cling film; refrigerate until cold.
3 Place 1 tablespoon of the lemon curd into each mould, cover; freeze until firm. Combine remaining lemon curd with cream, cover; refrigerate lemon cream until serving.
4 Remove moulds from the freezer, spread enough remaining ice-cream over lemon curd to fill moulds; cover, freeze bombes until firm.
5 Preheat oven to very hot.
6 Cut four rounds from sponge cake, large enough to cover top of each mould.
7 Beat egg whites in small bowl with electric mixer until soft peaks form; add extra sugar, 1 tablespoon at a time, beating until sugar dissolves between additions.
8 Turn one bombe onto one round of sponge cake on oven tray; peel away cling film. Spread a quarter of the meringue mixture over to enclose bombe completely; repeat with remaining bombes, sponge and meringue mixture. Bake bombes, uncovered, in very hot oven about 3 minutes or until browned lightly. Serve immediately with lemon cream.
serves 4
TIP Bombes can be prepared the day before serving to the stage at which they are ready to be baked; store in the freezer.

Press ice-cream around inside of moulds

Spoon then spread ice-cream over lemon curd

Spread meringue all over each bombe

watermelon and strawberry ice-block

lemonade, lemon and mint ice-block

spiced coffee ice-block

honey, banana and yogurt ice-block

watermelon and strawberry ice-block

preparation time 10 minutes (plus freezing time)
cooking time 5 minutes (plus cooling time)
serves 4

⅓ cup (80ml) water
2 tablespoons sugar
250g piece watermelon, peeled, deseeded,
    chopped coarsely
80g strawberries, chopped coarsely
2 teaspoons lemon juice

1 Combine the water and sugar in small saucepan; stir over low heat until sugar dissolves. Bring to a boil; boil, uncovered about 2 minutes or until mixture thickens slightly. Transfer syrup to small bowl; refrigerate until cold.
2 Blend or process cold syrup, watermelon, strawberries and juice until smooth. Pour mixture into four ⅓-cup (80ml) ice-block moulds. Freeze overnight until firm.

lemonade, lemon and mint ice-block

preparation time 5 minutes (plus freezing time)
serves 4

1½ cups (375ml) lemonade
1 teaspoon finely grated lemon rind
1 tablespoon lemon juice
2 teaspoons finely chopped fresh mint

1 Combine ingredients in medium freezerproof jug; freeze mixture about 1 hour or until partially frozen. Stir; pour mixture into four ⅓-cup (80ml) ice-block moulds. Freeze overnight until firm.

spiced coffee ice-block

*preparation time 5 minutes (plus cooling and
  freezing times)*
serves 4

2 teaspoons instant coffee
2 teaspoons drinking chocolate
2 teaspoons caster sugar
¼ teaspoon ground cinnamon
1 tablespoon boiling water
⅔ cup (160ml) cream, whipped lightly

1 Combine coffee, drinking chocolate, sugar and
cinnamon in medium jug. Add the water, stirring until
sugar dissolves, cool 5 minutes; gently stir in cream.
Pour mixture into four ⅓-cup (80ml) ice-block moulds.
Freeze overnight until firm.

honey, banana and yogurt ice-block

preparation time 5 minutes (plus freezing time)
serves 4

1 large banana (230g)
⅔ cup (190g) vanilla yogurt
1 tablespoon honey

1 Blend or process ingredients until mixture is smooth
and creamy. Pour into four ⅓-cup (80ml) ice-block
moulds. Freeze overnight until firm.

Enjoy scrumptious cakes like these little lime muffins with a freshly brewed cup of coffee or a pot of afternoon tea, in fact whenever the mood takes you. Or indulge your chocolate cravings with any of the delicious cakes, cookies, truffles, brownies and slices featured here.

cakes, bakes
and sweet treats

amaretti

choc-hazelnut cookie sandwiches

caramel chocolate cookies

almond shortbread drops

amaretti

preparation time 15 minutes (plus standing time)
cooking time 15 minutes
makes 20

1 cup (125g) ground almonds
1 cup (220g) caster sugar
2 egg whites
¼ teaspoon almond essence
20 blanched almonds (20g)

1 Lightly grease two baking trays.
2 Beat ground almonds, sugar, egg whites and essence in small bowl with electric mixer for 3 minutes; stand 5 minutes.
3 Spoon mixture into piping bag fitted with 1cm plain tube. Pipe directly onto prepared trays in circular motion from centre out, to make biscuits about 4cm in diameter.
4 Top each biscuit with a nut. Cover trays of unbaked biscuits loosely with foil; stand at room temperature overnight.
5 Preheat oven to moderate; bake biscuits in moderate oven about 12 minutes or until browned lightly. Stand amaretti 5 minutes; transfer to wire rack to cool.
TIP Amaretti can be baked the day they're made, however, they will spread a little more. For best results, stand the amaretti overnight.

choc-hazelnut cookie sandwiches

preparation time 25 minutes (plus refrigeration time)
cooking time 10 minutes
makes 30

80g butter, chopped
1 teaspoon vanilla essence
¼ cup (55g) caster sugar
1 egg
½ cup (50g) ground hazelnuts
¾ cup (110g) plain flour
¼ cup (25g) cocoa powder
1 tablespoon cocoa powder, extra

CHOC-HAZELNUT CREAM
100g dark chocolate, melted
50g butter
⅓ cup (110g) Nutella

1 Preheat oven to moderate. Lightly grease two baking trays.
2 Beat butter, essence, sugar and egg in small bowl with electric mixer until light and fluffy; stir in ground hazelnuts with sifted flour and cocoa. Enclose dough in cling film; refrigerate about 1 hour or until firm.
3 Meanwhile, make choc-hazel cream.
4 Roll dough between two sheets of baking parchment until 3mm thick. Using 4cm-fluted cutter, cut rounds from dough. Place rounds on prepared trays; bake in moderate oven about 8 minutes. Stand biscuits 5 minutes; transfer onto wire rack to cool.
5 Spoon choc-hazelnut cream into piping bag fitted with large fluted tube. Pipe cream onto one biscuit; sandwich with another biscuit. Place on wire rack set over tray; repeat with remaining biscuits and cream. When all sandwiches are on rack, dust with extra sifted cocoa.

CHOC-HAZELNUT CREAM
Beat cooled chocolate, butter and Nutella in small bowl with electric mixer until thick and glossy.

caramel chocolate cookies

preparation time 15 minutes
cooking time 20 minutes
makes 24

1 egg
⅔ cup (150g) firmly packed brown sugar
¼ cup (60ml) vegetable oil
½ cup (75g) plain flour
⅓ cup (50g) self-raising flour
¼ teaspoon bicarbonate of soda
100g dark chocolate, melted
250g Cadburys Caramel chocolate squares

1 Preheat oven to moderate. Lightly grease two baking trays.
2 Beat egg, sugar and oil in small bowl with electric mixer until mixture changes in colour. Stir in sifted dry ingredients and dark chocolate; stir until mixture becomes firm.
3 Centre one Caramel square on 1 heaped teaspoon chocolate mixture; roll into ball, enclosing Caramel. Place balls on prepared trays, allowing 6cm between each cookie; bake in moderate oven about 10 minutes. Stand cookies 5 minutes; transfer to wire rack to cool.
TIPS One heaped teaspoon is equivalent to 3 level teaspoons.
Chocolate squares with strawberry or peppermint centres can be used instead of Caramel squares. Biscuit dough is suitable to freeze.

almond shortbread drops

preparation time 15 minutes
cooking time 20 minutes (plus cooling time)
makes 12

60g butter, chopped
½ cup (75g) plain flour
1 tablespoon rice flour
2 tablespoons icing sugar
12 blanched almonds

1 Preheat oven to moderately low (160°C/140°C fan-assisted).
2 Process butter, flours and icing sugar until mixture forms a ball. Knead gently on floured surface until smooth.
3 Roll 2 teaspoons of mixture into balls; place on greased baking tray about 3cm apart. Top each ball with an almond.
4 Bake in moderately low oven about 20 minutes or until browned lightly. Cool on tray.
TIP This recipe can be made a week ahead.

refrigerator cookies

preparation time 20 minutes (plus refrigeration time)
cooking time 10 minutes
makes 50

250g butter, softened
1 cup (160g) icing sugar
2½ cups (375g) plain flour

1 Beat butter and sifted icing sugar in small bowl with electric mixer until light and fluffy. Transfer to large bowl.
2 Stir flour, in two batches, into butter mixture. Knead dough on lightly floured surface until smooth. Divide dough in half; roll each half into a 25cm log. Enclose in cling film; refrigerate about 1 hour or until firm.
3 Meanwhile, preheat oven to moderate (180ºC/160ºC fan-assisted).
4 Cut rolls into 1cm slices; place on greased oven trays 2cm apart. Bake, uncovered, in moderate oven about 10 minutes or until browned lightly. Turn cookies onto wire racks to cool.
TIPS The thinner the slice, the crisper the cookie. Keep this dough, rolled into a log shape and tightly sealed in cling film, in your fridge for up to three days or in your freezer for up to three months. The frozen dough should be defrosted in the refrigerator before slicing and baking.

variations

VANILLA
Beat 1 teaspoon vanilla extract into butter and sugar mixture.

CHOCOLATE AND HAZELNUT
Beat 2 tablespoons sifted cocoa powder into butter and sugar mixture, then stir in ⅓ cup (35g) ground hazelnuts and ¼ cup (45g) finely chopped milk chocolate chips before adding the flour. Bring back to room temperature before slicing.

LEMON
Beat 1 teaspoon finely grated lemon rind into butter and sugar mixture.

ORANGE
Beat 1 teaspoon finely grated orange rind into butter and sugar mixture.

pistachio shortbread mounds

preparation time 25 minutes
cooking time 25 minutes
makes 40

½ cup (75g) roasted shelled pistachios
250g butter, chopped
1 cup (160g) icing sugar
1½ cups (225g) plain flour
2 tablespoons rice flour
2 tablespoons cornflour
¾ cup (90g) ground almonds
⅓ cup (55g) icing sugar, extra

1 Preheat oven to low. Lightly grease two baking trays.
2 Toast nuts in small heavy-based frying pan until lightly browned; remove from pan. Coarsely chop ⅓ cup (50g) of the nuts; leave remaining nuts whole.
3 Beat butter and sugar in small bowl with electric mixer until light and fluffy; transfer mixture to large bowl. Stir in sifted flours, ground almonds and chopped nuts.
4 Shape level tablespoons of mixture into mounds; place mounds on prepared trays, allowing 3cm between each mound. Press one reserved nut on each mound; bake in low oven about 25 minutes or until firm. Stand mounds 5 minutes; transfer to wire rack to cool. Serve mounds dusted with extra sifted icing sugar.
TIP Rice flour, also known as ground rice, is a very fine powder made from pulverised long-grain or glutinous rice. It's used to make noodles and breads, and helps thicken cakes and puddings.

passionfruit butter bites

preparation time 20 minutes
cooking time 15 minutes
makes 37

250g unsalted butter, chopped
1 teaspoon vanilla essence
½ cup (80g) icing sugar
1½ cups (225g) plain flour
½ cup (75g) cornflour

PASSIONFRUIT BUTTER
80g unsalted butter
⅔ cup (150g) icing sugar
1 tablespoon passionfruit pulp

1 Preheat oven to moderately low. Line two baking trays with baking parchment.
2 Beat butter, essence and sugar in medium bowl with electric mixer until light and fluffy; stir in sifted dry ingredients, in two batches.
3 Roll rounded teaspoons of mixture into balls; place on prepared trays, allowing 3cm between each biscuit. Using fork dusted with a little flour, press tines gently onto each biscuit to flatten slightly; bake in moderately low oven about 12 minutes or until biscuits are firm. Stand biscuits 5 minutes; transfer to wire rack to cool. Serve biscuits sandwiched with passionfruit butter.

PASSIONFRUIT BUTTER
Beat butter and sugar in small bowl with electric mixer until light and fluffy; stir in passionfruit pulp.
TIP One rounded teaspoon is equivalent to 2 level teaspoons.

oatflake cookies

preparation time 30 minutes
cooking time 25 minutes per tray (plus cooling time)
makes 25 biscuits

1 cup (90g) rolled oats
1 cup (150g) plain flour
1 cup (220g) caster sugar
¾ cup (60g) desiccated coconut
125g butter, chopped
1 tablespoon golden syrup
1½ teaspoons bicarbonate of soda
2 tablespoons boiling water

1 Preheat oven to low (150°C/130°C fan-assisted). Lightly grease baking trays.
2 Combine oats, flour, sugar and coconut in large bowl.
3 Combine butter and syrup in small saucepan; stir over low heat until smooth.
4 Combine soda and the boiling water in small bowl, add to butter mixture; stir into dry ingredients while still warm.
5 Place level tablespoons of mixture onto trays about 5cm apart; press lightly. Bake about 25 minutes. Loosen cookies on trays while warm; cool on trays.
TIP Cookies can be made up to two weeks ahead; store in an airtight container.

almond crisps

preparation time 25 minutes
cooking time 10 minutes per tray (plus cooling time)
makes 15

125g butter, chopped
¼ cup (55g) caster sugar
1 cup (150g) self-raising flour
¼ cup (30g) ground almonds
2 tablespoons flaked almonds

1 Preheat oven to moderately hot (200°C/180°C fan-assisted). Lightly grease baking trays.
2 Beat butter and sugar in small bowl with electric mixer until smooth. Stir in flour and ground almonds.
3 Roll level tablespoons of mixture into balls; place onto trays about 5cm apart. Flatten slightly with a floured fork to 1cm thick; sprinkle with flaked almonds.
4 Bake about 10 minutes or until browned. Stand crisps on trays 5 minutes; transfer to wire racks to cool.
TIP Crisps can be made up to two weeks ahead; store in an airtight container.

fudgy-wudgy chocolate cookies

preparation time 15 minutes
cooking time 10 minutes (plus cooling time)
makes 24

125g butter, chopped
1 teaspoon vanilla extract
1¼ cups (275g) firmly packed brown sugar
1 egg
1 cup (150g) plain flour
¼ cup (35g) self-raising flour
1 teaspoon bicarbonate of soda
⅓ cup (35g) cocoa powder
½ cup (75g) raisins
¾ cup (110g) macadamia nuts, toasted, chopped
  coarsely
½ cup (95g) dark chocolate chips
½ cup (75g) chocolate buttons

1 Preheat oven to moderate (180°C/160°C fan-assisted). Line three oven trays with baking parchment.
2 Beat butter, extract, sugar and egg in medium bowl with electric mixer until smooth. Stir in sifted flours, soda and cocoa powder; stir in raisins, nuts and chocolate chips and buttons.
3 Drop rounded tablespoons of mixture onto trays about 4cm apart; press each cookie with hand to flatten slightly.
4 Bake 10 minutes. Stand cookies on trays 5 minutes; transfer to wire rack to cool.
TIPS Cookies can be made up to one week ahead; store in an airtight container.
Other nuts, such as walnuts or pecans, can be used instead of macadamias.

mini chocolate éclairs

preparation time 10 minutes
cooking time 30 minutes
makes 16

CHOUX PASTRY
20g butter
¼ cup (60ml) water
¼ cup (35g) plain flour
1 egg

PASTRY CREAM
1 cup (250ml) milk
½ vanilla pod, split
3 egg yolks
⅓ cup (75g) caster sugar
2 tablespoons cornflour

60g dark chocolate, melted

1 Preheat oven to hot. Lightly grease two oven trays.
2 Make choux pastry and pastry cream.
3 Spoon choux pastry into piping bag fitted with 1cm plain nozzle. Pipe 5cm lengths of choux pastry 3cm apart onto prepared trays; bake in hot oven 7 minutes. Reduce heat to moderate; bake further 10 minutes until éclairs are browned lightly and crisp. Carefully cut eclairs in half, remove any soft centre; bake further 5 minutes or until éclairs are dried out. Cool to room temperature.
4 Spoon cooled pastry cream into piping bag fitted with 1cm plain tube; pipe cream onto 16 éclair halves; top with remaining halves. Place éclairs on foil-covered tray; spread with melted chocolate.

CHOUX PASTRY
Combine butter with the water in small pan; bring to a boil. Add flour; beat with wooden spoon over heat until mixture comes away from side of saucepan and forms a smooth ball. Transfer mixture to small bowl; beat in egg with electric mixer until mixture becomes glossy.

PASTRY CREAM
Bring milk and vanilla pod to a boil in small pan. Discard vanilla pod. Beat egg yolks, sugar and cornflour in small bowl with electric mixer until thick. With motor operating, gradually beat in hot milk. Return mixture to pan; stir over heat until mixture boils and thickens. Cool.

sugared pastry twists

preparation time 5 minutes
cooking time 15 minutes
makes 96

1 sheet ready-rolled puff pastry, thawed
1 egg white
3 teaspoons caster sugar
½ teaspoon ground cinnamon

1 Preheat oven to moderate.
2 Brush pastry with egg white; sprinkle evenly with combined sugar and cinnamon.
3 Using a fluted pastry wheel, cut pastry sheet in half. Cut each half crossways into 5mm strips.
4 Twist each pastry strip; place on lightly greased oven tray. Bake in moderate oven about 15 minutes or until pastry browns lightly.

mint slice bites

preparation time 20 minutes
cooking time 30 minutes
makes 36

125g butter, chopped
200g dark chocolate, chopped coarsely
½ cup (110g) caster sugar
2 eggs, beaten lightly
1¼ cups (185g) plain flour
1½ cups (240g) icing sugar
1 teaspoon butter, extra
¼ teaspoon peppermint essence
2 tablespoons milk, approximately
50g dark chocolate, melted, extra

1 Preheat oven to moderate. Grease deep 19cm-square cake tin; line base with baking parchment.
2 Combine butter and chocolate in medium saucepan; stir over low heat until chocolate melts. Stir in caster sugar and egg then flour. Spread mixture into prepared tin; bake in moderate oven about 20 minutes. Stand cake in tin 15 minutes; turn onto wire rack to cool.
3 Meanwhile, combine icing sugar, extra butter and essence in small heatproof bowl; gradually stir in enough milk to make mixture form a thick paste. Stir mixture over small saucepan of simmering water until icing is of spreadable consistency. Spread icing over cake; allow to set at room temperature.
4 Using serrated knife, trim crisp edges from cake. Cut cake into 3cm squares; drizzle each square with melted extra chocolate.

walnut brownie mini muffins

preparation time 15 minutes (plus standing time)
cooking time 20 minutes (plus cooling time)
makes 24

½ cup (50g) walnuts, toasted, chopped finely
80g butter
150g dark eating chocolate, chopped coarsely
¾ cup (150g) firmly packed brown sugar
1 egg, beaten lightly
⅓ cup (50g) plain flour
¼ cup (60g) soured cream
3 x 50g packet Rolos

1 Preheat oven to moderate. Lightly grease two non-stick 12-hole 1½-tablespoon (30ml) mini muffin trays; divide walnuts among holes.
2 Stir butter and chocolate in small saucepan over low heat until smooth. Stir in sugar; cool to just warm.
3 Stir in egg, then flour and soured cream; spoon mixture into prepared tray. Press one Rolo into centre of each muffin; spread mixture so that Rolo is completely enclosed. Bake in moderate oven 15 minutes. Using a sharp-pointed knife, loosen sides of brownies from pan; stand 10 minutes. Remove muffins gently from pan.
TIP These treats are best served while still warm.

pecan and chocolate brownies

preparation time 15 minutes
cooking time 25 minutes
makes 8

80g butter, chopped
150g dark eating chocolate, chopped
¾ cup (165g) firmly packed brown sugar
2 eggs, beaten lightly
1 teaspoon vanilla extract
⅔ cup (100g) plain flour
1 tablespoon cocoa powder
50g dark eating chocolate, chopped, extra
¼ cup (30g) chopped pecans

1 Preheat oven to moderately hot (200°C/180°C fan-assisted). Grease eight holes of a 12-hole (⅓-cup/80ml) muffin tray; line bases with rounds of baking parchment.
2 Combine butter, chocolate and sugar in medium heavy-based saucepan; stir over low heat until smooth.
3 Transfer mixture to large bowl; stir in egg, extract, sifted flour and cocoa, then extra chocolate. Divide mixture among holes of prepared tray. Sprinkle with nuts; bake in moderately hot oven about 20 minutes. Stand muffins in tray for a few minutes before turning onto wire rack to cool.
TIP Brownies can be made three days ahead; store in an airtight container.

mini lime muffins

preparation time 20 minutes
cooking time 15 minutes (plus cooling time)
makes 30

6 egg whites
185g butter, melted
1 cup (125g) ground almonds
1½ cups (240g) icing sugar
½ cup (75g) plain flour
1 tablespoon finely grated lime rind
1 tablespoon lime juice
30 whole blanched almonds (60g)

1 Preheat oven to moderately hot. Grease 30 x 1½-tablespoon (30ml) mini muffin tin holes.
2 Place egg whites in medium bowl; whisk lightly until combined. Add butter, ground almonds, sifted icing sugar and flour, then rind and juice. Whisk until just combined. Divide mixture among prepared tins; top mixture in each hole with an almond.
3 Bake in moderately hot oven about 15 minutes. Turn onto wire racks to cool, right way up. Serve warm or at room temperature.
TIPS This recipe can be made 2 days ahead.
Recipe suitable to freeze; butter suitable to microwave.

pistachio and hazelnut cakes with toffee shards

preparation time 20 minutes
cooking time 30 minutes
serves 8

6 egg whites
185g butter, melted
¾ cup (75g) ground hazelnuts
¼ cup (35g) roasted shelled pistachios,
   chopped coarsely
1½ cups (240g) icing sugar
½ cup (75g) plain flour
2 teaspoons rosewater
⅓ cup (50g) roasted shelled pistachios, extra

TOFFEE SHARDS
⅔ cup (160ml) water
1⅓ cups (300g) caster sugar

1 Preheat oven to moderately hot. Grease eight ½-cup (125ml) oval or rectangular cake tins; stand on oven tray.
2 Place egg whites in medium bowl; whisk lightly with fork until combined. Add butter, ground hazelnuts, nuts, sugar, flour and rosewater; using wooden spoon, stir until just combined.
3 Pour mixture equally among prepared tins; top with extra nuts. Bakein moderately hot oven about 30 minutes. Stand cakes 5 minutes; turn, top-side up, onto wire rack. Serve cakes warm or at room temperature with toffee shards and thick cream, if desired.

TOFFEE SHARDS
Using wooden spoon, stir ingredients in small saucepan over heat, without boiling, until sugar dissolves; bring to a boil. Reduce heat; simmer, uncovered, without stirring, about 10 minutes or until toffee is golden brown. Remove from heat; allow bubbles to subside. Pour hot toffee onto lightly oiled oven tray;do not scrape the toffee from pan, or it might crystallise. Allow toffee to set at room temperature; break into shards with hands.

maple pecan cake

preparation time 15 minutes
cooking time 1 hour
serves 10

cooking-oil spray
1 cup (100g) pecans
⅓ cup (80ml) maple syrup
1¼ cups (310ml) boiling water
1¼ cups (235g) coarsely chopped dried figs
1 teaspoon bicarbonate of soda
60g butter
¾ cup (150g) firmly packed brown sugar
2 eggs
1 cup (150g) self-raising flour
MAPLE BUTTERSCOTCH SAUCE
1 cup (250ml) maple syrup
½ cup (125ml) cream
100g butter, chopped

1 Preheat oven to moderate. Grease deep 20cm-round cake tin; line base with baking parchment. Spray parchment with oil.
2 Arrange nuts over base of prepared pan; drizzle with maple syrup.
3 Combine the water, figs and soda in bowl of food processor. Cover with lid; stand 5 minutes. Add butter and sugar; process until almost smooth. Add eggs and flour; process until just combined. Pour mixture into prepared tin; bake in moderate oven about 55 minutes. Stand cake 5 minutes; turn onto wire rack. Serve with maple butterscotch sauce and, if desired, vanilla ice-cream.

MAPLE BUTTERSCOTCH SAUCE
Stir ingredients in small saucepan over heat until smooth; bring to a boil. Boil, uncovered, about 2 minutes or until mixture thickens slightly.
TIPS Either maple syrup or maple-flavoured syrup can be used in this recipe.

warm apple cake with brandy butterscotch sauce

preparation time 30 minutes
cooking time 40 minutes
serves 8

125g butter, chopped
½ cup (110g) caster sugar
2 eggs
⅔ cup (100g) self-raising flour
⅓ cup (50g) plain flour
1 tablespoon milk
3 medium granny smith apples (450g)
½ cup (160g) apricot jam, warmed
BRANDY BUTTERSCOTCH SAUCE
½ cup (100g) firmly packed brown sugar
½ cup (125ml) whipping cream
100g butter, chopped
2 tablespoons brandy

1 Preheat oven to moderately low. Grease and line base and sides of two 8cm x 25cm shallow cake tins.
2 Beat butter and sugar in small bowl with electric mixer until light and fluffy. Beat in eggs, one at a time, beating until combined between each addition. Stir in sifted flours and milk; spread mixture into prepared tins.
3 Peel, core and halve apples; slice halves thinly. Push apple slices gently into surface of cake mixture.
4 Brush apple with strained jam; bake cakes in moderately low oven about 40 minutes. Stand cakes 10 minutes; turn, top-side up, onto wire rack to cool. Serve pieces of cake warm, drizzled with brandy butterscotch sauce.

BRANDY BUTTERSCOTCH SAUCE
Combine ingredients in small saucepan. Stir over heat, without boiling, until sugar dissolves; bring to a boil. Reduce heat; simmer, uncovered, without stirring, about 3 minutes or until mixture thickens slightly.
TIP Peel, core and cut apples just before using to prevent the flesh browning.

bread and butter pudding cake

preparation time 40 minutes (plus standing time)
cooking time 1 hour 20 minutes (plus cooling time)
serves 12

⅓ cup (55g) sultanas
⅓ cup (55g) raisins
⅓ cup (50g) coarsely chopped dried apricots
¼ cup (35g) currants
⅓ cup (65g) chopped dried figs
2 tablespoons mixed peel
¼ cup (60ml) brandy
2 tablespoons orange juice
2 small brioche (200g)
80g butter, melted
¼ cup (80g) apricot jam, warmed
1 tablespoon icing sugar

SPONGE
4 eggs
½ cup (110g) caster sugar
¾ cup (110g) self-raising flour
50g butter, melted

CUSTARD
300ml whipping cream
1 cup (250ml) milk
2 eggs
4 egg yolks
½ cup (110g) caster sugar

1 Combine dried fruits, peel, brandy and juice in medium bowl, cover; stand overnight.
2 Preheat oven to moderately hot (200°C/180°C fan-assisted). Grease and flour deep 22cm-round cake tin.
3 Make sponge. Make custard.
4 Decrease oven to moderately low (160°C/140°C fan-assisted).
5 Grease same cleaned cake tin; line base and side with baking parchment, extending parchment 5cm above edge of tin. Cut each brioche vertically into six slices; brush slices on both sides with a quarter of the combined butter and jam.
6 Using serrated knife, split cake into three layers; place bottom layer in prepared tin, brush with another quarter of the jam mixture. Using 6cm cutter, cut eight rounds from middle layer; brush rounds on both sides with another quarter of the jam mixture, reserve. Chop remaining cake layer coarsely.
7 Layer half of the brioche then fruit mixture, chopped cake and remaining brioche slices in tin. Pour over remaining jam mixture. Pour hot custard over layered ingredients; top with reserved rounds. Bake, uncovered, in moderately low oven 30 minutes. Cover with foil; bake further 30 minutes; turn, top-side up, onto serving plate. Dust with sifted icing sugar.

SPONGE
Beat eggs and sugar in small bowl with electric mixer until thick and creamy; transfer to large bowl. Gently fold in triple-sifted flour and butter. Pour mixture into prepared tin; bake, uncovered, in moderately hot oven about 20 minutes. Turn cake onto wire rack immediately to cool. (Can be made ahead to this stage. Cover; refrigerate overnight.)

CUSTARD
Stir cream and milk in small saucepan over heat until almost boiling. Whisk eggs, yolks and sugar in large bowl. Whisking constantly, gradually add hot cream mixture to egg mixture; whisk until combined.
TIP You can use a purchased sponge cake, if you prefer.

chocolate peppermint cake

preparation time 20 minutes (plus refrigeration time)
cooking time 1 hour
serves 20

125g unsalted butter, chopped
2 teaspoons instant coffee powder
¾ cup (180ml) water
100g dark chocolate, chopped coarsely
1 cup (220g) caster sugar
1 egg, beaten lightly
¾ cup (110g) self-raising flour
½ cup (75g) plain flour
2 tablespoons cocoa powder

PEPPERMINT CREAM
125g unsalted butter, chopped
3 cups (480g) icing sugar
2 tablespoons milk
½ teaspoon peppermint essence
green food colouring

CHOCOLATE GANACHE
300g dark chocolate, chopped coarsely
1 cup (250ml) cream

1 Preheat oven to low. Grease two 8cm x 25cm cake tins; line bases and sides with baking parchment.
2 Stir butter, coffee, the water, chocolate and sugar in medium pan over heat until smooth. Transfer to medium bowl. Whisk in egg, sifted flours and cocoa. Divide mixture equally between prepared tins; bake in low oven about 45 minutes. Stand cakes 5 minutes; turn, top-side up, onto wire rack to cool.
3 Using serrated knife, split cooled cakes in half. Place bottom layers on wire rack over tray. Spread each with about a quarter of the peppermint cream; top with cake tops. Place remaining peppermint cream in piping bag fitted with 2cm fluted tube. Pipe remaining cream along centre of each cake top; refrigerate 1 hour.
4 Using metal spatula and working quickly, pour chocolate ganache over cakes, smoothing sides. Stand at room temperature until ganache sets.

PEPPERMINT CREAM
Beat butter in bowl with electric mixer until as pale as possible. Gradually beat in icing sugar, milk, essence and enough colouring to tint to the desired shade of green.

CHOCOLATE GANACHE
Combine chocolate and cream in small saucepan; stir over low heat until smooth.

chocolate fruit cake

preparation time 20 minutes
cooking time 1 hour
serves 12

125g butter, chopped
¾ cup (150g) firmly packed brown sugar
50g dark chocolate, chopped coarsely
½ cup (125ml) water
¼ cup (60ml) dark rum
¼ cup (30g) coarsely chopped walnuts
½ cup (75g) currants
1 cup (160g) sultanas
1 cup (170g) coarsely chopped raisins
½ cup (40g) mixed peel
¾ cup (110g) plain flour
2 tablespoons cocoa powder
2 tablespoons self-raising flour
½ teaspoon mixed spice
2 eggs, beaten lightly
80g dark chocolate, melted, extra
¼ cup (60g) soured cream

1 Preheat oven to low. Grease 20cm-ring cake tin; line base with baking parchment.
2 Combine butter, sugar, chocolate and the water in medium saucepan; stir over heat until sugar dissolves. Remove from heat; stir in rum, nuts and fruit. Add sifted dry ingredients and egg; stir until combined.
3 Spoon mixture into prepared tin; bake in low oven about 1 hour. Cool cake in tin.
4 Just before serving, combine cooled extra chocolate and soured cream in small bowl; stir until smooth. Turn cake onto serving plate, top-side up; spread chocolate mixture over top of cake.
TIP The chocolate fruit cake can also be baked in a 14cm x 21cm loaf tin; bake in a low oven about 1½ hours.

rich fruit cake

preparation time 40 minutes (plus standing time)
cooking time 2 hours (plus cooling time
serves 36

⅓ cup (55g) pitted prunes, halved
1½cups (240g) sultanas
1½ cups (230g) currants
½ cup (125ml) sweet sherry
½ cup (125ml) brandy
125g butter, softened
½ cup (110g) firmly packed brown sugar
3 eggs
1 tablespoon instant coffee granules
¼ cup (60ml) hot water
¼ cup (80g) plum jam
1 cup (150g) plain flour
¾ cup (110g) self-raising flour
1 tablespoon cocoa powder
1 teaspoon ground cinnamon
½ teaspoon mixed spice
½ teaspoon ground nutmeg
1½ cups (300g) glacé cherries
1½ cups (250g) halved, pitted dates
1 cup (170g) mixed peel
2 cups (240g) coarsely chopped walnuts

1 Combine prunes, sultanas and currants in large bowl, stir in sherry and brandy. Cover tightly with cling film; store in a cool, dark place overnight or up to a week, stirring every day.
2 On the day of baking, preheat oven to low (150°C/ 130°C fan-assisted). Grease deep 22cm-round or deep 19cm-square cake tin; line base and sides of tin with four thicknesses of baking parchment, extending parchment 5cm above edge(s).
3 Beat butter and sugar in small bowl with electric mixer only until combined. Add eggs quickly, one at a time, beat only until combined between each addition.
4 Transfer mixture to large bowl; stir in the combined coffee and the water and jam, then the sifted dry ingredients in two batches. Drain prune mixture, reserve liquid. Add prune mixture, cherries, dates, peel and walnuts to cake mixture.
5 Spread mixture into tin. Bake about 2 hours.
6 Brush reserved prune liquid over hot cake; cover with foil, cool in tin overnight.
TIPS Fruit for soaking can be prepared up to two weeks ahead.
Cake can be made up to three months ahead; store in an airtight container in the refrigerator, or freeze for up to 12 months.

white chocolate mud cake

preparation time 50 minutes
cooking time 1 hour 45 minutes (plus cooling time)
serves 12

250g butter, chopped
180g white eating chocolate, chopped coarsely
1½ cups (330g) caster sugar
¾ cup (180ml) milk
1½ cups (225g) plain flour
½ cup (75g) self-raising flour
½ teaspoon vanilla extract
2 eggs, beaten lightly

WHITE CHOCOLATE GANACHE
½ cup (125ml) whipping cream
360g white eating chocolate, chopped finely

CHOCOLATE CURLS
200g dark eating chocolate, melted
200g white eating chocolate, melted
200g milk eating chocolate, melted

1 Preheat oven to moderately low (170°C/150°C fan-assisted). Grease deep 20cm-round cake tin; line base and side with baking parchment.
2 Combine butter, chocolate, sugar and milk in medium saucepan; stir over low heat until melted. Transfer mixture to large bowl; cool 15 minutes.
3 Stir in sifted flours, extract and egg; pour into tin. Bake about 1 hour 40 minutes; cool cake in tin.
4 Meanwhile, make white chocolate ganache and chocolate curls.
5 Turn cake onto serving plate, top-side up. Spread ganache all over cake; top with chocolate curls.

WHITE CHOCOLATE GANACHE
Bring cream to a boil in small saucepan, pour over chocolate in medium bowl; stir with wooden spoon until chocolate melts. Cover bowl; refrigerate, stirring occasionally, about 30 minutes or until spreadable.

CHOCOLATE CURLS
Spread dark, white and milk chocolate separately on marble slab or work top. When chocolate is almost set, drag ice-cream scoop over surface of chocolate to make curls. Set chocolate can be scraped up, re-melted and used again.

lemon soured cream cake

preparation time 35 minutes
cooking time 1 hour 30 minutes (plus cooling time)
serves 12

250g butter, softened
2 tablespoons grated lemon rind
2 cups (440g) caster sugar
6 eggs
2 cups (300g) plain flour
¼ cup (35g) self-raising flour
¾ cup (180g) soured cream

1 Preheat oven to moderately low (170°C/150°C fan-assisted). Grease deep 27cm-round cake tin; line base with baking parchment.
2 Beat butter, rind and sugar in large bowl with electric mixer until light and fluffy; beat in eggs one at a time. Stir in half the sifted flours and half the soured cream, then stir in remaining flours and remaining soured cream until smooth.
3 Spread mixture into tin; bake about 1½ hours. Stand cake 5 minutes before turning onto wire rack to cool. Dust with sifted icing sugar before serving, if desired.
TIP Cake can be made a week ahead; store in an airtight container.

moist orange cake

preparation time 25 minutes
cooking time 45 minutes (plus cooling time)
serves 8

155g butter, softened
2 teaspoons finely grated orange rind
⅔ cup (150g) caster sugar
3 eggs
1¼ cups (185g) self-raising flour
¼ cup (60ml) milk
1 tablespoon desiccated coconut

ORANGE ICING
1 cup (160g) icing sugar
1 teaspoon butter, softened
1 tablespoon orange juice, approximately

1 Preheat oven to moderate (180°C/160°C fan-assisted). Grease deep 20cm-round cake tin; line base with baking parchment.
2 Combine butter, rind, sugar, eggs, sifted flour and milk in large bowl; beat on low speed with electric mixer until combined. Increase speed to medium, beat about 3 minutes or until mixture is lighter in colour and smooth.
3 Spread mixture into tin; bake about 45 minutes. Stand cake in yin 5 minutes before turning onto wire rack to cool.
4 Meanwhile, make orange icing.
5 Spread cold cake with orange icing; sprinkle with coconut.

ORANGE ICING
Sift icing sugar into small heatproof bowl, stir in butter and enough juice to make a stiff paste. Stir over hot water until icing is spreadable.
TIP Can be made two days ahead; keep in an airtight container.

mississippi mud cake

preparation time 10 minutes
cooking time 1 hour 20 minutes (plus cooling time)
serves 9

250g butter, chopped
150g dark eating chocolate, chopped
2 cups (440g) white sugar
1 cup (250ml) hot water
⅓ cup (80ml) whisky
1 tablespoon instant coffee granules
1½ cups (225g) plain flour
¼ cup (35g) self-raising flour
¼ cup (25g) cocoa powder
2 eggs, beaten lightly

1 Preheat oven to moderately low (170°C/150°C fan-assisted). Grease 23cm-square shallow cake tin; line base and sides with baking parchment.
2 Combine butter, chocolate, sugar, the water, whisky and coffee in medium saucepan; stir over low heat until mixture is smooth, cool. Stir in sifted flours and cocoa then egg.
3 Pour into tin; bake about 1¼ hours. Let stand 10 minutes; turn onto wire rack to cool. Serve dusted with sifted icing sugar, if desired.

vanilla butter cake

preparation time 30 minutes
cooking time 50 minutes (plus cooling time)
serves 9

125g butter, chopped
¾ cup (180ml) milk
3 eggs
1 tablespoon vanilla extract
1 cup (220g) caster sugar
1½ cups (225g) self-raising flour

1 Preheat oven to moderate (180°C/160°C fan-assisted). Grease deep 19cm-square cake tin; line base with baking parchment.
2 Combine butter and milk in small saucepan, stir over heat until butter is melted. Remove from heat; cool to room temperature.
3 Beat eggs and extract in small bowl with electric mixer until thick and creamy; gradually add sugar, beat until dissolved between each addition.
4 Transfer mixture to large bowl, stir in half the sifted flour and half the butter mixture, then remaining flour and remaining butter mixture.
5 Pour into tin; bake about 45 minutes. Stand cake in tin 5 minutes; turn, top-side up, onto wire rack to cool. Dust cold cake with sifted icing sugar, if desired.
TIP Cake can be made three days ahead; store in an airtight container.

sponge cake

preparation time 20 minutes
cooking time 20 minutes (plus cooling time)
serves 10

4 eggs
¾ cup (165g) caster sugar
⅔ cup (100g) wheaten cornflour
¼ cup (30g) custard powder
1 teaspoon cream of tartar
½ teaspoon bicarbonate of soda
300ml whipping cream
1 tablespoon icing sugar
½ teaspoon vanilla extract
¼ cup (80g) strawberry jam, warmed
250g strawberries, sliced thinly
1 tablespoon icing sugar, extra

1 Preheat oven to moderate (180°C/160°C fan-assisted). Grease two deep 22cm-round cake tins; sprinkle with flour, shake away excess.
2 Beat eggs and caster sugar in small bowl with electric mixer about 5 minutes or until thick and creamy; transfer to large bowl.
3 Sift dry ingredients twice onto baking parchment before sifting over egg mixture; gently fold ingredients together.
4 Divide mixture evenly between tins; bake about 20 minutes. Turn sponges immediately onto baking-parchment-lined wire rack; turn top-side up to cool.
5 Beat cream, icing sugar and extract in small bowl with electric mixer until firm peaks form. Place one cold sponge on serving plate; spread first with jam, then with cream mixture. Top with strawberry slices, then with remaining sponge. Dust with sifted extra icing sugar.
TIP When folding flour into egg mixture, you can use a large metal spoon, a rubber spatula, a whisk or use one hand like a rake.

carrot and banana cake

preparation time 20 minutes
cooking time 1 hour 15 minutes (plus cooling time)
serves 10

1¼ cups (185g) plain flour
½ cup (75g) self-raising flour
1 teaspoon bicarbonate of soda
1 teaspoon mixed spice
½ teaspoon ground cinnamon
1 cup (220g) firmly packed brown sugar
¾ cup (80g) coarsely chopped walnuts
3 eggs, beaten lightly
2 cups coarsely grated carrot
1 cup mashed banana
1 cup (250ml) vegetable oil

CREAM CHEESE FROSTING
90g packaged cream cheese
90g butter
1 cup (160g) icing sugar

1 Preheat oven to moderately low (170°C/150°C fan-assisted). Grease base and side of 24cm-round springform cake tin; line base with baking parchment.
2 Sift flours, soda, spices and sugar into large bowl. Stir in walnuts, egg, carrot, banana and oil; pour mixture into prepared tin.
3 Bake about 1¼ hours. Cool cake in tin.
4 Meanwhile, make cream cheese frosting.
5 Top cold cake with cream cheese frosting.

CREAM CHEESE FROSTING
Beat cream cheese and butter in small bowl with electric mixer until as white as possible; gradually beat in icing sugar.
TIPS You will need about four medium carrots (480g) and two large overripe bananas (460g) for this recipe. Pecans can be substituted for walnuts, if desired.

moist coconut cake with coconut ice frosting

preparation time 25 minutes
cooking time 1 hour (plus cooling time)
serves 10

125g butter, softened
½ teaspoon coconut essence
1 cup (220g) caster sugar
2 eggs
½ cup (40g) desiccated coconut
1½ cups (225g) self-raising flour
300g soured cream
⅓ cup (80ml) milk

COCONUT ICE FROSTING
2 cups (320g) icing sugar
1⅓ cups (110g) desiccated coconut
2 egg whites, beaten lightly
pink food colouring

1 Preheat oven to moderate (180°C/160°C fan-assisted). Grease deep 22cm-round cake tin; line base with baking parchment.
2 Beat butter, essence and sugar in small bowl with electric mixer until light and fluffy. Beat in eggs, one at a time.
3 Transfer mixture to large bowl. Stir in half the coconut and half the sifted flour, half the soured cream and half the milk, then add remaining coconut, flour, soured cream and milk; stir until smooth.
4 Spread mixture into tin; bake about 1 hour. Stand cake in tin 5 minutes before turning onto wire rack to cool.
5 Meanwhile, make coconut ice frosting.
6 Top cold cake with coconut ice frosting.

COCONUT ICE FROSTING
Combine sifted icing sugar in bowl with coconut and egg whites; mix well. Tint pink with a little colouring.

pear and almond cake with passionfruit glaze

preparation time 30 minutes
cooking time 50 minutes
serves 10

185g butter, chopped
½ cup (110g) caster sugar
3 eggs
1½ cups (185g) ground almonds
¼ cup (35g) plain flour
420g can pear halves in natural juice, drained

PASSIONFRUIT GLAZE
⅓ cup (80ml) passionfruit pulp
⅓ cup (80ml) light corn syrup
1 tablespoon caster sugar

1 Preheat oven to moderately low. Grease 22cm springform cake tin; line base and side with baking parchment.
2 Beat butter and sugar in medium bowl with electric mixer until light and fluffy. Add eggs, one at a time, beating until combined between each addition. Stir in ground almonds and flour.
3 Spread mixture into prepared tin; top with pear halves. Bake in moderately low oven about 50 minutes; stand cake 5 minutes. Remove from tin; turn, top-side up, onto wire rack. Pour passionfruit glaze over cake.

PASSIONFRUIT GLAZE
Stir combined ingredients in small saucepan over heat, without boiling, until sugar dissolves. Bring to a boil; reduce heat. Simmer, uncovered, without stirring, about 2 minutes or until thickened slightly; cool.
TIP Cake and glaze can be made a day ahead and refrigerated, covered separately, until required.

coffee hazelnut torte

preparation time 20 minutes (plus cooling time)
cooking time 1 hour 30 minutes
serves 16

6 egg whites
1¼cups (275g) caster sugar
½ cup (75g) roasted hazelnuts, chopped coarsely
1 cup (80g) roasted flaked almonds
1 tablespoon cocoa powder

COFFEE CREAM
⅔ cup (160ml) water
1 cup (220g) caster sugar
1 teaspoon gelatine
2 tablespoons milk
1 tablespoon instant coffee powder
250g unsalted butter, softened
1 teaspoon vanilla essence

1 Preheat oven to low. Line three baking trays with baking parchment; draw a 22cm-diameter circle on each tray.
2 Beat egg whites in medium bowl with electric mixer until soft peaks form. Gradually add sugar, beating after each addition, until sugar dissolves; fold in hazelnuts.
3 Spread mixture equally on drawn circles; bake in low oven about 1 hour or until firm. Cool meringues in oven with door ajar.
4 Place one meringue on serving plate; spread with a quarter of the coffee cream. Top with another meringue; spread with a third of the remaining coffee cream.
Top with last meringue; coat side of cake with remaining coffee cream. Press almonds over cream all around torte; dust with sifted cocoa.

COFFEE CREAM
Combine the water, sugar, gelatine, milk and coffee powder in small saucepan; stir over heat, without boiling, until sugar and gelatine dissolve. Cool to room temperature. Beat butter and essence in small bowl with electric mixer until light and fluffy. With motor operating, gradually beat in sugar mixture until fluffy (this will take about 10 minutes).
TIP Trace around a cake pan to get a circle that is the right size.

chocolate roulade with coffee cream

preparation time 20 minutes
cooking time 10 minutes
serves 8

1 tablespoon caster sugar
200g dark chocolate, chopped coarsely
¼ cup (60ml) hot water
1 tablespoon instant coffee powder
4 eggs, separated
½ cup (110g) caster sugar, extra
1 teaspoon hot water, extra
300ml whipping cream
2 tablespoons coffee-flavoured liqueur
1 tablespoon icing sugar

1 Preheat oven to moderate. Grease 25cm x 30cm swiss roll tin; line base with baking parchment. Place a piece of baking parchment cut the same size as swiss roll tin on board or work top; sprinkle evenly with caster sugar.
2 Combine chocolate, the water and half of the coffee powder in large heatproof bowl. Stir over large saucepan of simmering water until smooth; remove from heat.
3 Beat egg yolks and extra caster sugar in small bowl with electric mixer until thick and creamy; fold egg mixture into warm chocolate mixture.
4 Meanwhile, beat egg whites in small bowl with electric mixer until soft peaks form; fold egg whites, in two batches, into chocolate mixture. Spread into prepared tin; bake in moderate oven about 10 minutes.
5 Turn cake onto sugared paper, peeling baking parchment away; use serrated knife to cut away crisp edges from all sides. Cover cake with tea towel; cool.
6 Dissolve remaining coffee powder in the extra water in small bowl. Add cream, liqueur and icing sugar; beat with electric mixer until firm peaks form. Spread cake evenly with cream mixture. Roll cake, from long side, by lifting paper and using it to guide the roll into shape. Cover roll; refrigerate 30 minutes before serving.
TIP Be sure you beat the egg yolk mixture until thick, and the egg whites only until soft peaks form. Overbeating will dry out the egg whites and make them difficult to fold into the chocolate mixture.

Fold egg whites into chocolate mixture

Turn cake onto sugared paper

Use the sugared paper to help roll cake

lemon tartlets

preparation time 40 minutes (plus refrigeration time)
cooking time 30 minutes (plus cooling time)
makes 12

1 sheet ready-rolled butter puff pastry
20g butter, melted
1 teaspoon caster sugar
2 tablespoons icing sugar
1 egg, separated
⅓ cup (75g) caster sugar, extra
10g butter melted, extra
⅓ cup (80ml) milk
1 teaspoon finely grated lemon rind
1½ tablespoons lemon juice
2 tablespoons self-raising flour

1 Cut pastry sheet in half; stand on a board for 5 minutes or until partially thawed. Liberally grease a 12-hole, deep patty tin with a pastry brush dipped in the melted butter. Cut 12 x 10cm squares of baking parchment.

2 Sprinkle half of pastry with caster sugar, top with remaining pastry half. Roll pastry stack up tightly from the short side. Refrigerate until firm.

3 Cut pastry log into 12 x 1cm-wide pieces. Place one pastry piece, spiral-side down, on board dusted with sifted icing sugar; refrigerate remaining pastry. Roll out pastry piece into a 10cm round. Cut a round from the pastry using a 9cm cutter. Press the round into a patty tin hole. Repeat with the remaining pastry pieces. Freeze for 10 minutes.

4 Preheat oven to hot (220°C/200°C fan-assisted).

5 Place baking parchment squares over pastry in tin; place about a tablespoon of dried rice or beans over parchment. Bake 10 minutes in hot oven; remove parchment and rice. Reduce temperature to moderately low (160°C/140°C fan-assisted), bake further 10 minutes in moderately low oven or until base of pastry is browned lightly and crisp. Cool.

6 Reduce oven temperature to low (140°C/120°C fan-assisted).

7 Meanwhile, beat egg yolk and 2 tablespoons of extra sugar in small bowl with electric mixer until thick and creamy; fold in extra butter, milk, rind and juice, then sifted flour.

8 Beat egg white in small, clean bowl with electric mixer until soft peaks form. Gradually add remaining extra sugar; beat until sugar dissolved. Fold into lemon mixture in two batches; divide among pastry cases.

9 Bake in low oven about 10 minutes or until just set. Remove tartlets from tin; cool on wire rack.

10 Serve tartlets dusted with sifted icing sugar, if desired.

TIP This recipe is best made on the day of serving.

lime meringue tartlets

preparation time 25 minutes
cooking time 15 minutes
makes 20

2 eggs, separated
2 tablespoons caster sugar
1 teaspoon finely grated lime rind
1½ tablespoons lime juice
20g butter
20 x 4cm ready-made pastry shells
½ cup (110g) caster sugar, extra
⅔ cup (50g) shredded coconut

1 Combine egg yolks, sugar, rind, juice and butter in small heatproof bowl. Stir constantly over small saucepan of simmering water until mixture thickens slightly and coats the back of a spoon; remove from heat. Cover; refrigerate curd until cold.
2 Preheat oven to hot.
3 Divide curd evenly among pastry shells. Beat egg whites in small bowl with electric mixer until soft peaks form; gradually add extra sugar, 1 tablespoon at a time, beating until sugar dissolves between additions. Gently fold in ½ cup (35g) of the coconut.
4 Spoon meringue evenly over curd to enclose filling. Sprinkle tarts with remaining coconut; bake in hot oven about 5 minutes or until meringue is browned lightly. Refrigerate until ready to serve.
TIPS Pastry shells are made from shortcrust pastry and can be found at some supermarkets.
They may be frozen in an airtight container.

rich mocha fudge

preparation time 20 minutes
cooking time 15 minutes (plus cooling and
  refrigeration time)
makes 30 pieces

1 cup (220g) caster sugar
⅔ cup (160g) soured cream
2 tablespoons glucose syrup
250g dark cooking chocolate, finely chopped
100g packet white marshmallows, roughly chopped
2 tablespoons coffee-flavoured liqueur
2 tablespoons dry instant coffee
2 teaspoons boiling water
30 chocolate-coated coffee beans

1 Grease 8cm x 25cm shallow cake tin; line base and two long sides with baking parchment.
2 Combine sugar, soured cream and glucose in small saucepan; stir over low heat, without boiling, until sugar dissolves. Using pastry brush dipped in hot water, brush down side of pan to dissolve any sugar crystals; bring to a boil. Boil, uncovered, without stirring, about 10 minutes or until syrup reaches 155°C when measured on a sugar thermometer.
3 Remove from heat; add chocolate and marshmallows, stir until melted. Stir in combined liqueur, coffee and the boiling water.
4 Spread mixture into prepared tin; cool. Cover; refrigerate until firm.
5 Cut into 30 small squares; top each piece with a chocolate-coated coffee bean.
TIPS The recipe can be made up to four weeks ahead. Store, covered, in the refrigerator.
You can use a hazelnut-flavoured liqueur instead of the coffee-flavoured liqueur and top each piece with a halved hazelnut, if preferred.

white chocolate snowball truffles

preparation time 40 minutes
cooking time 5 minutes (plus refrigeration time)
makes 30

¼ cup (60ml) cream
30g butter
250g white eating chocolate, chopped finely
½ cup (70g) slivered almonds, toasted
1 tablespoon almond liqueur
250g white eating chocolate, melted, extra
1 cup (90g) desiccated coconut

1 Heat cream and butter in small saucepan; bring to a boil. Place chopped chocolate in medium heatproof bowl; add cream mixture, stir until smooth.
2 Stir in the almonds and liqueur. Cover and refrigerate, stirring occasionally, for about 30 minutes or until mixture begins to thicken. Roll rounded teaspoons of the mixture into balls; place in a single layer on cling film-lined tray. Refrigerate until firm.
3 Dip truffles into melted chocolate; gently shake off excess chocolate. Roll wet truffles in coconut; return to tray. Refrigerate until firm.
TIP Truffles can be made two weeks ahead. Store in an airtight container in the refrigerator.

cream cheese-filled brandied dates

preparation time 30 minutes
cooking time 15 minutes
makes 24

24 fresh dates (500g)
¼ cup (60ml) brandy
125g cream cheese, softened
1 tablespoon icing sugar
¼ cup (35g) hazelnuts, toasted, chopped finely
½ cup (110g) caster sugar
¼ cup (60ml) water
50g dark chocolate, melted

1 Make a shallow cut lengthways in each date (do not cut through); remove and discard stones. Combine dates in medium bowl with brandy; stand 15 minutes.
2 Meanwhile, beat cheese and icing sugar in small bowl with wooden spoon; stir in nuts.
3 Drain brandy from dates into cheese mixture; stir until filling mixture is smooth.
4 Spoon filling mixture into piping bag fitted with small plain tube; pipe mixture into date cavities.
5 Combine caster sugar and the water in small saucepan, stir over heat, without boiling, until sugar dissolves; bring to a boil. Reduce heat; simmer, uncovered, without stirring, until mixture is golden in colour. Remove from heat; stand until bubbles subside.
6 Drizzle half of the dates with toffee and remaining dates with chocolate; allow to set at room temperature.
TIP Toffee is best made just before serving or up to 1 hour beforehand.

rich chocolate truffles

preparation time 20 minutes (plus standing time)
cooking time 5 minutes (plus cooling time)
makes 20

200g dark chocolate, chopped coarsely
2 tablespoons cream
1 tablespoon Cointreau
⅓ cup (35g) cocoa powder

1 Combine chocolate and cream in medium heatproof bowl over medium saucepan of barely simmering water; stir until smooth. Remove from heat; cool. Stir in liqueur. Cover; stand at room temperature 3 hours or until firm.
2 Roll 2 level teaspoons of the mixture into balls. Place sifted cocoa in medium bowl. Toss balls to coat in cocoa; shake away excess cocoa. Refrigerate truffles in an airtight container.
TIPS Grand Marnier can be substituted for the Cointreau.
This recipe can be made a week ahead; roll truffles in cocoa 3 hours before serving.

chocolate cups with mascarpone and berries

preparation time 30 minutes
makes 16

16 x 2.5cm paper cases
cooking-oil spray
100g dark eating chocolate, melted
½ cup (140g) mascarpone cheese
1 tablespoon orange-flavoured liqueur
100g fresh raspberries
100g fresh blueberries

1 Lightly spray paper cases with cooking-oil spray. Using small, new, cleaned brush, paint chocolate thickly inside each case. Place paper cases on tray; refrigerate about 5 minutes or until chocolate sets. Peel away and discard paper cases.
2 Meanwhile, combine mascarpone and liqueur in small bowl. Place 1 teaspoon of the mascarpone mixture in each chocolate case; top with berries.
TIPS We used Grand Marnier in this recipe, but you can use Cointreau or any other orange-flavoured liqueur, if you prefer.
You need a small, unused paintbrush for this recipe. Paper cases can be found in confectionery stores and some supermarkets.
Originally from Lombardy in southern Italy, mascarpone is a buttery-rich, cream-like cheese made from cow milk. Ivory-coloured, soft and delicate, with the texture of softened butter, mascarpone is one of the traditional ingredients in tiramisu and other Italian desserts.

Paint chocolate thickly inside the cases

Peel the cases away carefully

Fill chocolate cases with mixture

caramel chews

preparation time 10 minutes
cooking time 15 minutes
makes 50

125g butter, chopped
395g can sweetened condensed milk
2 tablespoons honey
¾ cup (150g) firmly packed brown sugar
100g dark chocolate, melted
¼ cup (35g) hazelnuts, toasted,chopped coarsely

1 Grease deep 15cm-square cake tin; line base and sides with baking parchment.
2 Combine butter, milk, honey and sugar in medium saucepan; stir over heat, without boiling, until sugar dissolves. Increase heat; cook, stirring, about 10 minutes or until glossy and caramel in colour.
3 Pour caramel into prepared tin; cool. Remove caramel from tin. Spread with chocolate; top with nuts. Allow chocolate to set at room temperature; cut into small squares to serve.
TIP You'll know that the caramel is ready to be removed from the heat when the mixture starts to come away from the base and side of the saucepan.

chocolate and peanut butter swirl

preparation time 15 minutes
cooking time 10 minutes
makes about 72

360g white chocolate, chopped coarsely
½ cup (140g) smooth peanut butter
400g dark chocolate, chopped coarsely

1 Grease 20cm x 30cm baking tin; line base and sides with baking parchment, extending 5cm above long edges of tin.
2 Stir white chocolate in small heatproof bowl over small saucepan of simmering water until smooth; cool 5 minutes. Add peanut butter; stir until smooth.
3 Stir dark chocolate in small heatproof bowl over small saucepan of simmering water until smooth; cool slightly.
4 Drop alternate spoonfuls of white chocolate mixture and dark chocolate into prepared tin. Gently shake tin to level mixture; pull a skewer backwards and forwards through mixtures several times for a marbled effect. Stand at room temperature about 2 hours or until set; cut into small pieces.
TIP You can melt the chocolate in a microwave oven; cook on MEDIUM (55%) about 1 minute, stirring twice while cooking.

glossary

AIOLI An addictive garlic mayonnaise, aïoli has inflamed the passions of so many people around the world that local aïoli festivals are held at garlic harvest time every year. With 'ail' meaning garlic and 'oli' meaning oil, this Provençal classic marries well with fish, meats and vegetables.

ALL-BRAN A low-fat, high-fibre breakfast cereal based on wheat bran.

ALLSPICE Also known as pimento or Jamaican pepper, allspice is so-named because it tastes like a combination of nutmeg, cumin, clove and cinnamon. It is available whole (a pea-sized dark-brown berry) or ground, and used in both sweet and savoury dishes. Available from most supermarkets and specialty spice stores.

ALMONDS

Blanched Brown skins removed.

Caramelised Toffee-coated almonds available from some supermarkets, gourmet food and specialty confectionery stores.

Essence Often interchangeable with extract; made with almond oil and alcohol or another agent.

Flaked Paper-thin slices.

Ground Also known as almond meal; nuts are powdered to a coarse flour-like texture, for use in baking or as a thickening agent. Flourless cakes use a nut meal as a substitute for flour.

Slivered Small pieces cut lengthways.

AMARETTI Small Italian-style macaroons (biscuit or cookie) made with ground almonds.

ANCHOVY FILLETS Salty, strong-flavoured small fish; most commonly available canned. Used in salads, vegetable dishes, pasta and on pizza.

APPLES, GREEN The Granny Smith apple is crisp and juicy with a rich green skin; good to eat and ideal for cooking.

APRICOTS Used in sweet and savoury dishes, they have a velvety, golden-orange skin and aromatic sweet flesh. Also available dried.

ARTICHOKES

Globe large flower-bud of a member of the thistle family, having tough petal-like leaves; edible in part when cooked.

Hearts tender centre of the globe artichoke. Purchase fresh, or in brine canned or in glass jars.

ASPARAGUS These fragile shoots are a member of the lily family; cook with care to avoid damaging the tips.

AUBERGINE Also known as eggplant; belongs to the same family as tomatoes, chillies and potatoes. Ranging in size from tiny to very large and in colour from pale green to deep purple; eggplant has an equally wide variety of flavours.

AVOCADO A fruit with a soft, buttery flesh and a mild flavour. Best eaten raw, when ripe; usually added to salads or made into a dip, such as the famous guacamole. Test for ripeness by gently pressing the stem end; it should feel tender or give slightly.

BACON RASHERS Also known as bacon slices; made from cured and smoked pork side.

BAKING POWDER Raising agent consisting mainly of two parts cream of tartar to one part bicarbonate of soda.

BAMBOO SHOOTS The tender shoots of bamboo plants harvested before they are two weeks old. Crisp in texture, they are often used in Asian cooking. Available fresh from Asian food stores and canned

from supermarkets. Where possible, use fresh shoots as their flavour far outweighs the canned variety. Rinse canned shoots well to rid them of all traces of the canning liquid.

BASIL An aromatic herb; there are many types, but the most commonly used is sweet basil. See also Thai basil.

BEANS

Borlotti also known as roman beans.

Broad Also known as fava, windsor or horse beans, broad beans are available dried, fresh, canned and frozen. Fresh and frozen, they are best peeled twice (discarding both the outer long green pod and beige-green tough inner shell).

Butter beans cans labelled butter beans are, in fact, cannellini beans. Confusingly butter is also another name for lima beans, sold both dried and canned; a large beige bean having a mealy texture and mild taste.

Cannellini Small white bean similar in appearance and flavour to great northern and navy or haricot beans. Sometimes sold as butter beans.

Green Sometimes called french or string beans (although the tough string they once had has generally been bred out), this long fresh bean is consumed pod and all.

Kidney Medium-sized red bean, slightly floury yet sweet in flavour; sold dried or canned.

Mexican-style A canned mixture of either haricot or pinto beans cooked with tomato, peppers, onion, garlic and spices.

Sprouts Also known as bean shoots; tender new growths of assorted beans and seeds germinated for consumption. The most readily available are mung bean, soy bean, alfalfa and mangetout sprouts.

BEEF

Blade steak From the shoulder blade.

Eye fillet Tenderloin, fillet.

Skirt steak Cut from the underside of the centre.

T-bone steak Sirloin steak with the bone in and fillet eye attached; also known as porterhouse.

BEETROOT Also known as beets or red beets; firm, round root vegetable.

BICARBONATE OF SODA Also known as baking soda.

BLACK ONION SEEDS Also known as kalonji or nigella, are angular purple-black seeds, creamy colour inside and possess a sharp, nutty taste. Are available in specialty spice, Middle-Eastern and Asian food stores.

BLIND BAKING A cooking term describing a pie shell or pastry case baked before filling is added. To bake blind, ease pastry into pan or dish, place on oven tray; cover pastry with baking paper, fill with dried beans, rice or proper baking 'beans' (also called pie weights). Bake in moderately hot (200°C/180°C fan-forced) oven 10 minutes, remove paper and beans; bake for another 10 minutes or until browned lightly. Cool before adding filling. Dried beans and rice used to weigh down the pastry are not suitable for eating; cool after use, then store in an airtight jar and reuse each time you bake blind.

BREADCRUMBS

Packaged Fine-textured, crunchy, purchased, white breadcrumbs.

Stale One- or two-day-old pieces of bread made into crumbs by grating, blending or processing.

BULGUR WHEAT Also known as burghul; hulled steamed wheat kernels, once dried are crushed into various size grains. Used in Middle-Eastern dishes.

BUTTERNUT SQUASH Pear-shaped member of the gourd family with golden skin and orange flesh.

CABBAGE

Chinese Also known as peking cabbage, wong bok or petsai. Elongated in shape with pale green, crinkly leaves; is the most common cabbage in South-East Asia. Can be shredded or chopped and eaten raw or braised, steamed or stir-fried. Available from supermarkets and greengrocers.

Savoy Large, heavy headed cabbage with crinkled dark-green outer leaves with a mild taste.

CAJUN SEASONING Used to give an authentic USA Deep South spicy Cajun flavour to food, this packaged blend of assorted herbs and spices can include paprika, basil, onion, fennel, thyme, cayenne and tarragon.

CAPERBERRIES The fruit formed after caper buds have flowered, caperberries are milder in taste than capers. They marry

well with seafood dishes and look fantastic on an antipasto platter. Sold pickled with stalks intact, they can be purchased from most delicatessens.

CAPERS The grey-green buds of a warm climate (usually Mediterranean) shrub; sold

either dried and salted or pickled in vinegar brine. Baby capers also are available.

CARDAMOM Native to India and used extensively in its cuisine, cardamom is a member of the ginger family and attains a sweet yet spicy flavour. This spice can be purchased in pod, seed or ground form from most supermarkets and spice stores.

CARAWAY SEEDS A member of the parsley family, caraway seeds have a nutty, anise-like flavour and are used in many Hungarian and German dishes. Available from most supermarkets and spice stores.

CASHEWS We used unsalted roasted cashews in this book.

CAYENNE PEPPER A hot powder made from the dried pods of pungent chillies, cayenne pepper has little aroma but a fiery taste. Available from most supermarkets and spice stores.

CELERIAC A member of the celery family, celeriac is a tuberous brown-skinned root with white flesh; tastes like an earthy, more pungent celery. Sometimes called knob celery, celeriac is the cooking celery of Northern Europe. Peeled and diced, it can be used raw in salads; steamed or boiled, it can be mashed like potato or diced and served as a cooked vegetable. At its best in winter, it is available from most greengrocers.

CELERY Grows as a cluster of long stalks; eaten raw or cooked.

CHEESE

Blue Mould-treated cheeses mottled with blue veining. Varieties include firm and crumbly Stilton-types to mild, creamy brie-like cheeses.

Cheddar The most widely eaten cheese in the world, cheddar is a semi-hard cow milk cheese. It ranges in colour from white to pale yellow and has a slightly crumbly texture if properly matured.

Feta Greek in origin; a crumbly textured goat's or sheep's milk cheese with a sharp salty taste.

Goat's Made from goat's milk, goat's cheese has an earthy, strong taste. Can be purchased in both soft and firm textures, in various shapes and sizes, sometimes rolled in ash or herbs. Available from most supermarkets and delicatessens.

Gorgonzola A creamy Italian blue cheese with a mild, sweet taste. Gorgonzola is as good an accompaniment to fruit as it is when used in cooking. Available from some supermarkets and delicatessens.

Grated pizza A commercial blend of varying proportions of processed grated mozzarella, cheddar and parmesan.

Gruyere A firm, cow-milk Swiss cheese having small holes and a nutty, slightly salty flavour. Emmental or appenzeller can be

used as a substitute. Available from some supermarkets and delicatessens.

Haloumi A firm, cream-coloured sheep-milk cheese matured in brine; has a minty, salty fetta flavour. It can be grilled or fried, briefly, without breaking down. Available from most supermarkets and Middle-Eastern food stores.

Mascarpone is a cultured cream product. Whitish to creamy yellow in colour, it has a soft, creamy texture, a fat content of 75%, and a slightly tangy taste.

Mozzarella a semi-soft cheese with a delicate, fresh taste; has a low melting point and stringy texture when hot.

Parmesan Also known as parmigiano; is a hard, grainy, cow-milk cheese. The curd is salted in brine for a month before being aged for up to two years in humid conditions.

Pecorino The generic Italian name for cheeses made from sheep milk. It's a hard, white to pale yellow cheese, usually matured for eight to 12 months. If unavailable, use parmesan.

Ricotta Soft white cow-milk cheese; roughly translates as 'cooked again'; made from whey, a by-product of other cheese making, to which fresh milk and acid are added. Ricotta is a sweet, moist cheese with a fat content of around 8.5% and a slightly grainy texture.

CHERRIES Soft stone fruit varying in colour from yellow to dark red. Sweet cherries are eaten whole and in desserts while sour cherries such as the bitter Morello variety are used in jams, preserves, pies and savoury dishes, particularly as an accompaniment to game birds and meats.

CHERVIL While this aromatic feathery green herb tastes somewhat like a blend of fennel and celery, it is a member of the carrot family. Traditionally used for its leaves alone, the roots are also edible. Available both fresh and dried but has the best flavour when fresh; like coriander and parsley, its delicate flavour diminishes the longer it is cooked. Chervil goes well with cream and eggs, and in white fish and chicken dishes.

CHICKEN

Breast With skin and bone intact.

Breast fillets Breast halved, skinned and boned.

Tenderloins Thin strip of meat lying under the breast.

Thigh Has skin and bone intact.

Thigh cutlets Thigh with skin and centre bone intact; sometimes known as a chicken chop.

CHICKPEAS Also known as hummus, garbanzos or channa; an irregularly round, sandy-coloured legume.

CHILLI

Dried flakes Deep-red, dehydrated chilli slices and whole seeds.

Jalapeño fairly hot green chillies. Available in brine bottled or fresh from specialty greengrocers.

Powder The Asian variety is the hottest, made from ground chillies; it can be used as a substitute for fresh chillies in the proportion of ½ teaspoon ground chilli powder to 1 medium chopped fresh chilli.

Thai red Small, hot and red in colour.

CHINESE CABBAGE Also known as peking or napa cabbage, wong bok and

petsai, the pale green, crinkly leaves of this elongated cabbage only require brief cooking.

CHINESE COOKING WINE A clear distillation of fermented rice, water and salt, it's about 29.5% alcohol by volume.

Used for marinades and as a sauce ingredient, It can be purchased from most Asian food stores.

CHIVES Related to the onion and leek; has a subtle onion flavour.

CHOCOLATE

Chips Available in milk, white and dark chocolate. These hold their shape in baking and are ideal as a cake decoration.

Dark eating Made of cocoa liquor, cocoa butter and sugar.

Milk Primarily for eating.

White Eating chocolate.

CHOCOLATE HAZELNUT SPREAD Also known as Nutella.

CHORIZO A salami-like sausage of Spanish origin, chorizo is made of coarsely ground pork and highly seasoned with garlic and chillies. Available from most delicatessens.

CIABATTA In Italian, it means 'slipper', which is the traditional shape of this crisp-crusted wood-fired bread. Available from most supermarkets or bakeries.

CINNAMON STICK Dried inner bark of the shoots of the cinnamon tree.

CLAMS We used a small ridge-shelled variety of this bivalve mollusc; also known as vongole.

COCOA POWDER Also called cocoa; dried, unsweetened, roasted then ground cocoa beans.

COCONUT

Cream Is obtained commercially from the first pressing of the coconut flesh, without the addition of water; the second pressing (less rich) is sold as the milk. Available in cans and cartons at supermarkets.

Desiccated Unsweetened, concentrated, dried finely shredded coconut flesh.

Flaked Dried flaked coconut flesh.

Milk Not the juice found inside the fruit, which is known as coconut water, but the diluted liquid from the second pressing from the white flesh of a mature coconut. Available in cans and cartons at supermarkets.

Shredded Thin strips of dried coconut.

COFFEE-FLAVOURED LIQUEUR Tia Maria, Kahlua or any generic brand.

COINTREAU Citrus-flavoured liqueur.

COLOURINGS Many types are available from cake decorating suppliers, craft shops and some supermarkets; all are concentrated. It's best to use a minute amount of any type of colouring first to determine its strength.

CORIANDER Also known as cilantro or chinese parsley; bright-green-leafed herb with a pungent flavour. Often stirred into or sprinkled over a dish just before serving for maximum impact. Also available ground.

Root and stem mixture Roots and stems of a bunch of coriander can be cleaned, chopped and used in various dishes, most notably, Thai curry pastes.

CORN KERNELS Also called niblets; available canned from supermarkets.

CORN SYRUP A thick sweet syrup made by processing cornstarch; available in light or dark varieties.

CORNFLOUR Also called cornstarch; used as a thickening agent in cooking.

COURGETTES Also known as zucchini.

COUSCOUS A fine, grain-like cereal product, originally from North Africa, made from semolina. Couscous can be used in salads, as a base for stews or, as the Egyptians do, as a dessert mixed with sugar, nuts and dried fruit. Available from most supermarkets and Middle-Eastern food stores.

CREAM We used fresh pouring cream, also known as pure cream. It has no additives, and contains a minimum fat content of 35%.

Soured Thick, smooth and slightly acidic cream; used to add richness to soups and stews, also dolloped on potatoes and soups.

Whipping A cream containing a thickener, with a minimum fat content of 35%.

CREAM CHEESE Commonly known as Philadelphia or Philly cheese. A soft, cow-milk cheese with a fat content of at least 33%. Available from supermarkets.

CREME FRAICHE A French variation of sour cream; is a mildly acidic, high fat, slightly nutty tasting thick cream. Crème fraîche and sour cream can be used interchangeably with sour cream in some recipes, but the former can also be whipped like cream and does not split or curdle when boiled. Available from most supermarkets and delicatessens.

CUMIN Also known as zeera or comino; is the dried seed of a plant related to the parsley family having a spicy, nutty flavour. Available in seed form or dried and ground from supermarkets.

CURRANTS Tiny, almost black raisins so-named after a grape variety that originated in Corinth, Greece.

CURRY POWDER A blend of ground spices used for convenience when making Indian food. Can consist of some of the following spices in varying proportions: dried chilli, cinnamon, cumin, coriander, fennel, fenugreek, mace, cardamom and turmeric. Available in mild or hot varieties.

CUSTARD POWDER Instant mixture used to make pouring custard.

DATES Fruit of the date palm tree with a sticky texture; sometimes sold already pitted and chopped.

DILL Green-coloured herb with feathery leaves and tiny green-yellow flowers. Commonly used in fish and egg dishes or finely chopped in salads.

FENNEL Also known as finocchio, bulb or Florence fennel, is also the name given to dried licorice-flavoured seeds. Eaten raw, braised, fried, roasted or stewed, it is mildly sweet and has a subtle licorice-like flavour. Fronds and top shoots are usually

discarded (unless used as a garnish) and the bulb trimmed at the base to extract the fibrous core. A large fennel bulb can be as big as a grapefruit, while baby fennel can be slightly flat and weigh as little as 100g.

FERRERO ROCHER A commercial sweet made from hazelnuts and milk chocolate.

FIG Small, soft, pear-shaped fruit with a sweet pulpy flesh full of tiny edible seeds. Also available dried.

FIVE-SPICE POWDER A fragrant ground mixture of cassia, clove, star anise, sichuan pepper and fennel seeds, five-spice, also known as chinese five-spice, can be used as a seasoning for stir-fries or as a rub for meats. Available from most supermarkets, Asian food stores or specialty spice stores.

FLOUR

Besan A fine, powdery flour made from dried ground chickpeas. Available from Asian and health food stores.

Buckwheat Although not a true cereal, flour is made from its seeds. Available from health food stores.

Plain An all-purpose wheat flour.

Self-raising Plain flour sifted with baking powder in the proportion of 1 cup flour to 2 teaspoons baking powder.

FRESH HERBS We have specified when to use fresh or dried (not ground) herbs in the proportion of one to four for fresh herbs; use 1 teaspoon dried herbs instead of 4 teaspoons (1 tablespoon) chopped fresh herbs.

GAI LARN Also known as gai lum, chinese broccoli and chinese kale, this vegetable is prized more for its stems than its coarse leaves. Can be eaten stir-fried on its own or tossed into various soups and noodle dishes. Available from most supermarkets, Asian food stores and greengrocers.

GALANGAL Also known as ka, galangal is a rhizome with a hot ginger-citrusy flavour that is used similarly to ginger as a seasoning and as an ingredient. Fresh ginger can be substituted for fresh

galangal but the flavour of the dish will not be exactly the same. Available from some greengrocers and Asian food stores.

GARAM MASALA A blend of spices, originating in Northern India; consists of cardamom, cinnamon, coriander, cloves, fennel and cumin, in varying proportions, roasted and ground together. Available from some supermarkets, Indian food stores and specialty spice stores.

GELATINE We used powdered gelatine; also available in sheet form known as leaf gelatine.

GHEE Clarified butter; with the milk solids removed, this fat can be heated to a high temperature without burning.

GINGER

Fresh Also known as green or root ginger; is the thick gnarled root of a tropical plant. Can be kept peeled, covered with dry sherry in a jar and refrigerated, or frozen in an airtight container.

Ground Also called powdered ginger; used as a flavouring in cakes, pies and puddings but not instead of fresh ginger.

GNOCCHI Italian 'dumplings' made of potatoes, semolina or flour.

GOLDEN SYRUP A by-product of refined sugarcane; pure maple syrup or honey can be substituted.

GRAND MARNIER Orange-flavoured liqueur based on cognac brandy.

GREEN GINGER WINE Beverage 14% alcohol by volume, has the taste of fresh ginger. Substitute dry (white) vermouth, if preferred.

GREMOLATA An Italian gremolata is traditionally a blend of finely chopped lemon rind, parsley and garlic. Sprinkled over osso buco just before serving warms the gremolata, enlivening it just enough

to send a sharp aromatic message to the diner's tastebuds.

HARISSA A North African paste made from dried red chillies, garlic, olive oil and caraway seeds, can be used as a rub for meat and as an ingredient in sauces and dressings. It is available ready-made from some supermarkets and Middle Eastern food stores.

HAZELNUTS Also known as filberts; plump, grape-size, rich, sweet nut with a brown inedible skin that is removed by rubbing heated nuts together vigorously in a tea towel.

HONEY The variety sold in a squeezable container is not suitable for the recipes in this book.

HORSERADISH A plant grown for its pungent, spicy roots; they are generally grated and used as a condiment, particularly with roast beef or fish, or in sauces. Is also available bottled or dried.

ICE-CREAM We used an ice-cream with 5g of fat per 100ml.

KAFFIR LIME LEAVES They are used, fresh or dried, as a flavouring, like bay leaves, throughout Asia. Sold fresh, dried or frozen, the dried leaves are less potent so double the number called for

in a recipe if you substitute them for fresh leaves. Available from most greengrocers and Asian food stores.

KALAMATA OLIVES Purplish-black Greek olives cured in vinegar and sometimes preserved in olive oil.

KIWI FRUIT Also known as chinese gooseberry.

LAMB

Backstrap The larger fillet from a row of loin chops or cutlets.

Boned shoulder Boneless section of the forequarter. Also available rolled and secured with string or netting.

Cutlet Small, tender rib chop.

Fillet The smaller piece of meat from a row of loin chops or cutlets.

French-trimmed shanks Also known as drumsticks or Frenched shanks; all the gristle and narrow end of the bone is discarded then the remaining meat trimmed from the forequarter leg.

Leg Cut from the hindquarter.

Rack Row of cutlets.

Trim Boneless cuts free from external fat.

LEEK A member of the onion family, with a mild flavour. Its thick white stem must be washed thoroughly before use; separate its layers and rinse away any trapped dirt. Leeks can be boiled, steamed or braised; is most famously used in vichyssoise.

LEMONADE A carbonated soft drink.

LEMONGRASS A tall, clumping, sharp-edged aromatic tropical grass that both smells and tastes of lemon. Generally only the stem end of the plant is used in cooking. It is sold fresh in most supermarkets, greengrocers and Asian food stores.

LENTILS Dried pulses often identified by and named after their colour (red, brown, yellow). Also known as dhal.

LETTUCE

Butter Have small, round, loosely formed heads with soft, buttery-textured leaves ranging from pale green on the outer leaves to pale yellow-green on the inner leaves. Has a sweet flavour.

Cos Also known as romaine lettuce; is the traditional Caesar salad lettuce.

Mizuna A wispy, feathered green salad leaf that originated in Japan. Available from most supermarkets and greengrocers.

LIMONCELLO Italian lemon-flavoured liqueur; originally made from the juice and peel of lemons grown along the Amalfi coast.

LYCHEES Originating in China over 1000 years ago, lychees are a delicious fresh fruit with a light texture and flavour. Peel away rough skin, remove seed and they're ready to eat. Available, fresh and canned, from most supermarkets and greengrocers.

MACADAMIAS Native to Australia, a rich and buttery nut; store in refrigerator because of its high oil content.

MADEIRA A fortified wine originally from the Portuguese island of the same name. Types range from golden and dry to rich, sweet and dark; can be served as an aperitif but is also an excellent cooking wine.

MALIBU Coconut-flavoured rum.

MANGETOUT ('eat all') Also known as snow peas. Mangetout tendrils, the growing shoots of the plant, are available from most supermarkets and greengrocers.

MANGO, GREEN Sour and crunchy, green mangoes are just immature fruit that can be eaten as a vegetable in salads, curries and stir-fries. They will keep, wrapped in plastic, in the refrigerator up to two weeks. Available from most greengrocers.

MAPLE SYRUP A thin syrup distilled from the sap of the maple tree. Maple-flavoured syrup is not an adequate substitute for the real thing.

Maple-flavoured syrup made from sugar cane rather than maple-tree sap; used in cooking or as a topping but cannot be considered an exact substitute for pure maple syrup.

MARJORAM Strong-flavoured herb traditionally used in Italian and Greek cooking; use sparingly.

MARSALA A sweet fortified wine.

MARSHMALLOWS Pink and white; made from sugar, glucose, gelatine and cornflour.

MAYONNAISE A paste consisting of oil, egg and vinegar.

MILK

Buttermilk Sold alongside fresh milk products in supermarkets; is commercially made similarly to yogurt. It is low in fat and is a good substitute for dairy products such as cream or soured cream; good in baking and in salad dressings.

Evaporated Unsweetened canned milk from which water has been extracted by evaporation. Also available skim with a fat content of 0.3%.

Sweetened condensed From which 60% of the water has been removed; the remaining milk is sweetened with sugar.

MIRIN A Japanese champagne-coloured cooking wine made of glutinous rice and alcohol expressly for cooking and should not be confused with sake. There is a seasoned sweet mirin called manjo mirin made of water, rice, corn syrup and alcohol. Available from some supermarkets and Asian food stores.

MIXED SPICE A blend of ground spices usually consisting of cinnamon, allspice, cloves and nutmeg. Available from most supermarkets and specialty spice stores.

MUSHROOMS

Button Sometimes called champignons, are the youngest variety, and usually the smallest. The body of this mushroom is firm and tightly closed against the stem, with none of the gill-like 'veil' exposed.

Cup Slightly bigger and darker in colour than the button, with its veil (or velum) just starting to open. Cups are among the most versatile, having a distinctive flavour without being overpowering. Perfect for soups, stir-fries and sauces, and delicious sautéed in a frying pan.

Flat Large, flat mushrooms with a rich earthy flavour and meaty texture; ideal for filling and barbecuing as a meal on its own rather than just another ingredient.

Oyster Also called abalone mushrooms, available in a wide variety of colours, have a subtle, delicate flavour and work well with veal, seafood and poultry.

Portobello Large, dark brown mushrooms with full-bodied flavour, ideal for filling or barbecuing.

Shiitake Called the king of mushrooms in their native Japan; available both fresh and dried. Fresh shiitake need to have their woody stems removed before

they're used; their rich flavour and dense, substantial texture are shown to best advantage when braised or fried then eaten on their own. When dried, shiitake must be reconstituted by being soaked in water before use in stir-fries and various one-pot dishes.

Chestnut Are light to dark brown mushrooms with full-bodied flavour. They hold their shape upon being cooked. Button or cups can be substituted.

MUSSELS Buy from a reliable fresh fish supplier. Must be tightly closed when bought, indicating they are alive. Before cooking, scrub shells with a strong brush and remove 'beards'. Discard any shells that do not open after cooking.

MUSTARD

American Usually served with hot dogs, is mild with a smooth texture and is often flavoured with sugar and spices.

Black seeds Also known as brown mustard seeds, are more pungent than the white (or yellow) seeds and are used in most prepared mustards.

Dijon Is a pale-yellow to brown French mustard often flavoured with white wine.

Wholegrain Also known as seeded mustard, is a coarse-grain mustard made from black and yellow mustard seeds and dijon-style mustard.

NAM JIM Is a generic term for a Thai dipping sauce; most versions include fish sauce and chillies, but the remaining ingredients are up to the individual cook.

NOODLES

Bean thread Also known as bean thread vermicelli, cellophane noodles or glass noodles.

Egg noodles Made from wheat flour and eggs; strands vary in thickness.

Rice A common form of noodle used throughout South East Asia. Chewy and pure white, they do not need pre-cooking before use.

Rice stick Also known as sen lek, ho fun or kway teow; come in different widths. Dried noodles made from rice flour and water; available flat and wide or very thing (vermicelli). Should be soaked in boiling water to soften.

NUTELLA Chocolate-hazelnut spread.

OCEAN TROUT A farmed fish with pink, soft flesh, it is from the same family as the Atlantic salmon.

OIL

Groundnut Pressed from ground peanuts; most commonly used oil in Asian cooking because of its high smoke point (capacity to handle high heat without burning).

Olive Made from ripened olives. Extra virgin and virgin are the best; extra light or light refers to the taste not fat levels.

Sesame Made from roasted, crushed, white sesame seeds; a flavouring rather than a cooking medium.

Vegetable Any number of oils sourced from plants rather than animal fats.

ONIONS

Red Also known as Spanish, red Spanish or Bermuda onion; a sweet-flavoured, large, purple-red onion.

Spring Crisp, narrow green-leafed tops and a round sweet white bulb.

ORECCHIETTE Originally a homemade specialty from the Italian region of Puglia, orecchiette translates as 'little ears', a shape this short pasta resembles. If not available, use any small pasta you like — penne, farfalle or little shells.

OYSTERS A bivalve mollusc; when buying, look for oysters that are plump and glossy and smell fresh.

PAK CHOY Also known as bok choy or chinese chard; has a fresh, mild mustard taste. Stems and leaves can be stir-fried, braised or stirred through soup. **Baby pak choy**, also known as pak kat farang, shanghai pak choy or chinese chard, is

small and more tender than pak choy. It has a mildly acrid, distinctively appealing taste and is one of the most commonly used Asian greens. Available from supermarkets and greengrocers.

PANCETTA An unsmoked bacon; pork belly cured in salt and spices then rolled into a sausage shape and dried for several weeks. Usually used, either sliced or chopped, as an ingredient rather than eaten on its own. Available from some supermarkets and delicatessens.

PANETTONE A sweet Italian yeast bread with raisins and candied orange, is usually tall and cylindrical and translates as 'big bread'. Available from some supermarkets and delicatessens.

PAPPARDELLE A wide, ribbon-like pasta with scalloped sides, pappardelle is sometimes sold as lasagnette or even lasagne. Available from some supermarkets and delicatessens.

PAPRIKA Ground, dried red capsicum (bell pepper), available sweet and hot from supermarkets and specialty spice stores.

PASSIONFRUIT Also known as granadilla; a small tropical fruit, native to Brazil, comprised of a tough outer skin encasing edible black sweet-sour seeds.

PASTE Some recipes in this book call for commercially prepared pastes of various strength and flavours; use whichever one you feel suits your spice-level tolerance best.

Green curry The hottest of the traditional pastes; great in chicken and vegetable curries, and a great addition to stir-fries and noodle dishes.

Red curry Probably the most popular curry paste; a hot blend of different flavours that complements the richness of

pork, duck and seafood, also works well in marinades and sauces.

Shrimp A strong-scented, almost solid preserved paste made of salted dried shrimp. Used as a pungent flavouring in many South-East Asian soups and sauces. Available from Asian food stores.

Tandoori Consisting of garlic, tamarind, ginger, coriander, chilli and spices.

Vindaloo A fiery paste consisting of coriander, cumin, turmeric, chilli, ginger, garlic, tamarind and lentil flour.

PATTY-PAN SQUASH Round squash with a frilled edge, available in yellow and green.

PEANUT BUTTER Peanuts ground to a paste; available in crunchy and smooth varieties.

PEARL BARLEY Barley that has had the husk discarded and has been hulled and polished, similarly to rice.

PECANS Native to the United States and now grown locally; golden-brown, buttery

and rich. Good in savoury and sweet dishes; especially good in salads.

PEPPERS Also called bell pepper or capsicum; available red, green, yellow or orange or purplish black. Seeds and membranes should be discarded before use.

PESTO Made from garlic, oil, vinegar, pine nuts, basil, herbs and spices. Available bottled from supermarkets.

PINE NUTS Also known as pignoli, pine nuts are not in fact a nut but a small, cream-coloured kernel from pine cones. Used commonly in pesto and salads, pine nuts often appear in Middle-Eastern and Indian cooking. Available from supermarkets and nut stores.

PISTACHIOS Pale green, delicately flavoured nut inside hard off-white shells.

To peel, soak shelled nuts in boiling water 5 minutes; drain, pat dry with absorbent paper. Rub skins with cloth to peel.

PITTA BREAD Round, dinner-plate sized Lebanese bread eaten on its own; roughly torn and used to scoop up dips and salads; or filled with a combination of meats and salad vegetables and rolled into a substantial sandwich.

POLENTA A flour-like cereal made from dried corn (maize) sold ground in several different textures and available at most supermarkets. Can be eaten soft and creamy, or chilled and grilled.

PORK

American-style ribs Well-trimmed, long mid-loin ribs used in traditional American barbecue spare ribs. Grilling, barbecuing or roasting are the best methods for this cut; wonderful when brushed with a sweet baste for perfect sticky ribs.

Fillet Skinless, boneless eye-fillet cut from the loin.

Loin From pork middle.

Neck Sometimes called pork scotch, boneless cut from the foreloin.

Spare ribs Also known as belly ribs or rashers, pork spare ribs have no bone and an equal proportion of fat and meat.

POUSSIN A small chicken, no more than six weeks old, weighing a maximum of 500g.

PRAWNS Also known as shrimp. To 'peel and devein', remove the head by holding it in one hand and twisting the body with the other; peel away the legs and shell from the body, but leave the tail intact, if you like, for decorative purposes. Remove and discard the centre vein from the back of each prawn, using a small sharp knife or your fingers.

PRESERVED LEMON Lemons preserved in salt and lemon juice. A common ingredient in North African cooking. Available from most Middle-Eastern food stores and delicatessens.

PROSCIUTTO Salted, air-cured and aged, prosciutto is usually eaten uncooked. Available from some supermarkets and delicatessens.

PUMPKIN Also known as squash; is a member of the gourd family and used as an ingredient or eaten on its own. Various types can be substituted for one another.

RAISINS Dried, sweet grapes.

READY-ROLLED PASTRY Packaged sheets of frozen puff and shortcrust pastry. Available from supermarkets.

RICE

Arborio Commonly used for making risottos; a round-grain rice well-suited to absorb a large amount of liquid. Its high starch content help give risottos their creamy texture. It is perfectly cooked when the rice is al dente; tender on the outside, but slightly firm in the centre. Available from most supermarkets.

Jasmine Sometimes sold as Thai fragrant rice, Jasmine rice is so-named due to its sweet aroma. Available from supermarkets and Asian food stores.

White Is hulled and polished, can be short- or long-grained.

RISONI Risoni, like orzo, is a very small rice-shaped pasta. It is great added to soups, baked in a casserole or as a side dish when served with a main course. Available from supermarkets.

ROCKET Also called arugula; a pepper-tasting green leaf used similarly to baby spinach leaves, eaten raw in salad or used in cooking.

Baby leaves Are both smaller and less peppery than the larger variety.

ROLOS Soft caramel-filled chocolates.

ROTI Also known as chapati, an unleavened flat bread used in place of cutlery to pick up wet curries when eating an Indian meal.

SAFFRON One of the most expensive spices in the world, true saffron comes only from the saffron crocus, that can

produce several flowers a year. Available from supermarkets and specialty spice stores.

SAKE Japan's favourite rice wine, sake is used in cooking, marinating and as part of dipping sauces. If unavailable, dry sherry, vermouth or brandy can be used as a substitute. When consumed as a drink, it can be served cold or warm. Available from liquor stores.

SALSA The Spanish word for sauce. A typical Mexican raw sauce is called salsa cruda; one made with green tomatoes or any combination of all-green herbs or vegetables is called salsa verde.

SAMBAL OELEK Also spelt ulek or olek, this spicy Indonesian condiment is usually made of chillies, shrimp paste, sugar and salt. Available from most supermarkets and Asian food stores.

SASHIMI Japanese method of slicing raw fish. When purchasing fish for sashimi, ensure it has a firm texture and a pleasant (but not 'fishy') sea-smell.

SAUCES

Fish Also called nam pla or nuoc nam, fish sauce is made from pulverised salted fermented fish, most often anchovies. It has a pungent smell and strong taste, so use sparingly. Available from supermarkets and Asian food stores.

Hoisin A thick, sweet Chinese barbecue sauce, hoisin is made from salted fermented soy beans, onions and garlic. It can be used as a marinade or a baste, or as a flavouring for stir-fried, braised or roasted foods. Available from supermarkets and Asian food stores.

Kecap manis An Indonesian sweet, thick soy sauce made with palm sugar, used in marinades, dips, sauces and dressings, as well as a table condiment. Depending on the brand, the soy's sweetness comes from either molasses or palm sugar. Available from supermarkets and Asian food stores.

Oyster Made from oysters and their brine, cooked with salt and soy sauce then thickened; available from most supermarkets and Asian food stores. Vegetarian oyster sauce, made from water, mushroom extract, soya beans, salt, sugar and starch, is available from most Asian food stores.

Soy Also known as sieu, is made from fermented soy beans. Several variations are available in most supermarkets and Asian food stores.

Sweet chilli The comparatively mild, thin sauce made from red chillies, sugar, garlic and vinegar; often used as a condiment.

Tabasco Brand name of extremely fiery sauce made from vinegar, hot red peppers and salt.

Tomato Also called ketchup; flavoured condiment made from tomatoes, vinegar and spices.

Worcestershire A thin, dark-brown spicy sauce used as a seasoning for meat, gravies and cocktails and as a condiment.

SCALLOPS A bivalve mollusc with fluted shell valve; we use scallops having the coral (roe) attached.

SESAME SEEDS The most common are black and white; a good source of calcium. To toast, spread seeds evenly on oven tray, toast briefly in moderate (180°C/160°C fan-forced) oven.

SHALLOTS Also called French shallots, golden shallots or eschalots; small, elongated, brown-skinned member of the onion family. Grows in tight clusters similar to garlic.

SHERRY Fortified wine consumed as an aperitif or used in cooking. Sold as fino (light, dry), amontillado (medium sweet, dark) and oloroso (full-bodied, very dark).

SICHUAN PEPPERCORNS Also known as szechuan or chinese pepper, a mildly hot spice that comes from the prickly ash tree. Although it is not related to the peppercorn family, small, red-brown

aromatic sichuan berries look like black peppercorns and have a distinctive peppery-lemon flavour and aroma. Available from Asian food stores and specialty spice stores.

SPINACH Also known as english spinach and, incorrectly, silverbeet. Its tender green leaves are good uncooked in salads or added to soups, stir-fries and stews just before serving. **Baby spinach leaves**, young leaves mostly used raw in salads, are also available.

SPLIT PEAS Also known as field peas; green or yellow pulse grown especially for drying, split in half along a centre seam. Used in soups, stews and, occasionally, spiced and cooked on their own.

SPONGE FINGER BISCUITS Also known as savoy biscuits, lady's fingers or savoiardi biscuits, they are Italian-style crisp fingers made from sponge cake mixture.

SPRING ROLL WRAPPERS Sometimes called egg roll wrappers; they come in various sizes and can be purchased fresh or frozen from Asian supermarkets. Made from a delicate wheat-based pastry, they can be used to make gow gees and samosas as well.

SQUID HOOD A type of mollusc; also known as calamari. Buy squid hoods to make preparation easier.

STAR ANISE The dried, star-shaped seed pod can be used whole as a flavouring and the seeds used alone as a spice; both can be used ground. While

it does have a slight liquorice-like taste, it should not be compared to or confused with anise, being far more spicily pungent, with overtones of clove and cinnamon. Available from supermarkets and Asian food stores.

STOCK Available in cans or tetra packs. Stock cubes or powder can be used. As a guide, 1 teaspoon of stock powder or 1 small stock cube mixed with 1 cup (250ml) water will give a fairly strong stock. Be aware of the salt and fat content of cubes, powders and prepared stocks.

SUGAR

Brown A very soft, fine granulated sugar retaining molasses for its characteristic colour and flavour.

Caster Also known as superfine or finely granulated table sugar.

Icing Also known as confectioners' sugar or powdered sugar; granulated sugar crushed together with a small amount (about 3%) cornflour added.

Palm Also called nam tan pip, jaggery, jawa or gula melaka; made from the sap of the sugar palm tree. Light brown to black in colour; usually sold in rock-hard cakes. If unavailable, use brown sugar. Available from some supermarkets and Asian food stores.

SUGAR SNAP PEAS Also called honey snap peas; fresh small pea that can be eaten whole, pod and all, similarly to snow peas. Available autumn to spring from supermarkets and greengrocers.

SULTANAS Also known as golden raisins; dried seedless white grapes.

SUMAC A deep-purple-red astringent spice coarsely ground from berries growing on shrubs that flourish wild around the Mediterranean, sumac adds a tart, lemony flavour to dips and dressings and goes well with poultry, fish and meat. Available from Middle Eastern food stores and specialty spice stores.

SWORDFISH An oily firm-fleshed fish.

TAHINI A sesame seed paste most often used in hummus, baba ghanoush and other Lebanese recipes. Available from Middle Eastern food stores and health food stores.

TAMARIND Tamarind is the product of a native tropical African tree. Dried tamarind is reconstituted in a hot liquid which gives a sweet-sour, astringent taste to food.

TEQUILA Colourless alcoholic liquor of Mexican origin made from the fermented sap of the agave, a succulent desert plant.

THAI BASIL Also known as horapa, Thai basil has smallish leaves and purple stems, a sweet licorice aniseed taste and is one of the basic flavours that typify Thai cuisine. Available from greengrocers.

TOFU Also known as bean curd, tofu is an off-white, custard-like product made from the milk of crushed soy beans. Available fresh as soft or firm, and processed as fried or pressed dried sheets.

TOMATOES

Canned Peeled tomatoes in natural juice. Available whole, crushed and diced.

Cherry Also known as Tiny Tim or Tom Thumb tomatoes; are small and round.

Paste Triple-concentrated tomato puree used to flavour soups, stews, sauces and casseroles.

Plum Also called egg or roma, these are smallish, oval-shaped tomatoes much used in Italian cooking or salads.

Semi-dried Partially dried tomato pieces in olive oil; softer and juicier than sun-dried, these are not a preserve so don't keep as long as sun-dried.

Sun-dried We used sun-dried tomatoes packaged in oil, unless otherwise specified.

TORTILLA Pronounced tor-tee-yah; are made either of wheat flour or ground corn meal, and can be purchased fresh, frozen or vacuum-packed. Available from supermarkets.

TURKISH BREAD Also known as pide; turkish bread comes in long (about 45cm) flat loaves as well as individual rounds. Made from wheat flour and sprinkled with sesame or black onion seeds. Available from most supermarkets and Middle-Eastern bakeries.

TURMERIC A member of the ginger family, turmeric is a root that is dried and ground, resulting in the rich yellow powder used in most Asian cuisines. It is intensely pungent in taste but not hot. Available from supermarkets and Asian or Indian food stores.

TZATZIKI Greek yogurt and cucumber dip; sometimes contains mint and/or garlic.

VANILLA POD Dried long, thin pod from a tropical golden orchid grown in Central and South America and Tahiti. The black seeds inside the bean are used to impart a luscious vanilla flavour in baking and desserts.

VEAL Meat from a young calf, identified by its creamy pink flesh, fine texture and delicate taste.

Schnitzels thinly sliced steak.

Shin Usually cut into 3cm- to 5cm-thick slices; also called osso buco and used in the famous Italian slow-cooked casserole of the same name.

VIETNAMESE MINT Not a mint at all, but a pungent, peppery narrow-leafed member of the buckwheat family. It is a common ingredient in Thai foods. Available from most greengrocers.

VINEGAR

Apple cider Made from fermented apples.

Balsamic Originally from Modena, Italy, there are now many balsamic vinegars on the market ranging in pungency and quality depending on how, and how long, they have been aged. Quality can be determined up to a point by price; use the most expensive sparingly.

Raspberry Raspberry is one of the most common varieties, and it can be used in a great many ways other than as part of a vinaigrette. Sprinkle it over a bowl of cooked vegetables or a fresh fruit salad to bring up the flavours and add a note of piquancy, or use it in a marinade or

sauce for meat, poultry or game — it's particularly suited to duck.

Red wine here are many white wine vinegars available that have had fruit or herbs macerated in them. **Sherry** Natural vinegar aged in oak according to traditional Spanish system; mellow wine vinegar named for its colour.

Rice Colourless vinegar made from fermented rice and flavoured with sugar and salt.

Sherry Natural vinegar aged in oak according to Spanish traditional system.

White Made from spirit of cane sugar.

WALNUTS A rich, buttery and flavourful nut. Should be stored in the refrigerator because of its high oil content.

WATER CHESTNUTS Resemble chestnuts in appearance, hence the

English name. They are small brown tubers with a crisp, white, nutty-tasting flesh. Their crunchy texture is best experienced fresh, however, canned water chestnuts are more easily obtained and can be kept about a month, once opened, under refrigeration.

WHITEBAIT Small, silver-coloured fish eaten whole; no gutting is required. Rinse thoroughly and drain well before using.

WONTON WRAPPERS Also known as wonton skins; made of flour, eggs and water they come in varying thicknesses. Usually sold packaged in large amounts and found in the refrigerated section of Asian grocery stores and some supermarkets; gow gee, egg or spring-roll pastry sheets can be substituted.

YEAST Allow 2 teaspoons (7g) dried granulated yeast to each 15g fresh yeast.

YOGURT We used plain, unflavoured yogurt, unless otherwise specified.

index

conversion charts

MEASURING EQUIPMENT

The cup and spoon measurements used in this book are metric: one measuring cup holds approximately 250ml; one metric tablespoon holds 20ml; one metric teaspoon holds 5ml.

HOW TO MEASURE

The most accurate way of measuring dry ingredients is to weigh them. When using graduated metric measuring cups, shake dry ingredients loosely into the appropriate cup. Do not tap the cup on a bench or tightly pack the ingredients unless directed to do so. Level top of measuring cups and spoons with a knife. When measuring liquids, place a clear glass or plastic jug with metric markings on a flat surface to check accuracy at eye level. We use large eggs having an average weight of 60g.

WARNING This book may contain recipes for dishes made with raw or lightly cooked eggs. These should be avoided by vulnerable people such as pregnant and nursing mothers, invalids, the elderly, babies and young children.

DRY MEASURES

METRIC	IMPERIAL
15g	½oz
30g	1oz
60g	2oz
90g	3oz
125g	4oz (¼lb)
155g	5oz
185g	6oz
220g	7oz
250g	8oz (½lb)
280g	9oz
315g	10oz
345g	11oz
375g	12oz (¾lb)
410g	13oz
440g	14oz
470g	15oz
500g	16oz (1lb)
750g	24oz (1½lb)
1kg	32oz (2lb)

OVEN TEMPERATURES

These oven temperatures are only a guide for conventional ovens.
For fan-forced ovens, check the manufacturer's manual.

	°C (CELSIUS)	°F (FAHRENHEIT)	GAS MARK
Very low	120	250	½
Low	150	275-300	1-2
Moderately low	170	325	3
Moderate	180	350-375	4-5
Moderately hot	200	400	6
Hot	220	425-450	7-8
Very hot	240	475	9

LIQUID MEASURES

METRIC	IMPERIAL
30ml	1 fluid oz
60ml	2 fluid oz
100ml	3 fluid oz
125ml	4 fluid oz
150ml	5 fluid oz (¼ pint/1 gill)
190ml	6 fluid oz
250ml	8 fluid oz
300ml	10 fluid oz (½ pint)
500ml	16 fluid oz
600ml	20 fluid oz (1 pint)
1000ml (1 litre)	1¾ pints

LENGTH MEASURES

METRIC	IMPERIAL
3mm	⅛in
6mm	¼in
1cm	½in
2cm	¾in
2.5cm	1in
5cm	2in
6cm	2½in
8cm	3in
10cm	4in
13cm	5in
15cm	6in
18cm	7in
20cm	8in
23cm	9in
25cm	10in
28cm	11in
30cm	12in (1ft)

ACP Books
General manager Christine Whiston
Test kitchen food director Pamela Clark
Editorial director Susan Tomnay
Creative director Hieu Chi Nguyen
Director of sales Brian Cearnes
Marketing manager Bridget Cody
Business analyst Rebecca Varela
Operations manager David Scotto
International rights enquiries Laura Bamford
lbamford@acpuk.com

ACP Books are published by ACP Magazines a division of PBL Media Pty Limited

Group publisher, Women's lifestyle Pat Ingram
Director of sales, Women's lifestyle Lynette Phillips
Commercial manager, Women's lifestyle Seymour Cohen
Marketing director, Women's lifestyle Matthew Dominello
Public relations manager, Women's lifestyle Hannah Deveraux
Creative director, Events, Women's lifestyle Luke Bonnano
Research Director, Women's lifestyle Justin Stone
ACP Magazines, Chief Executive officer Scott Lorson
PBL Media, Chief Executive officer Ian Law

Produced by ACP Books, Sydney.
Published by ACP Books, a division of ACP Magazines Ltd, 54 Park St, Sydney; GPO Box 4088, Sydney, NSW 2001.
phone (02) 9282 8618 fax (02) 9267 9438.
acpbooks@acpmagazines.com.au
www.acpbooks.com.au
Printed and bound in China.

Australia Distributed by Network Services,
phone +61 2 9282 8777 fax +61 2 9264 3278
networkweb@networkservicescompany.com.au
United Kingdom Distributed by Australian Consolidated Press (UK),
phone (01604) 642 200 fax (01604) 642 300
books@acpuk.com
New Zealand Distributed by Netlink Distribution Company,
phone (9) 366 9966 ask@ndc.co.nz
South Africa Distributed by PSD Promotions,
phone (27 11) 392 6065/6/7 fax (27 11) 392 6079/80
orders@psdprom.co.za
Canada Distributed by Publishers Group Canada
phone (800) 663 5714 fax (800) 565 3770
service@raincoast.com

A catalogue record for this book is available from the British Library.
ISBN 978-1-903777-38-1
© ACP Magazines Ltd 2008
ABN 18 053 273 546
This publication is copyright. No part of it may be reproduced or transmitted in any form without the written permission of the publishers.